3/3/60

DATE DUE

DEC 1 '67

10651497

Mark all else

Principles of Christian Ethics

PRINCIPLES OF
CHRISTIAN ETHICS

By

C. B. EAVEY, Ph.D.

ZONDERVAN PUBLISHING HOUSE
GRAND RAPIDS   MICHIGAN

PREFACE

This book is written with the conviction that the ground of man's existence is the eternal God. Though he sojourns on earth in a physical body, man is not a mere physical and temporal being. He is fundamentally and essentially a creature of spiritual nature originating in God and not from below. Man is therefore something infinitely greater than a collection of natural forces. He is not a machine; he is not an animal; he is more than body; he is more than tradition, history, and all else. Within him is an element which transcends everything material and temporal. This element is the soul or spirit, which comes from God, links man to God during the days of his short pilgrimage on earth, and returns to God, its eternal home.

It is a gross misrepresentation of the facts of human life to deny the reality of the spiritual, to reject all things pertaining to the life of the spirit, and to put in their places a positivistic and relativistic philosophy and mode of living. Man does this because he is proud. His pride leads him to believe that whatever is the cause of the problems he meets, it is not man himself. Most prone is man to reject any suggestion of his being wrong. Most expert is he at explaining away what he does not like and rationalizing his sins. Very difficult is it for him to see in himself defects and blemishes.

The Bible teaches that man is in rebellion and sin against God, who created him good and upright. When man chose to go his way instead of rendering obedience to God, he broke the law of his own nature and sold himself to sin, a disease which ravages his whole being. So long as man refuses to recognize his corruption, he will seek out many devices to solve the problems of his life. But he will always fail, because he is wrong within himself and in his relationship to his Creator. By fighting God, by resisting and disobeying Him, he robs himself of the good he seeks. Whatever he may do, until he is restored to obedient relationship to God through Christ, he will never be right in himself.

Man is a moral being. Perpetually he is confronted with possibilities of moral choice, and these possibilities make him uneasy. However materialistic an individual becomes, he must constantly make decisions in moral situations. The moral structure is undeniably a part of every human being. Whatever scientists may say about social conditioning and the effect of cultural influences, however much relativists may deny its reality, the moral life is still part of the equipment of all normal people. This life cannot be explained by physical determinism; the only way to account for it is to see it as coming from God in whom man exists and moves.

There is an urgent need at the present time for a better understanding of the principles basic to ethical action, of higher ideals of moral practice, and of a deeper sense of moral responsibility. This book is written for persons who are willing to ponder the problems of life and who want to think more about questions bearing upon everyday conduct. It is of little import whether or not the reader accepts the ideas of the author of the book, but it is highly necessary that interest in ethics be aroused and that Christian people especially develop a sincere purpose to make their ethical living less superficial.

The aim of the author has been to understand and so to write that the reader will understand the essential message of our Lord Jesus Christ. During the years, the author has received largely from the thoughts and the interpretations of other writers. Not always has it been possible to trace to their source the ideas of others which have become a part of his own thinking. In this book, however, there appears nothing that was not subjected to the author's own thinking and that was not tested, as far as possible, in his own experience.

The author is keenly aware that he has received far more freely than he has been able to give. If this book conveys to its readers even a little from the wealth of helpful content found in ethical thought of all time, the author's efforts will not have been in vain.

The book is sent forth with the hope that many, who are sincerely desirous of living a good life in the sight of God and before their fellow men, will derive profit and inspiration from thinking upon what is contained in it.

This volume is the first of two on the general subject, "Christian Ethics," one on "Principles of Christian Ethics" and a second, to be released later, on "Practical Christian Ethics." Designed as companion volumes, these will offer a complete course in Christian Ethics, both the theoretical (principles) and the practical aspects.

C. B. EAVEY

Wheaton, Illinois

ACKNOWLEDGMENTS

Permisssion of the publishers to quote as indicated from the following sources is gratefully acknowledged:

From *The Dawn of World Redemption*, by Erich Sauer, pages 24 and 54. Used by permission of the author and of the publishers, The Paternoster Press, 11 Great James Street, Bedford Row, London, W.C. 1, England; and William B. Eerdmans Publishing Company, Grand Rapids, Michigan.

From *Christianity and Ethics*, by Archibald Browning Drysdale Alexander, pages 50 and 174. Used by permission of the publisher, Charles Scribner's Sons, New York.

From *Christian Ethics*, by Samuel Phillips Newman Smyth, pages 293-295, 479, 480. Used by permission of the publisher, Charles Scribner's Sons, New York.

From *The Crisis of Our Age*, by P. A. Sorokin, pages 97, 98. Used by permission of the publisher, E. P. Dutton and Company, New York.

From *Perfect Freedom*, by T. C. Hammond, pages 61 and 205. Used by permission of the publisher, The Inter-Varsity of Evangelical Unions, London, England.

CONTENTS

Preface

Acknowledgments

Chapter I Introduction 13

Chapter II The Bible and Ethics 31
The Nature and the Purpose of God
The Perversity and the Sinfulness of Man
The Grace of God through Christ

Chapter III The Bible and Ethics (Continued) 58
The Work of Jesus Christ
The Kingdom of God
The Holy Spirit and Ethics
Conclusion

Chapter IV The Place of Ethics in the Christian Life.... 91
General Ethics and Christian Living
Reason in Ethics
Christian Ethics in Action

Chapter V The Goal of Life 122
Goals in General Ethics
The Goal in Christian Ethics

Chapter VI The Knowledge of Good and Evil 137
Three Answers to the Question
The Answer of Christian Ethics

Chapter VII The Standard of Conduct 157
Theories Concerning the Standard
The Moral Standard of the Universe

Chapter VIII The Motives of Conduct 182
The Nature of Motivation
Pleasure, Pain, and Reason in Motivation
The Christian Life and Motive

Chapter IX   Freedom 213
              Factors That Complicate the Problem
              Action and Freedom
              Freedom a Growth
              The Conditions of Freedom
              Christian Freedom

Chapter X   The Responsibility of the Christian............244
              The Doctrinal and Theoretical Basis of
                Responsibility
              Meeting Responsibility
              Discipline

Principles of Christian Ethics

CHAPTER I

Introduction

ETHICS IS THE SYSTEMATIC study of standards of right and wrong in conduct. It is that part of science and philosophy which is concerned with the sources, the principles, and the practices of forming and using judgments of right and wrong. Conduct is behavior selected and directed by a person in the light of his principles of right and wrong. Conduct is, therefore, an outward expression of character, which, in turn, has its roots in personality or the self. We cannot, then, limit ethics to *doing*; it is not only a description of the outward acts of man, but it deals also with the sources of action, the motives, and especially the ends which guide a man in his conduct. In short, it stresses *being* as well as doing. "Ethics is quite as much a study of character as it is of conduct."

Christian ethics treats of the sources, the principles, and the practices of right and wrong in Christian conduct. Christian conduct is behavior performed with a view to pleasing God by a person who is living to Christ. Such an one did not always have Christ at the center of his life. He began to live to Christ when the Holy Spirit convinced him of sin and when through grace he was brought to see the dying Saviour making a propitiation for his guilt. Ever since he was born again, for him to live means Christ. The aim and the end of his life is Christ. For Christ's glory he lives; in defense of Christ's gospel he would die. Christ is the pattern of his life and the model after which he molds his character, but He is more: Christ is possessor of his personality, "his very breath, the soul of his soul, the heart of his heart, the life of his life." Christ lives in him and the life he now lives, he lives by faith in the Son of God who loved him and gave Himself for him.

Christian ethics, then, is no mere setting forth of the ethical

13

teachings of the historical Jesus and His apostles. It presents
no abstract theory of virtue and duty but proceeds from a vital
relationship with the living Christ. Christian ethics, it is true,
accepts, with ethics in general, whatever light nature and reason
bring to bear upon ethical problems. But it adds to this the
clearer light that comes from divine revelation. And by virtue
of the experience of living relationship into which he has entered as an outcome of this revelation, the Christian seeks
direction for conduct in the guidance of the indwelling Holy
Spirit, who is given according to the promise of the ascended
Lord.

History shows that man is a doer of deeds which are distinguished by their ethical qualities. Records of the earliest
times give evidence of human actions with specific qualities
which are judged with approval or disapproval, alike by the individual and by the members of the group in which he lives.
The judgment passed, whether by the doer or by others, is
influenced by the extent to which the act is recognized to be
the product of the individual's power to will freely. An act
done under known compulsion is not judged in the same way
as an act recognizably performed with complete freedom of
choice. Both this power to do or refuse to do and the judgment
conditioned thereby, indicate that a standard exists which ought
to govern man's conduct but that it may not be allowed to do
so. In other words, though a man may not obey them, moral
laws are essential to his nature.

The Universality of Moral Laws

Moreover, moral laws are just as universal as physical laws.
Amid all the differences in cultural level, from the most savage
to the most highly civilized, men, as individuals and as groups,
judge actions according to standards that are moral. And
everywhere at all times, despite apparent laxity or elasticity of
moral standards, there is a certain similarity in the essence,
if not in the form, of their moral judgments. Furthermore,
moral laws are characterized by permanency instead of tempo-
rariness. The fundamental moral law never changes. Right
is right and wrong is wrong, whatever men may say, whatever
change customs undergo, in spite of boasted progress, however

many human laws are made, whatever may prevail in practice. Basic moral law is just as fixed, just as unchanging and functions just as surely, as the law of gravity or any other physical law.

That men anywhere live without recognition of moral law is not a scientific fact. Some of the most primitive peoples ever discovered hold and practice a high moral code. Only in recent times has it been maintained that men began far down on an exceedingly low level and gradually worked up to a boasted present perfection, much more imagined than actual.

Undeniably, man has made progress in many realms and departments of life. However, the simple fact is that he has not made corresponding progress in the realm of the spiritual and the moral. In spite of advancement along educational, cultural, scientific, economic, and political lines, our modern world is desperately ill, and man is probably more miserable than he has ever been. Howard Vincent O'Brien has this to say about present-day life: "Wherever you look, there's something missing. I think it is *morals*. We strive to get as much as possible for doing as little as possible; and we strive to gouge out of the buyer the most for the least. Simple honesty is rare enough for amazed comment. The thief has become respectable. The shadow of corruption hangs over the land. And poor witless clowns think they can do something about it by making agreements and passing laws. But the soul of man is sick. It will take more than this to cure him."

Yet in his pride man is determined to defend himself and to think highly of himself. Most unwilling is he to admit that the cause of the troubles of life is in himself. Every one of us knows from personal experience how difficult it is to face the suggestion that we are not right. All of us are experts in explaining away our wrong acts and rationalizing our sins. We are prone to argue that man is right — all right. We have never learned with Augustine that "no man can suffice to himself either for beginning or for completing any good work" or with Jeremiah that "cursed is every man that has hope in man." More and more we refrain from digging beneath the surface of life; more and more we stress facts, ignoring the truth that facts, however numerous and however important, can never substitute for moral values and moral standards. Less and less are we concerned with the simple wisdom of life, with the things of true worth. In short, we are taken up more and more with the physical world, with temporal things, and with superficialities, and less and less with moral reality.

Not always has the vision of a state of happiness and perfection been held so lightly. Before the minds of men became enamored with fallacies such as prevail today, emphasis was centered on moral factors. Not always has it been considered that man is driven by blind, irresistible forces operating apart from all reactions to standards of right and wrong. In the words of Ovid, the perfection of an earlier age which gave way to an age in which "modesty, truth and honor fled, in place of which succeeded fraud, deceit, treachery, violence, and an insatiable itch to amass wealth" was recognized as basically a moral perfection. It was seen as dependent on the absence of evil and as characterized by that striving to reach the goal of living without which man cannot be satisfied.

If men have no vision to inspire and guide them in their living, they cannot be anything but perplexed, confused, discouraged, and unhappy when they see going on in the world so much they cannot reconcile with their ideal of what ought to be. With nothing to keep them on their course, uncertainty, uneasiness, fear, anxiety, and flight from reality into mental disease, are almost inevitable. The idea that men, like animals, are under the rule of biological necessity, that moral laws are relative and no moral judgments have objective validity, that right and wrong are different for different people at different times, that morality is a matter of private opinion with no standards to be applied to all men, that custom, tradition, social approval, or legal enactment determines morality, that happiness or personal pleasure is the end which should guide one in his actions, that to find out what one should do he need only appeal to nature, that the fundamental values upon which our civilization is founded are worthless and should be scrapped — no conception such as any of these can give life a meaning and a purpose.

Ethics an Inquiry into the Meaning and Purpose of Life

Ethics can be defined as the science of the end of life — the science that inquires into the meaning and purpose of life. It is concerned with the ultimate problems of human conduct. It holds up a standard, or norm, of life. It is not occupied only with bare facts as the physical sciences are but also with values, with what ought to be, with the ideal in character and conduct. It is therefore usually called a *normative* science. This is not to say that ethics has no interest in actual conditions; it has to do with both moral reality and moral ideality. It is *normative* in the sense that it sets up norms or standards of what should be considered the goal of human endeavor. It is sometimes called the search for ideals of right and goodness.

Man has always been engaged in this search. That is to say, ethics had its origin in the innate morality of man. A most outstanding characteristic of man is his power of thought. Created a moral agent, able to discern between right and wrong, capable of expressing ethical judgments, with desire to know and to do the good, and endowed with capacity to think, man cannot but inquire into the meaning and purpose of life. Such inquiry was the beginning of the science of ethics. This science is essentially an activity of human beings, thinking about moral matters in the light of their experiences and their understanding of themselves and their relationships. Obviously, early thinking in this field, as in all other fields, was somewhat unsystematized. Consequently, this natural ethics could scarcely be called a system of ethics. Nevertheless, it represents a real attempt to deal in thought with moral reality in the form of the ideals and aspirations man discovers in himself and which he is impelled to strive to fulfill, and with the sense of obligation that the consciousness of these ideals and goals arouse in him.

In the long course of years, as the thought of men developed on the continuing basis of its own accretions, philosophical ethics came into being. For well over two thousand years philosophers in the West, beginning with Socrates, Plato, and Aristotle, have been expressing their views and developing in a more systematic way the science of ethics. Many systems of ethics have been founded. All these systems rest ultimately upon the idea that the life examined by thought and reason in the light of inherent moral principles is the only life worth living. This idea was advanced by the first Greek philosophers. Also, though they differ in some ways, all the great ethical systems agree in emphasizing basic principles such as justice, fair play, good will, honesty, and truthfulness — principles whose value has been demonstrated through thousands of years of human experience.

The Five Main Problems of Ethics

The main ethical problems with which the minds of men have grappled from the beginning are five in number. Discussions on these problems constitute the major portion of the content of philosophical ethics. Varying conceptions of the best answers to the questions involved in these problems are the basis of the different systems of ethics.

The oldest and perhaps the most important ethical question is, *What is the highest ideal that man can have as his ultimate standard of right conduct?* As was said above, ethics is primarily concerned with the *ideal* of life. The ideal has reference to a better state of being than the actual. Man is forever and always aware that he is not as he should be, that some condition of life higher and better than the one already attained exists for himself individually and for society as a whole. There is no ethical life apart from an ideal. Some conception of what is finally and ultimately good — the supreme good, the *summum bonum* of human existence, the highest for which a man should live — is a moral necessity of man's being. The answer to this question is, therefore, the test of every system of morals.

The second problem is expressed in the question, *What is the source of our knowledge of the highest good?* "To know the ultimately real" is an aim of every one and engages, more or less, the thought of every person. Though aware that our knowledge is founded on a set of principles which we *naturally* know, not something we originate in our own thinking, we are impelled to seek out the source or origin of these principles. Deep within ourselves we know that there is a good and a right toward which we tend. We know fully as well that when we do evil or wrong, we go against something within us, that evil, in a very fundamental sense, is not natural. The answer any person gives the question as to whence comes this knowledge of good and evil depends upon his epistemological point of view.

The third main problem is the problem of authority. Its question is, *What is our final authority for what is right and what is wrong?* The essential mark of human conduct is control, for conduct is chosen and directed behavior. Man is not driven by physical necessity; behavior subjected to physical necessity is not human behavior in the true sense of the word "human," for it is not under control. Any necessity in human behavior is a moral necessity, one in which there is choice, with the possibility of mistake or success. Man's nature is a moral nature endowed with the power of choosing its paths to the goal of living. Acts directed to the goal of living are good acts; acts directed away from the goal of living are bad acts; every truly human act is under control, carried on either for the right or for the wrong. Ethics has to do with the laws of wholesome living; it is not directly concerned with artificialities, shallow desires, or the denial of life and its ends. It seeks to know the authority for the making of the choices of life.

The fourth problem of ethics relates to the motives of the agent of moral action. *Why does he act as he does? What motives prompt his conduct?* Every human action in itself is morally good, morally bad, or morally indifferent, according as it leads to, away from, or contributes in no way to, the attainment of an ethical end or goal. Thus a just act is always good in itself; an unkind act is always bad in itself; going for a ride is in itself indifferent. But beyond the ethical quality of the act itself, there is the morality also of the motive of the person who does it. He may be meting out justice for the purpose of perpetrating harm upon a fellow man whom he hates; he may help a poor man with a view to influencing him to engage in crime; he may go for a ride in order to commit a burglary. Why one does an act gives his deed ethical content, for virtue resides in the intention or motive as well as in the result.

The fifth chief problem of ethics concerns the freedom of the will. *Is man at all times and under all circumstances completely*

free to choose and to do as he chooses? Ethics recognizes man
as a being endowed with the power of self-determination, as one
who is responsible for his motives, intentions, dispositions, and
actions. Good and evil, right and wrong, are the direct business of the will. To be engaged with them is its task, just as
it is the task of the eyes to see and of the intellect to know.
Without the power of self-determination, the idea of a supreme good to seek would have no meaning. Where there is
no freedom of choice, there is no action that is either good or
bad. It is in his will that man ascends to the heights of goodness or descends to the lowest depths of evil.

The Place of Law in Attaining the Goal of Living

To fulfill his nature, man must live morally. All ethical
thought has for its foundation the realization that the steps
by which life moves to its goal are personal actions, proceeding
under the control of reason and will and directed by moral law.
In every truly human act, even the smallest, there is morality,
because morality is the fulfilling or the breaking of the law
that governs human nature. We study physics to gain knowledge of the laws of force and matter so that we can adjust our
life to surroundings. We study ethics to gain understanding of
the laws of human life and conduct that we may adjust our
lives to our moral conditions of living.

The ultimate end of the conduct of each individual is the
attainment of the goal of living. With a nature that is moral,
free, and rational, with power to control his actions and to go
to his end or away from it, man is guided by natural moral
law. It is impossible to live life without law. We must have
law, and we must have understanding of the nature of law, for
we must live life, and we cannot live it unless we have understanding of what life is and means. Without law, life is nothing
and means nothing.

Life and law are inseparably interrelated. Life is motion to
a goal. Law is direction of the motion that is life to the goal
of life. Law is nothing but direction; it is not life; therefore
law and morality are also inseparably interrelated. In fact,
morality is only conformity with the rule which regulates life,
and that rule is moral law. This law is inherent in man, a

part of his very nature. We have to think about life because we must live life. We can ignore neither law nor morality because both enter too definitely into human life to be overlooked. Our attitude to life determines our attitude to law.

Law is a friend to man; it exists for the purpose of keeping him on the right road; it functions to prevent disaster. We cannot reach the goal of life by rendering wholehearted devotion to physical or scientific laws and by making a host of human laws, if we at the same time resent law, flout law, demand release from law, and try to do away with the only foundation law has. We cannot escape human responsibility by acknowledging the order of nature and inconsistently insist on making man the sole exception to that order, the only creature not subject to the government and direction of natural law. Like everything else in the universe, man must be directed by a law that perfects his nature. Man's nature is free; physical law and physical necessity do not govern his actions. Only one law can operate in this moral nature to direct it to the goal of living, and this is moral law.

Natural Moral Law and the Great Eternal Law

From nothing, nothing comes. Order cannot originate from disorder; government never arises from anarchy; natural moral law did not just happen to come on the scene of life. As was said above, our view of life determines our view of law. So long as we are confused about the goal of life and doubt or openly deny that there is such a goal, human life will have little meaning. So long as human action is meaningless, we will live paradoxically, with an absurd faith in law, devoting ourselves with abandon to law, but yet despising and resenting law. On the other hand, if we are convinced that there is a purpose in living and that the life of an individual is a motion of progress to the goal for which he was made, we will realize that progress is the outcome of systematic direction, that government is the foundation of all order, and that a great eternal law is the source of all law and of all truth. Then it will be easy for us to accept the fact that natural moral law in man is but the expression of this eternal law.

Thomas Aquinas defined this eternal law as "the type of

divine wisdom which directs all actions and motions." God is
the active agent who brought the universe into being, the creator and the perpetual re-creator of all things. The world of
things, far from being made up of forces that can be measured
or of energies that struggle without direction, is a ceaseless expression of the present thought and continuing action of God.
The universe and all that is in it is very definitely governed by
God; His will controls and directs the energy of the universe.
Government, or direction to an end, is the effect of law. The
ultimate end of the universe and the direction given it by God
is eternal. The universal principles from which He proceeds
in governing the universe comprise the eternal law.

God exists. He is a supremely intelligent, infinitely wise,
completely omnipotent, ever loving, altogether perfect Being.
Man can neither deny His reality nor explain the world without Him. There would be no science without His government,
or philosophy apart from first principles which have their beginning in Him. The great men in philosophy subscribe to
the existence of a God, the reality of human spirit, and the
immortality of the soul. The highest good Plato identifies with
God and holds that man's end is to be found in knowledge of
Him and in communion with Him. Every great western philosopher holds the same views. True it is, there is much variety
in their conceptions of God and the human spirit, but no
philosopher of major importance has denied God or human
spirit. From the irrefutable evidence of His handiwork, as Paul
declares, the existence and nature of the divine Architect is
plainly visible to those whom He created and to whom He
consigned the lordship of the earth. And Paul states also that,
even in his natural state, man is constituted for the moral life
and is not without some knowledge of right and wrong nor of
the source whence it comes.

As the universe is nothing apart from its Creator, so the
finite spirit of man can make nothing of itself, except in relation to the supreme creative Spirit in which all finite existence is grounded. Physical things are not God's chief creation.
His real creation is spirit. As finite spirits created by God, we
have thoughts and feelings and wills of our own, as well as a
measure of self-control, or the power of self-direction. In short,

we have a certain selfhood and a degree of moral independence which makes us real persons. On the other hand, we cannot regard ourselves as self-sufficient and completely independent, because we too often have experiences which demonstrate our finiteness. We cannot understand how these two facts are put together; we only know that we must admit both. Only as the life of God dwells within the finite spirit is it possible to reach the goal — a good and happy life. In this indwelt life lies the moral perfection and the blessedness of man, the finite being.

The law that is in God is the eternal law; the same law is also in finite creatures but is called natural law. God established nature and governs nature. Everything in the universe exists in God and is governed or directed by God. All direction is to an end and each single thing is directed according to its nature. A rosebush does not develop like an apple tree nor does a puppy become able to climb a tree as does a kitten. Like every other creature, man is a part of nature, and, as is the case with every other creature, he is governed according to his nature — the nature of a free moral being who is responsible for his conduct. In those respects in which he has plant nature or animal nature, man is subject to the physical laws, which operate in those kingdoms. But in so far as he is a real person, he is in control of his acts, he must direct himself, he cannot be merely acted upon and remain free. The law through which God governs him is a moral law, not a physical law.

Only God fully understands the eternal law. No finite being can comprehend the infinite. We know this law through its effects. Every person knows something of the eternal law. The origin of all truth is in this eternal law of God. The truth is recognized in some measure by every human being; through the use of reason the fundamental principles of thought and action come naturally to each of us. The eternal law, as law, is known in its effects by every person, at least in its effect within himself, as the law functions in directing him. To deny a knowledge of the eternal law would be to deny natural moral law, for the eternal law as it operates in men is the natural moral law. Such denial must be made in the face of all the evidence given by reason, experience, and history. Moreover, it makes man the only creature in God's created universe without a law proper to his nature.

Any human law that is really a law derives from the eternal law of God. Every human law is a law only as it is in harmony with natural moral law. The natural law is the way of nature and of good for man; any human or civil law, to qualify as law, must be in conformity with the moral law natural to man; and natural moral law is the eternal law from the side of man.

Natural moral law is an intrinsic law, not a law brought to bear upon man from without. In common with all creatures, man has natural inclinations. In addition, he has the faculty of reason which not only recognizes natural limitations but also works upon them. For man an action is natural only if it is in harmony with reason. The outcome of the reacting of reason to or upon natural inclination is a natural dictate or command of reason. All of this is from within, coming from nature. Thus the natural moral law is an intrinsic rule by which man, through the application of reason, participates actively in his own direction to the goal of life.

Law a Friend to Man

Law is not something forced upon man, not something to be feared and avoided, not something to be fled from as undesirable, not a barrier limiting our activities, not something intended to take the joy out of life, not a thing to be evaded whenever possible. Nor is law something to be worshiped, something with magic power, an antidote to be used when we do not wish to accept responsibility, or a rule to be enforced for the purpose of easing conscience. Law flows from man's nature and is necessary for the protection of his liberty because he is a free being. Law exists for one purpose: to guide man to his final goal, which is happiness. Law is man's friend, ever present and ever ready to direct him as he travels the rough journey of life. Without law life would not be life.

God a Reality in the Lives of Men

God is the ultimate source of ethical law and morality. Not only does He know and will the morality which is for us, but it constitutes a part of His very essence; it belongs to His being as eternal fact. Moral law is the revelation of an ideal that exists eternally in His mind. Moral truth comes from Him, not from the thought and investigation of man. The moral law and the knowledge of it is in men, even when they do not know Him as the origin thereof. That God has a connection with men in general, including those not in fellowship with Him through Christ, is evident from the words of Paul to the Athenians: "For in him we live, and move, and have our being." Furthermore, he quoted, with approval, Greek poets who had said, "For we are also his offspring" (Acts 17:28). Peter, addressing Gentiles who, presumably, had never before heard the Gospel of salvation, said, "But in every nation he that feareth him, and worketh righteousness, is accepted with him" (Acts 10:35).

Augustine stresses in these words the reality of God in the life of men: "That which is now called the Christian religion existed among the ancients, and has never failed from the beginning of the human race, until Christ came in the flesh, whence the true religion, which was already in existence, began to be called Christian." To Augustine, the City of God and the earthly state mingled together from the creation of man and will continue to mingle together through all time. God has always been present in the life of the world, though He be unperceived and, often, unacknowledged. This is clearly shown in the first verses of John's Gospel and in the opening verses of the First Epistle of John.

The good that men do, even when they do not know God and even when they deny His existence, they do through His power, because to God all power belongs. Wholly apart from any direct and acknowledged operation of the grace of God in his heart and life, man has within himself ideals and aspirations that he strives to fulfill. The awareness of these ideals and goals gives rise to the sense of obligation. Ignorant of the fact though he may be, confused though he may be, however much he may deny the truth, whatever else he may feel obligated to, the ultimate cause of this sense of obligation is the eternal law and its author, God.

The Ethics of the Natural Man and the Ethics of the Christian

This means that the teachings of the Bible, experience, and reason all agree in recognizing that the natural man has moral cognition. Natural ethics, or ethics developed informally in a rather unsystematized manner, and Christian ethics are not opposed. God, who moved in the first creation and who ever continues to move in all created things, appeared in Christ and cannot be in contradiction to Christianity. True it is, sin entered into the first creation and originated a contradiction of what might be called "original Christian morality." But even in man under sin, there is still ethical knowledge which can and does find expression in practice and which condemns sin.

However, natural ethics and Christian ethics are not identical. The chief difference is that the former is unable to get beyond the moral requirement, the sense of obligation. It has no remedy for what is fundamentally wrong in man. Christian ethics is founded on a new life, the life of the Spirit of God, the source of the second creation. The operation of faith in the atoning merits of a crucified Redeemer delivers man from sin and brings him into the kingdom of God, a kingdom where the Spirit of God rules. Under this rule there is a continual overcoming of sin and error. Natural ethics inclines to disregard the reality of sin in human life and consequently moves in an unreal realm.

The revelation of God in Christ is the factor which dominates and influences the Christian's entire outlook and gives a wholly new value to all his aims and actions. However, Christian ethics does not do away with the reason of man and his natural reactions. Christian truth is entirely reasonable; to the reason of man the appeals of Christianity are directed. God does not do violence to the nature of his highest created being by ignoring that in him which makes him superior to other creatures. "Come now, and let us reason together" is His call. The experience of the new birth wrought within by faith is founded upon the inward consciousness of truth. Faith does not suspend the operation of reason but frees reason from error and sin, thus enabling it to operate more perfectly. Besides, since Christian ethics embodies in itself natural ethical knowledge, it can enlighten and purify this knowledge by removing therefrom unwholesome conceptions while not going contrary to natural reason. The natural virtues have their value for Christian character; ennobled and enhanced through Christian experience, they are in line with Christian virtue.

Philosophical Ethics and Christian Ethics

Definite relationships exist also between philosophical ethics and Christian ethics. Philosophical ethics is ethics as developed and systematized by men who have brought to bear upon ethical matters more thought than the average person has given them or is able to give them. Whatever fancies and extravagancies may appear in any of the systems thus founded, there is no essential contradiction between true philosophical ethics and Christian ethics. In a Christian society, philosophical ethics is bound to be influenced by Christian teachings. So while the philosophical ethicist may be trying to work only in the light of nature and reason, he is subject to the effects of the Christian revelation. The best systems of ethics have been wrought out in those lands where Biblical teaching was common. Logically as well as actually, Christian ethics contains more than philosophical ethics as such, because it deliberately includes, in addition to what man can develop by thinking and reasoning, the clearer light shed upon ethical life by God in revelation.

There is one fundamental difference between the two: Christian ethics maintains the reality of the experience of Christ in the life of the Christian, from which experience comes a body of conduct bearing distinct marks of its origin. No philosophical reasoning can therefore satisfy the Christian heart and conscience, if it ignores what, to the Christian, is the supreme reality in his experience. He has had a vision of God in Christ Jesus; ever after, Jesus is for him the end for life and for conduct. Having experienced forgiveness of sin, he has fellowship with God and with a group of believers whose conduct also bears the marks of a new life in Christ. The basis of Christian ethics is therefore the forgiven life expressing itself in a transformation of all ideals and in a transvaluation of all values. Thereafter, whatever reason and thought do is done upon a foundation of the results of a transforming experience.

Philosophical ethics and Christian ethics are related because they have a common material. Even for Christian morality there is no other world, no purely spiritual arena, for conduct. The Christian, though his citizenship is in heaven, is an inhabitant of this world, the world of the first creation deformed by sin. His conduct is involved with duties to his body, his family, his fellow men, his employer or his employees, his society, and his state. All of these were present before Christianity appeared and continue to be present apart from Christianity. Philosophical ethics approves what promotes their welfare and rejects the opposite, and Christian ethics must recognize the validity of the moral principle thus applied. Besides this likeness in material, there is also a formal likeness between the two. Both philosophical ethics and Christian ethics can operate only through the faculties of thought and will. Both must acknowledge the necessity of personal self-determination as the basis for moral action.

General Ethics, Natural and Philosophical Ethics Combine

The total of ethical knowledge formulated by man, apart from special revelation, is comprised under the term, general ethics. It includes as a minor part of its content the findings of natural ethics, or the relatively unsystematized results of the ethical thinking of average people. By far the major part of its content consists in the results of the more systematic thinking and reasoning of men who have applied themselves to formal study of ethical matters. General ethics, then, represents the knowledge of moral principles of which human reason is capable, apart from revelation. This statement does not imply that morality is a product of the thought and reason of man. On the contrary, morality is something that is recognized, or discovered, by reason. Because men are moral by nature, they think about morality; they do not become moral beings because they think. The cause of our being is also the ultimate cause of our moral knowledge, that is, God.

The Relation between Christian Doctrine and Christian Ethics

There remains for consideration one final introductory matter, namely, the relation between Christian dogmatics and Christian ethics. The former is a study of the doctrines drawn from the

Bible and developed through the application of thought and reason. The latter represents a critical effort of Christian thought to discover and systematize moral principles and to apply such principles for the sake of gaining greater consistency and precision in Christian conduct. For many centuries of the Christian era, ethics was a part of theology. Finally, in the course of time, Christian ethics became a separate science in distinction from dogmatics.

Christian ethics may be regarded as that part of Christian theology which treats the principles of human response to divine action in creation, revelation, and redemption. Dogmatics might be thought of as theoretical theology and ethics as practical theology. Actually, the two are so closely interrelated that it is not possible to distinguish between them, except in thought. Ethics has its basis in doctrine, and every doctrine has its ethical aspect or quality. Christian ethics is founded, not on some one doctrine but on the whole of systematic theology, that is, God and the totality of His acts. Paradoxically, therefore, ethics stands in a relation of dependence on doctrine, yet it is a science different from dogmatics and relatively independent. Though not all theologians have so thought, it is probably best that the two be treated separately for this reason: when treated together as a single science, one or the other is likely to be slighted due to the special interest of the person who deals with the subject.

QUESTIONS

1. What is your definition of ethics?
2. What is conduct? How is it related to character? What is Christian conduct?
3. What is the connection between revelation and ethics?
4. Why is an act done under compulsion not an ethical act?
5. Does violation of moral law harm one as much as violation of physical law?
6. Do you agree that man has made less progress in the realm of the spiritual and the moral than in other departments of life? If so, why? If not, why not?
7. Is or is not pride the basic cause of man's lack of concern with moral reality?
8. How do you react to the idea that ethics is an inquiry into the meaning and purpose of life?

9. Explain why natural ethics does not constitute a system of ethics.
10. Just what is philosophical ethics?
11. Can you think of main problems of ethics other than the five listed?
12. What is a truly human act? How does it differ from an act that is not truly human?
13. Show the place of natural moral law in attaining the goal of living.
14. Explain: "Without law, life is nothing and means nothing."
15. Is it possible to conceive of any instance in which law is not a friend to man?
16. How are natural moral law and the great eternal law related one to the other?
17. Can there be government without law? If not, why not?
18. How is a finite person related to God, the infinite Person?
19. How does God govern man according to his nature?
20. Illustrate: "Every person knows something of the eternal law."
21. Is a human law that is not derived from the eternal law of God really a law? Explain your answer.
22. Show that natural moral law is an intrinsic law.
23. Do all men — non-Christian and Christian — "live, and move, and have their being" in God?
24. Are all men — non-Christian and Christian — subject to moral law? If not, why not?
25. In what sense are natural ethics and Christian ethics not identical?
26. Is it correct to say that the Christian is under natural moral law?
27. What does Christian ethics have that philosophical ethics does not have?
28. Explain: the Christian must be moral in a world.
29. Define general ethics.
30. How is Christian doctrine related to Christian ethics?

CHAPTER II

The Bible and Ethics

THE BIBLE is not given us as a treatise on ethics, yet it has ever so much to say about human conduct. The Bible is God's own record of the history of salvation wrought by Himself through Christ. In it are truths that are unfolded nowhere else. It is one harmonious whole; it is a system of prophecy worked out in history according to divine plan. Its goal is Christ; its theme is the kingdom of God.

Through all ages the minds of men have grappled with the threefold problem of man's origin, what he now is, and what he shall be. Numerous, varied, fanciful, incomplete, and unsatisfying have been the answers. In mystery the thinking of man begins, in mystery it proceeds, and in mystery it ends. Man is to himself the riddle of the universe. But God has given the answer plainly. Through the ages His one increasing purpose runs as He makes concrete in creative deeds His eternal thoughts. The history of mankind is the story of His dealings with man. The answer God gives is Himself, His own being in the person of His only-begotten Son. "In the beginning was the Word, and the Word was with God, and the Word was God." The Son of God, the eternal Word, is the center of divine revelation, for He is the center of a circle, whose circumference is the whole human race. In Christ will mankind attain its final and blessed goal.

In God everything has its beginning, for He is the Creator of all things. His Son "is the image of the invisible God, the firstborn of every creature: For by him were all things created, that are in heaven, and that are in earth, visible and invisible" (Col. 1:15, 16). "All things were made by him; and without him was not any thing made that was made" (John 1:3).

What God begins, He completes; nothing can frustrate His final, eternal purpose. He is at present carrying on through Christ His process of redeeming man who in self-will chose not to align himself with God's original way of developing His final purpose in creation. In God shall all be ultimately consummated. After everything has been put in subjection to Christ, "then shall the Son also himself be subject unto him that put all things under him, that God may be all in all" (I Cor. 15:28). Thus God reveals Himself in Christ, the eternal Word, through whom He accomplishes His purpose according to plan.

The eternal Word is revealed through the spoken Word, which became the written Word. The written Word became the Bible. So the Bible is God's Word and, therefore, the final word about God and man, about spiritual and eternal things. Being the Word of the living God, it is "the infallible rule of faith and practice."

Faith Basic in Conduct

Faith determines practice, or conduct. The old view that it does not matter what a person believes so long as he does good is unsound because his idea of what is good depends upon what he believes. This is true, at least in general, on even the intellectual and natural level. If one believes as a communist, he behaves as a communist; if one is a Republican, he stands for Republican principles; if one is a sincere adherent of a certain religious faith or denomination, he lives and worships according to its teachings; if one is a nominal Christian, his conduct is that of one not wholeheartedly devoted to Christ. Likewise, the living faith of a true Christian issues in conduct which is Christian. "A good tree cannot bring forth evil fruit, neither can a corrupt tree bring forth good fruit," said Jesus (Matt. 7:18). Of course, a man does not always do what he knows he ought to do, nor is he always able to reduce his faith to practice due to the fact that he may lack clear recognition of the implications for conduct of his belief. But in general our conduct, or at least our conceptions of what our conduct should be, are shaped by our faith. Experience plainly teaches that when faith begins to weaken, conduct soon sinks to a lower standard of practice.

The Christian life begins with personal faith in the Lord Jesus Christ as the Son of God whom the Bible sets forth as the only Saviour from sin and its consequences. But that is only the beginning, not the end. Christian faith is no mechanical idolization of the letter but a progressive development resulting in increasing knowledge of God, through Christ, and in increasing understanding of His ways and purposes. The Bible clearly reveals the nature of God, showing us His holiness and our accountability to Him, thus causing us to reverence Him more highly. It portrays man as he is, giving us realization of the sinfulness of our human nature; thus it leads us to humble ourselves in contrition and repentance and to be thankful to God for His mercy. It shows us the grace of God who gave His Son to die on the Cross for our sake; thus it causes us to love Him more deeply. So, as the revelation causes faith to grow more and more, conduct becomes progressively more Christian.

THE NATURE AND THE PURPOSE OF GOD

God a Reality to All Human Beings

The first foundation stone of Christian faith is the doctrine of God. The first efficient cause was God. "God is the cause that causes all other causes to be." Not only is God the first cause but He is also the final cause or the end of all things. All things come from God through Christ; "without him was not any thing made that was made" (John 1:3). Being the cause of the world, He is its final end and the sole director or governor of the world to that end. God is the only self-sufficient Being; upon Him all depend and to Him all look; everything is dependent upon Him for its nature, its existence, its goal, and its direction to its end or goal. God is the one, eternal, absolute Spirit. In Him is life, the highest, the most perfect life. God is most real and He is more intimately nigh to each one of us than any human being.

Only as we know about God can we know the important things concerning either the world or ourselves. Manifestly, every one of us needs to know about the world, at least the main things like its origin, its meaning, and its relation to himself. Also, it is important that we know things about ourselves like our origin, the meaning of our lives, and our relation to things around us.

While the Bible tells us much about God, it makes no attempt to prove His existence. Not a single writer of either the Old or the New Testament argues for the existence of God. Everywhere, from the first verse of Genesis to the last verse of Revelation, this is taken for granted. Moreover, the Bible recognizes that men not only know God but that they also have certain ideas as to who He is and what He is (Rom. 1:18-23).

Man everywhere believes in the existence of a Supreme Being, or beings, to whom he is morally responsible and to whom he needs to make propitiation. This universal belief does not come from reason, because many who believe in God do so without having engaged formally in reasoning. Nor does it have its source in tradition, because tradition can hand down only what has been originated. Neither does it come from the Bible, because anyone who accepts the Bible as the revelation of God has already assumed the existence of God. All evidence points to the fact that this universal belief in God is essential to the nature of man and comes from moral intuition. To know that God is, man needs no proofs of His existence, else the Bible would have given us proofs.

Arguments or Proofs of the Existence of God

Nevertheless, the series of arguments or proofs of God developed by many thinkers through the ages does have great practical value in showing that faith in God is in harmony with reason. No one of these arguments taken alone can be regarded as conclusive proof, but together they so substantiate our intuitive conviction of God's existence as to furnish a basis which in itself is sufficient to bind the moral actions of man. The first of this series is the cosmological proof, or the argument from cause to effect. The world and what is in it, including man, had to have a cause or origin. It could not have come into being of itself. As we ourselves are intelligent creatures, its first cause must have been an intelligent Being. The teleological proof, or the argument from design, requires belief in One whose plans give purpose and goal to the world. The existence of a thing, especially of anything so complex as man and the world in which he lives, is evidence of the existence of an originating and superintending intelligence and will functioning in the making of that thing for a purpose. The ontological proof is based on the fact that man has an idea of an infinite and perfect Being; if this Being did not exist, man could have no thought of Him. The moral proof holds that since man has a moral nature and a conscience, there must be a moral Being and Lawgiver. The physico-theological proof, or the argument from congruity, requires belief in God as the Builder of all, for otherwise there would not be the order in the natural world and in our mental and moral nature that is manifest. The psychological proof requires belief in God as the only Being who can give us happy emotions, else the soul would find no rest in God.

Thus, while the Bible makes no attempt to prove the existence of God, the world without us and the world within us bear testimony that He is. The Bible does assume and declare that this great truth is known in the depth of man's being, and that God has left none without witness to Himself. "For the invisible things of him from the creation of the world are clearly seen, being understood by the things that are made, even his eternal power and godhead" (Rom. 1:20). So men are without excuse, "because that which may be known of God is manifest in them," for within themselves, "God hath shewed it unto them" (Rom. 1:19).

The Claim of God on Man

God created us, body, soul, and spirit; therefore He has an absolute claim on us. As His creatures, with no existence in our own right, we ought to be and to do what He wishes us to be and to do. We are not our own; we possess nothing absolutely, not even our own bodies. Anything we are, we are because of Him; anything we have, we hold in trust for Him who created us and all things. We are therefore obligated to use ourselves and anything we call our own only as He intends that they should be used. In so doing, we fulfill the natural moral law of our being and the great eternal law from which it derives.

God, who is altogether perfect and wholly good, created a good earth and a man in His own image. But upon this earth and into the nature of the man, whom He had created to reveal His glory, evil came. We do not understand how this was possible nor why God permitted it. The Bible as a record of salvation, which shows to man by means of prophecy and history the way to redemption, gives nothing more than a few hints as to the origin of evil. That Satan exists as the "prince of this world" and "prince over the powers of the air" is confirmed by our Lord and Paul. It seems that, in the eternity before the creation of the earth and man, a kingdom of evil, opposed to the universal kingdom of God, had its origin in the fall of Satan. The Bible says nothing directly about this fall but from what is said by way of allusion it is inferred that, as a prince in heaven, he rebelled against God and was cast out of heaven because he sought to make himself equal to the Almighty in power (Isa. 14:12-15; Ezek. 28:12-15, 17).

At any rate, there is a personal devil as is indicated in numerous passages of the New Testament, recording the words of both Jesus and His apostles. This devil, Satan, has great intelligence and much power, even if he is a fallen spirit. Though we are not given the details, it seems that this one was arrayed against God and the working of righteousness before man ever came on the scene. So evil existed in another creature prior to the time of man; it did not originate primarily in man. He was tempted by a crafty, hostile power who was working to destroy the plan of God. Back of the time of man and his sojourn in Paradise is the great revolt of Satan and a mighty conflict between Satan and God.

The Purpose of God for Man

Man was put in Paradise for a purpose. The purpose of God in creating him was to make him, in a measure, a ruler like Himself. From Paradise as a center, man was to rule over the earth and everything in it, to subdue it, and lead the creation forward to redemption and perfection. Satan, the opponent of God, would not allow this to be done without attack. Created a spirit, a moral agent with a free will, man was obliged to undergo a moral conflict with the possibility of choosing to do evil. His nature implied a conflict, for the goal could be reached only as he conquered. Through victory in the temptation, he would have grown in moral stature and at the same time fulfilled God's purpose in ruling the earth.

The restriction placed upon man's liberty in reference to the fruit was not an arbitrary one but arose from the necessity of the case. Man was a responsible moral being created by God and, therefore, owing God service and obedience. The fact of his obligation to, and of his dependence upon, God must be suitably impressed upon him at the very outset for his own good and for bringing to pass the end which God had set. Adam and Eve were wholly free to choose their course of action. In loving-kindness, moved by the wish to give instead of to withhold, God imparted to them helpful information, constituting a warning to them to refrain from seeking to enter into the knowledge of good and evil.

It was as if God spoke to them as follows: "I am putting thee in Paradise with a nature that has in it the divine and the heavenly. Thou art my highest order of creation, so everything in the world is to be subject to thee as ruler. Having a nature inferior to thine, the world and the life in it are of a much lower order than thou art. Do thou not, therefore, my beloved children, desire to be partakers of anything in the world. Thou art to have nothing to do with it but to rule over it. In it are locked mysteries far too great for thee to comprehend. As a spirit which has kinship with Me, thou hast power to search into them. But the world stands not in thy sphere of existence; it is not heavenly and eternal as thou art. Be content, therefore, to keep thyself apart from it. Nourish thyself, as a heavenly being, with the heavenly food provided for thee. Rule over the world without desiring to partake of its nature, and fulfill for Me the purposes which I have for thee and for it. Lust not to know the good and the evil which the life of the world knows; be content to live in the innocence of non-experimental knowledge.

"Thou canst not be both a heavenly spirit and a creature of an earthly nature. Therefore, turn away thy desire and thy imagination from the fruit of the tree that can only give thee such knowledge as belongs to life on a worldly level. Nourish thyself instead on heavenly food from the tree of life. Be content with life in the spirit, for, if thou dost eat of the other fruit, it will open thy eyes so that thou canst see nothing but the earthly. Henceforth, though thou wilt be able to perceive what evil is, thou wilt only know the good as it would have been. In the moment that thou eatest of this fruit, all that is heavenly in thy spirit and thy body must die and no longer have power in thee. And thou wilt fall into a slavery of misery and torment, wretchedness and distress, such as will cause thee to try to hide even from thine own self."

The Will of God Is the Foundation of Right

From the fact that God is our Creator, it follows that a thing is right for one reason: *it is the will of God.* This is not to say that He forces His will upon man in an arbitrary manner, merely for the sake of exacting our obedience. His will is the expression of His character, and His character is what it is because of His personality and His nature. In short, His will is but the expression of the great eternal law of His own being. For Christian ethics, the duty of obedience rests upon divine commandment in two senses: it is both commanded by God in the Bible and taught by nature; it is at once revealed eternal law and natural law.

That is, a thing is not to be regarded as right simply because we think it is, much less because it seems to be expedient. What is right and what is wrong are quite independent of what we happen to think. The rightness of any action is not to be determined on the basis of whether its consequences may bring more pleasure than pain to myself or to others. The distinction between right and wrong is not a matter of taste and opinion. It is not a matter of how we may feel about things; it is not a matter of seeing after the sight of our physical eyes nor of hearing with our bodily ears. The distinction between right and wrong is rooted in the nature and will of God. The distinction between right and wrong is the distinction between those things which help and those things which hinder man in his progress toward the goal of living—the attainment of that end for which his nature destines him. What those things are which help man to attain the true end of his nature are determined fundamentally by God, the Creator of that nature. He established the law of life. Man cannot alter it, but he can refuse to follow it.

THE PERVERSITY AND THE SINFULNESS OF MAN

Adam and Eve, in spite of God's loving appeal, chose to disobey. They knew the difference between obedience and disobedience. Yet, when Satan, whose fall had brought evil into the universe, tempted them, they yielded and brought evil into the world. They did not originate the evil; they were led into it through temptation, or inducement, from without. After they had sinned, they recognized sin as something foreign to their nature and made a distinction between themselves and the evil, for they had unreasoned feelings of shame and fear that prompted them to cover their nakedness and to hide from God.

The Effect of Sin in Man's Nature

The appeal Satan used was, "Ye shall be as gods, knowing good and evil." Desiring to be wise, seeking to have knowledge such as God has, man chose, in the face of command and of warning as to outcome, to assert himself and to try to get wisdom. In the instant he disobeyed, he underwent a radical change of nature. The heavenly in his spirit and his body was extinguished in him. That divine element which made him superior to the world and safe from being harmed by it departed from him, and he became a being subject to all the outrageous flings of an earthly existence — evil and sin, blindness and self-deception, bondage and corruption, endless fears and conflicting desires, suffering and death. The knowledge of good and evil became his in distorted form: he knows only too well what evil is, but he knows good only as it would have been had he obeyed God. The result is a life of unsatisfied longing for the return of a glory that is departed.

There can be no government without law. Law is worthless without penalty. Penalty amounts to nothing unless it is enforced. The command of the law under which Adam and Eve were to live was obedience to God in refraining from eating of the forbidden fruit. The penalty of the breaking of the law was death. So death — spiritual, eternal, and physical — was theirs. At the moment they rebelled, they became victims of spiritual death, or eternal separation from God. At the same time, they became subject to physical death.

Separated from God, they lost the image of God, in which they had been created. That is, they lost a certain aspect of that image; they could not lose it in its totality. The Bible teaches that in man as created there was a resemblance to God subject to loss and a resemblance that is never lost. The image lost by Adam and Eve was the image of the spiritual and moral nature of God, possessed by beings who are holy as God is holy. There is an image of God even in fallen man (Acts 17:28; I Cor. 11:7; Jas. 3:9). As St. Bernard says, the image of God is not entirely lost. "The fine gold has become dim but it is still gold. The beauteous color has faded, but it is not altogether defaced. The will has enslaved itself to sin, but it remains a will." The bedimmed image is what makes man a moral personality with conscience, freedom of will, and capacity for moral judgment. Without this image, he would not be a man, he would not have a human nature. But, since the image of God in one aspect was lost, this human nature operates in a disturbed and abnormal manner.

It operates thus because, when Adam and Eve lost the image of God, they lost also their holy and righteous nature and became creatures of a fallen sinful nature. It is this fallen and sinful nature that has been inherited by every human being born of them. They could transmit to offspring only the nature they possessed. The fall of man was universal (Rom. 5:12-21; I Cor. 15:21,22). The disobedience of Adam and Eve wrought the moral ruin of the human race. They became sinners by sinfully disobeying; all other men sin because they are sinners, because they have a sinful nature. "There is none righteous, no, not one: There is none that understandeth, there is none that seeketh after God. They are all gone out of the way, they are together become unprofitable: there is none that doeth good, no, not one" (Rom. 3:10-12).

Man Not Entirely Lost to the Appeal of the Good

Yet man has perpetual yearning after the good of a lost paradise. That image of God which he has not lost causes his nature to operate with a view to completing itself — for the purpose of achieving the end for which he was created. There is a sense in which reason, apart from any special revelation from God, gives him perception of what that end is. At least in general, he knows how he should live to fulfill his nature. For example, there is common understanding of what is meant by the idea of a good life or a noble life. Everybody believes that normal people think truthfulness is right and lying is wrong. It is deemed reasonable to think that the intellect should be in control of the emotions, not that they should be left to run wild. It is generally agreed that the body should obey the mind, not the mind the body. Since the beginning of time, temperance and self-control have been regarded as virtues.

Likewise it has always been generally acknowledged that in human nature are higher principles and lower principles, and that the former should not be sacrificed to the latter. There has always been general recognition that justice, courage, prudence, temperance, and due consideration of one's fellows are the chief virtues. And it has always been recognized that the man in whose life these have ascendance is really a man, that he is fulfilling his true nature. On the other hand, it has been felt that the oppressor, the coward, the fool, the libertine, and the selfish person is hurting himself, that he is not living a full life, that he is less a man for being what he is and doing as he does. The sum of all this is that in man exists a natural moral law which he realizes is binding on his nature in a twofold sense: he has the obligation to obey it; when he does not obey it, he violates his nature and thereby fails to attain his end.

Reason, Unaided by Revelation, Not Sufficient to Bring Man in Line with God's Purpose

However, though man does, through reason unaided by revelation, have some perception of what he should strive for as the good, this moral law, present in man by virtue of his being a creation of God, does not suffice to bring man to the goal of life. In the first place, though this law exists, man's knowledge of it is incomplete and distorted. Human reason, clouded and weakened by unredeemed sin, functions in a most perverted manner. Ever since he fell, man has been prone to take evil for good and good for evil. It is impossible to set a limit to the power of man to deceive himself and to his ability to substitute rationalization for reason, to persuade himself that injustice is justice, that unchastity is an adventure, that desire is the voice of God, that the expedient is the right, that evil is good. Knowledge of this natural moral law in its more delicate implications and applications is dependent on a fineness of moral sensitivity which is often conspicuous by its absence. Passion, pride, self-interest, reputation, custom, ambition, envy, covetousness, and many tendencies of sinful fallen nature blind men to truths which should be self-evident.

Moreover, in the second place, man, with his sinful nature, is without power to follow fully and perfectly the good he knows and acknowledges. No words could express better the helplessness of fallen human nature in relation to the natural moral law — the expression in man of the eternal law of God — than do these words of the apostle Paul: "For we know that the law is spiritual: but I am carnal, sold under sin. For that which I do I allow not: for what I would, that do I not; but what I hate, that do I. If then I do that which I would not, I consent unto the law that it is good. Now then it is no more I that do it, but sin that dwelleth in me. For I know that in me (that is, in my flesh,) dwelleth no good thing: for to will is present with me; but how to perform that which is good I find not. For the good that I would I do not: but the evil which I would not, that I do. Now if I do that I would not, it is no more I that do it, but sin that dwelleth in me. I find then a law, that, when I would do good, evil is present with me. For I delight in the law of God after the inward man: But I see another law in my members, warring against the law of my mind, and bringing me into captivity to the law of sin which is in my members" (Rom. 7:14-23).

The Barrier of Sin

With Cardinal Newman, we all know that the human race "is out of joint with the purposes of its Creator." More than that, as individuals, each of us has "known sin." Wholly apart from particular evil deeds of which we are guilty, we have feelings of dissatisfaction with ourselves, the awareness of a lack within ourselves. Even when we feel free of *sins,* we are not able to get away from the consciousness of *sin.* It is of no use to substitute words like maladjustment, illness, complex, compulsion, frustration, and mental disorder for the word "sin" to denote what is wrong with man. Sin is not a mere defect. It is a false position; it is love of self in opposition to God. Its root is evil in the heart; it is a condition of heart, out of which issue all the deeds of the life. It is something for which the individual has personal responsibility. It implies that right relationship with God is the solution of man's moral problem.

Sin, then, is not a matter of doing, or not doing, but a fundamental self-centeredness which alienates man from God. Acts of sin are the result of the sinful condition of the nature of man. The remedy is redemption, regeneration of the heart, through Christ. Regardless of how "good" one's behavior is, the problem of sin in the heart remains. However highly our actions are approved by ourselves and others, sin is ever present with us. Our sinfulness is something for which we are responsible, yet it is something inseparable from our being. The choice of our first parents to get for themselves knowledge of good and evil enslaved us to a constant misuse of our freedom in the lifelong search for moral good which the world they lusted after can never furnish. We are all born in sin in the sense that we are perpetually inclined to put self instead of God on the throne. Our corrupt nature continually predisposes us to displace God in our being, to disapprove "of fully recognizing God any longer" (Rom. 1:28).

THE GRACE OF GOD THROUGH CHRIST

In wonderful grace which is beyond the power of finite mind to comprehend, God did not set man aside when he, through disobedience and sin, failed his test. This defection on the part of His created spirits did not thwart the final purpose of God. Though man is a sinner, though he grievously offended, God's love for man persists. Even as he stands before the seat of judgment for his sin, where God pronounces upon him the penalty required by eternal law, He makes the first promise of the gospel of redeeming love, a promise in which is contained the entire plan and history of salvation (Gen. 3:15). Had man not fallen, the need for redemption would not have arisen. Man would have gone along his way in a course of upward development attended by ever increasing blessing. But with the entrance of sin into man's nature, it became necessary for God to develop His final purpose in ways different from those He would otherwise have used. The presence of sin and evil, which man is powerless to overcome, necessitates a new creation through the power of God.

God Must Deal with Man as a Creature Blinded by Sin

To consummate the plan of salvation, God must deal with man as a creature who had denied His sovereignty, thrust God from the throne of his heart, and made self the ruler of his being. Man's own self is the center of his life. He loves this self above all else. He looks to it for his happiness; he thinks it is good; he exalts it and worships it. All his thoughts revolve around it. Along with this self is ranged the world which man chose in preference to God. Since self and the world cannot fill the void in his being left there by the departure of God, his soul is filled with a perpetual hunger causing his life to be nothing but "an extremity of want continually desiring, and an extremity of desire continually wanting." This insatiable hunger for self-assertion and the world, for temporal possessions and sinful pleasure, is the basis of restless, opposed passions which torment the life of fallen man.

Yet, blinded by sin, man is not aware of his deplorable state (Job 42:3; Prov. 21:2; John 9:39-41; Eph. 4:18; Rev. 3:17). So long as he sees good within himself and makes self his god, he will never look to his Creator for redemption. Man must learn through experience his utter helplessness. Accordingly, God's plan of salvation, worked out progressively in time covering thousands of years, is designed to give man opportunity to learn that his way is not in himself. The educative purpose is that, trying his strength in all directions, man may come finally to the twofold realization, through repeated failure, of his own insufficiency and of the sufficiency of God. Again and again, man is tested in respect to obedience to some specific revelation of the will of God. Because he persists in continual rebellion against God, each stage of testing ends with a judgment of God upon him for disobedience.

Created in innocency, given a simple test, and warned of the consequences of disobeying, man deliberately disobeyed. The judgment was expulsion from the Garden of Eden (Gen. 3:24). Through the knowledge of good and evil he obtained by the fall, man's conscience awoke. So, he was made responsible for doing all known good and abstaining from doing all known evil. The result is stated in Genesis 6:5 — "every imagination of the thoughts of his heart was only evil continually." God sent upon man the judgment of the flood. Then He put him under the government of man by man. He made man responsible to govern the world for Him. Upon his failure to do so, there came the judgment of the confusion of tongues and the setting aside of the nations (Gen. 11:9). Next, a people chosen by God as His own was tested as to faith in, and willingness to act upon, the promises of God. The end was unbelief when Israel chose at Mt. Sinai to accept the law (Ex. 19:8). After Sinai, Israel was tested by law but the history of the nation is one long record of violation of law. This testing ended in the judgment of the captivities and the dispersion of Israel. Then God put man under grace (John 1:17), testing him as to whether he would accept or reject Christ. The result is that man rejects his Saviour. The tribulation under Antichrist is the judgment. Finally, there is the kingdom of glory, a kingdom in which God will appear triumphantly (Eph. 1:10); Rev. 11:15). The judgment upon those who will not accept His rule is destruction and fiery ruin (Matt. 25:34; Heb. 4:3; Rev. 13:8; 20:9).

God Respects Man's Personality and Freedom in Carrying Out His Eternal Purpose in Christ

"Known unto God are all His works from the beginning of the world" (Acts 15:8) — rather, as the original Greek signifies, "from the beginning of the ages," or from all eternity. Through the ages, God has been revealing to man His plan, as man has been able to receive the revelation. Certainly God had power to prevent man's fall and all his succeeding failures, for He has all power in heaven and in earth. But He also knows all things. It was known to Him that it was best, on the whole, not to violate man's nature by interfering with his freedom. He knew that "not as the offense, so also is the free gift," that the evil resulting from breaking the eternal law was not as the good man would derive from His unmerited favor and the gift imparted by grace through Christ. He saw that to permit the fall of the first man was by far the best for mankind in general; that much more good than evil would come to the posterity of Adam by his fall; that if sin abounded thereby over all the earth, yet grace would overflow to all men, reaching to every individual of the human race, dependent upon his choice.

All the dealings of God with mankind are designed to further His purpose in creation. This purpose is the unfolding, setting forth, and manifesting of the glory of God. All is from Him; He is the beginning. All is through Him; He is the perpetual re-creator and sustainer of everything. All is unto Him; He is the ultimate objective, the last as He is the first. He magnifies Himself by so ordering His work as to cause it to lead to Him and to have its end in Him (Num. 14:21; Ps. 102:16; Isa. 42:8; 43:7; 48:11; 60:2; Ezek. 39:21; Rom. 11:36; Eph. 1:6; Phil. 2:11; Col. 1:16; I Pet. 4:13).

God is the one absolute Spirit but He is also the Person of the highest, most perfect life. Not only does He have the natural attributes of omnipotence, omniscience, omnipresence, eternity and immutability, but He has also the moral attributes of holiness, righteousness and justice, mercy and longsuffering, and love. The manifestation of His glory is, therefore, a twofold one — a manifestation, showing forth His natural attributes and another, manifesting His moral qualities. The former are displayed in the material realm, that is, in the mineral, vegetable, and animal kingdoms. But the moral attributes, the qualities of the personality of God, can find expression only in connection with morally free personalities, that is, in a spiritual kingdom. Only in a spiritual being, a person with moral qualities, can God, the supreme Person, show His glory.

"But the essence of such spiritual life, and the essence of all true morality in general, is not only an outward, objective carrying out of law and a merely legal freedom from sin and guilt, *but a personal, organic* participation in the life of the Deity itself. For God, as the supreme lawgiver, has appointed the moral ordering of the world according to His nature, and He is *Love,* the most perfect love (I John 4:16). Therefore the moral appointment of free creatures must also be an appointment to *love,* and the supreme final purpose of world creation must consist in the self-unfolding and self-displaying of God as the Perfect, Holy, and Loving One, in the establishment of a fellowship of life and love between the Creator and the creature" (Erich Sauer: *The Dawn of World Redemption,* p. 24).

God Preparing the Soul of Man to Realize His Eternal Purpose in Christ

Everything done by God with mankind since the fall of Adam, or even from before the foundation of the world, is for one purpose: to prepare the soul of man for this fellowship with Himself. Through testings, through human failure oft repeated, through judgments, He ever seeks to draw man back to Himself, to wean him away from a life centered in self — a fleshly life of self-love, self-esteem, and self-seeking that delights in the perishing satisfactions of this world — a life that has self instead of God for its object of love and devotion. After all possibilities are exhausted, after man has come to recognize his complete moral and spiritual bankruptcy, then will God's plan of salvation through Christ be seen as the only possible plan. And finally, "according to his promise," there will appear "new heavens and a new earth, wherein dwelleth righteousness" (II Pet. 3:13).

God has never left Himself without a people. Whenever He was obliged to bring judgment upon men for their life and doings, there has always been left in the world a small remnant. God has always had men such as Enoch, Noah, Abraham,

Joseph, Job, Moses, David, Daniel, and the prophets, who had Him for their King and who were essentially loyal to Him even though they did not obey His eternal law implicitly. Though unnoticed and even despised and persecuted by the world, it is the few from the many who are the salt of the earth. It is through them that God advances His kingdom. In carrying forward His purpose, God uses the insignificant and the unnoticed to the end that self may be brought to nought. He "hath chosen the foolish things of the world to confound the wise; and God hath chosen the weak things of the world to confound the things which are mighty; And base things of the world, and things which are despised, hath God chosen, yea, and things which are not, to bring to nought things which are: That no flesh should glory in his presence" (I Cor. 1:27-29).

So the history of man is a constant succession of repeated beginnings under grace ending in just as constant failure of the human element. Withal, the revelation is carried forward progressively because each time God begins anew, He starts in advance of the previous level of beginning. (Isa. 65:17; Hos. 2:23; Eph. 1:10). "But this is all God's work, not 'human progress,' no ascent of the creature out of the depths into the heights, but a condescension of the Creator out of the heights into the depths; no development of human powers until the unfolding of the highest, ideal humanity, but a leading on to divine, eternal goals through mighty acts of divine intervention in love and power. Thus then, through divine acting from above to beneath, will the earthly being be led from beneath to above, until finally God's glory is manifested in things created and everything earthly is transfigured in the heavenly" (Erich Sauer: *The Dawn of World Redemption,* p. 54).

Through opportunity to follow conscience, fallen man learned what sin had wrought in his nature — that estrangement from God so affected this nature as to make his imagination, his purposes, and his desires "only evil continually." Under government of man by man, he found out how vain is the attempt to conquer evil in his own strength. With Abraham began a completely new age, the actual revelation of redemption through faith. Abraham was the first recipient of the Old

Testament revelation which led directly to Christ and which is the root of the olive tree of the kingdom of God (Rom. 11: 16-24). The history of the faith of Abraham, Isaac, Jacob, and Joseph, who as a type of Christ suffered and triumphed in humiliation and exaltation, points forward to Christ Himself as the One who enables man through faith to triumph over evil, sin, and self.

"In thee shall all families of the earth be blessed," was the promise to Abraham (Gen. 12:3). God chose Abraham, the "father of all them that believe" (Rom. 4:11), to be the progenitor of a covenant people, Israel. This people God set apart for a twofold task: to be the recipient of His revelation and the source whence would come the Redeemer of the world; to be the channel through which all the peoples of the world should receive the revelation of salvation.

In thus limiting revelation to one nation, God did not depart from peoples other than Israel. He has never left Himself without witness to any people. He speaks to all men in the works of creation through which both He Himself and His moral requirements may be known of men (Rom. 1:19-21). He speaks to all men through conscience which either accuses or defends them (Rom. 2:14, 15). Then there is the language of wisdom even in those lands that have not been reached with the light of His special revelation. In the nature of man remain general moral elements from the moral qualities with which he was created. "There is a spirit in man: and the inspiration of the Almighty giveth them understanding" (Job 32:8). From Him comes to the human mind knowledge in general, as in the case of Socrates, Plato, Confucius, Lao Tze, Zarathustra, and many other poets and thinkers of the nations. Also, man has the language of human government. With no ruling authority any society would soon be a chaos of evil and ruin. God instituted an order, and rulers are His instruments (Rom. 13:4). Finally, men have history. God speaks through human history which He guides. His setting aside of the Gentile nations does not at all signify that He has abandoned them. He is the God "of the Gentiles also" (Rom. 3:29). God displays His glory in a particular history of revelation to the end that mankind in general may eventually see that glory manifested in His eternal salvation for all men.

The Functioning of the Law in Furthering God's Purpose in Christ

The history of this salvation is carried forward to Christ through the time man was under the Law. The Bible teaches that the Mosaic Law "was our schoolmaster to bring us unto Christ, that we might be justified by faith" (Gal. 3:24). "Now to Abraham and his seed were the promises made. He saith not, And to seeds, as of many; but as of one, And to thy seed, which is Christ" (Gal. 3:16). Once Christ came, "we are no longer under a schoolmaster," or one who disciplines and corrects (Gal. 3:25).

Right standing with God is a matter of faith. "No man is justified by the law in the sight of God" (Gal. 3:11). Then, why was the law given after the promise had been made to Abraham? It was added for the sake of transgressions, that is, to give to sin the character of transgression, in order that sin might be made manifest as transgression. Men had sinned before the time of Moses, but their sins were not charged to their account in the absence of law (Rom. 5:13). Also, the law increased transgressions in the sense that it provoked men to do that which it prohibited, thus demonstrating the depravity of human nature (Rom. 7:8, 11-13). A second reason for the giving of the law was that it might serve temporarily "till the seed should come to whom the promise was made" (Gal. 3:19). That is, the law was merely preparatory to Christ, having its goal in Him and disappearing when He came. "For Christ is the end of the law for righteousness to every one that believeth" (Rom. 10:4).

The law was given, in the third place, for instruction. It sets forth the standards of right conduct. By its definite rules, it shatters the complacency arising from practice founded upon human self-deception and man's cleverness in convincing himself that wrong is right, that desire is the voice of duty. It instructs as to the nature of sin, giving him knowledge that sin is missing the mark, disobedience, transgression, rebellion. Through bringing man to the realization of the guiltiness of sin, it shows also the guilt of the sinner. The conduct which

God demands of men, He demands out of His holiness and righteousness. The holiness of God is the basic thought of the law. Over against the majesty of the law, the weakness, the sinfulness, and the helplessness of man appear in bold relief. When man realizes that sin dwelling in him is determining his actions, his pride and self-sufficiency are shattered. Thus the manifestation of the holiness of God and His law leads man to perceive that he is lost and impels him to acknowledge his need of grace, pointing him to Christ the Saviour.

The Mosaic Law is one law, an indivisible unit binding on man in respect to every single one of its provisions (Deut. 27: 26; Matt. 5:18; Gal. 3:10; Jas. 2:10). It was given to Israel in three divisions: the commandments or moral rules, setting forth the righteous will of God (Ex. 20:1-26); the "judgments" or the rules governing social life (Ex. 21:1-23:33); and the "ordinances" or the rules regulating worship (Ex. 25:1-31:18). Within the whole law, the commandments and the ordinances constitute one complete, inseparable whole. The breaking of any commandment of the moral law necessitated the bringing by the sinner of an offering, as specified in the ordinances, in order to remove the guilt and condemnation incurred.

The appointments of worship set forth symbolically the Old Testament fellowship with God and typically the New Testament fellowship with God through Christ. The moral rules showed the gulf that existed between a holy God and the sinner. The chief purpose of the ceremonial service of God was fellowship. The offering of sacrifices meant a certain forgiveness of sins (Lev. 4:20; 5:10) and, as a consequence, restoration of fellowship with God whose law the sinner had broken. The idea of sacrifice is not only propitiation but also reconciliation, not mere meeting of legal demands but a return to fellowship.

However, the Mosaic sacrifices made this reconciliation with God possible only through a "covering up" of sin. These sacrifices could not take away sins, "for it is not possible that the blood of bulls and of goats should take away sins" (Heb. 10:4, 11). Nothing but the blood of Christ could do this (Heb. 9:14, 26). So there was not an absolute forgiveness of sins and an unlimited fellowship under the law; it was only an outward purifying and a limited fellowship, pointing forward to the true forgiveness and unlimited fellowship with God through Christ. Therefore, before the sacrifice of Christ on the Cross, men were under the judgment of moral laws, which gave them knowledge of sin and guilt before God and under ceremonial laws, the observance of which set them free, yet continually reminded them of sin and guilt (Heb. 10:3).

The Two Parts of the Law Constitute an
Inseparable Whole Pointing to Christ

However, as has already been stated, these belong together as two parts of an inseparable whole. Only one law was given Israel and that law had only one goal, Christ. When He came into the world, He said, "Sacrifice and offering thou wouldest not, but a body hast thou prepared me: In burnt offerings and sacrifices for sin thou hast no pleasure. Then said I, Lo, I come (in the volume of the book it is written of me,) to do thy will, O God" (Heb. 10:5-7). Christ fulfilled the moral laws by bringing to pass "grace," the unmerited favor of God in the complete forgiveness of sins; He fulfilled the ceremonial laws by bringing to pass "truth," the substance instead of the shadow (John 1:17). Now those who come to worship are made perfect for complete and unlimited fellowship with God because in Christ is the reality itself of those blessings of which "the law, having a shadow of good things to come, and not the very image of the things, can never with those sacrifices which they offered year by year continually make the comers thereunto perfect" (Heb. 10:1).

"In the Old the New is concealed, in the New the Old is revealed," said Augustine. Though each is distinct, the Old and the New Testaments are one in the revelation by God of one single divine work of reconciliation and restoration to fellowship with Himself of man who rebelled against the great eternal law. Christ is the fulfillment of the first promise He made to man and the completion of that which He promised in His covenant with Abraham. The whole of the Old Testament record in history and in prophecy is a record of the work of God in Christ reconciling the world unto Himself. Especially in the Mosaic sacrifices is the work of Christ set forth; in their original form they are symbols of Him; in their fulfillment they are types of Him (Heb. 8:5; 9:23-25). These sacrifices show forth the work of Christ from birth to the Cross and beyond the Cross into heaven itself where He exercises His eternal priesthood.

Christ not merely fulfills but goes far beyond all that is included in the law. Under the economy of the law there were many sacrifices; millions and millions of them were made from Moses to Christ, not one of which could do more than give the conscience temporary relief. Christ by one sacrifice "hath perfected forever them that are sanctified" (Heb. 10:14).

The Function of Promise or Prophecy in Furthering God's Purpose in Christ

The law is one of two chief aspects of revelation in the Old Testament; the second aspect is promise or prophecy. Prophets are those who bring to men the message of God. They are interpreters, expounders, tellers forth, though not always in advance. "For the prophecy came not in old time by the will of man: but holy men of God spake as they were moved by the Holy Ghost" (II Pet. 1:21). In the Old Testament, according to Dr. Evans, appear more than thirty-eight hundred times expressions embodying the meaning of the words, "Thus saith the Lord." The history of prophecy had its earliest beginnings in the time of Adam and reaches into the present age of the Church. The origin, the content, and the goal of all prophecy is Christ. In the prophets, Christ as "Logos" spoke concerning Himself as the Messiah who is "the crown and shining star of all prophecy." As Luther says, the prophets spoke and acted "in the name of the coming Christ."

A word that is very prominent in the messages of the prophets in general is "judgment." They declare divine judgment upon past and present and future, upon evil in low places and high places, upon sin in the lives of evil men and good men, upon individuals and nations, upon God's chosen people and the nations of the world. They denounce in scathing terms sins and moral evils, such as adultery, murder, rebellion, violence, avarice, usury, oppression, bribery, pride, haughtiness, deceit, hatred, idolatry, insincerity, and self-righteousness.

For the prophets, doing the will of God is the rule for the life of man. This is a matter of religious devotion which is as moral as it is religious. They unsparingly scourge the sins of formalism and hypocritical observance which turn attention from real moral issues. The will of God applies quite as much to the doing of moral tasks as it does to the practices of worship. Ritualism, tradition, and custom are not substitutes for right conduct. One of the false conceptions most frequently denounced by the prophets is the idea that God stresses correctness in ceremonial rites more than He does moral conduct (Isa. 1:11-20; Jer. 2:1-21; Ezek. 18:1-9; Amos 5:1-27; Mic. 6:1-8). Thus in the messages of the prophets, as in all of the Old Testament, God stands out as a holy and righteous Being to whom His people are linked not by a bond of what is merely legally proper or ritually correct but by one of what is spiritually and ethically vital.

The prophets foretell the future even when not pronouncing judgment for wrongdoing. Thus they tell beforehand of the conversion of Israel and of the nations of the world. Conversion will be effected through the appearing of the Messiah in whom the brightness of the glory of God will finally show forth undimmed by the self-seeking of the creature. "To him (Jesus Christ) give all the prophets witness" (Acts 10:43). Christ is the center of the history of salvation; the Old Testament history of revelation is a "history of Christ" before He became man. The person of Christ in His humanity as to family, place, and time of birth are foretold in Old Testament prophecy. The work of Christ, in numerous details having to do with His first coming and in respect to the glory of His second coming and His subsequent reign, is portrayed in a most wonderful manner.

God, the Creator of the world, is "the King, eternal, immortal, invisible, the only wise God" (I Tim. 1:17). "For of him, and through him, and to him, are all things" (Rom. 11:36). He issued the decree of creation and redemption "according to the eternal purpose which he purposed in Christ Jesus our Lord." The end returns to Him because in the beginning lies the end in harmony with His purpose "who in everything carries out the plan of His will." This plan is that "at the coming of the climax of the ages, everything in heaven and on earth should be unified through Christ." In infinite wisdom He made known to Israel the "secret of His will" having foreordained them in accordance with His plan and purpose. Then He carried to the Gentiles the good news that means salvation, and those who received it, He "sealed with that holy spirit of promise, which is the earnest of our inheritance until the redemption of the purchased possession, unto the praise of his glory" (Eph. 1:9-14).

Holy Fellowship the Final Goal

His final goal God did not reveal in its fulness all at once but made it known gradually in a history of salvation that developed by stages. It matters little whether these stages be called dispensations, periods, epochs, or ages. What is important is the perception of the stages and insight into the spiritual and moral lessons, in particular and in general, which God wants to teach. Each stage or period is marked by definite special principles. Each has a special duty and a special lesson to be learned. With the ending of a period there is an annulment of some regulations until then valid. Some principles are general in nature, therefore applicable in all periods. It was God's design that man learn well these four general lessons: to conceive of God as He is, a Person who is holy and righteous and sovereign, the supreme Being whose purpose must ultimately be achieved; to accept his responsibility as a free moral agent with obligation to render implicit obedience to God, his sovereign; to come to the realization of his guilt when he fails and to see his failure as self-will and essentially a state of rebellion; to see Christ and the redemption effected by Christ as the way back to fellowship with God.

The God who is sovereign is also a Person. It is ours to do as He says. But even in the Old Testament, there are already indications of a relationship that is inwardly personal instead of externally legal. God speaks to righteous Abraham as a friend, not as a demanding ruler. He says to the Israelites, "I will walk among you, and will be your God, and ye shall be my people" (Lev. 26:12). Even after this people had gone far astray, His yearning desire was that He might live with them and walk with them (Ezek. 37:27). Various men of Old Testament times had intimate communion with their Creator. This sense of holy fellowship runs through the entire body of the Scriptures, and finally provision is made for its unending enjoyment. Dimly was it recognized by a few Old Testament men that the Spirit of God dwelt in them and worked a gracious influence in their lives. In the New Testament, this closer fellowship and communion with God is fully revealed in the Person of our Lord Jesus Christ, and each of God's children becomes a temple of the Holy Spirit, a true Person who lives and dwells in him and makes him a partaker of the divine nature.

Thus these things "happened unto them for ensamples: and they are written for our admonition, upon whom the ends of the world are come" (I Cor. 10:11). The Old Testament is an essential part of God's record of salvation. All of it was written *for* us, though not all of it was written *to* us. It is the same with the Old Testament as it is with certain portions of the Gospels: there are statements which do not apply immediately to us, such as, for example, the instructions given His disciples by Jesus for making ready the Passover or His directions to them for the seating of the five thousand. On the other hand, there are indirect moral teachings of the Old Testament which are *always* applicable to us. "All scripture is given by inspiration of God, and is profitable for doctrine, for reproof, for correction, for instruction in righteousness: That the man of God may be perfect, throughly furnished unto all good works" (II Tim. 3:16, 17).

QUESTIONS

1. If the Bible is not a treatise on ethics, why does it have so much to say on the subject of human conduct?
2. Explain: "In Christ will mankind attain its final and blessed goal."
3. How does faith determine conduct? Illustrate.
4. Do you see progressively Christian conduct in the Bible's record of God's dealings with men?
5. Why does the Bible not give us proofs of the existence of God?

6. Why are we responsible to God?
7. Need we know the origin of evil? Would we be any better off if we did?
8. Do you agree that the purpose of God in creating man was to make him, in a measure, a ruler like Himself? If you do not, why not?
9. Why was a restriction placed on man's liberty in the beginning?
10. What is the root of the distinction between right and wrong?
11. Is this a protection to man or not?
12. List as best you can the changes that took place in the nature of man as a consequence of his having sinned.
13. Do you think that a human being can fall so low as to be lost to all desire to do any good?
14. Are there universal principles of right and wrong living?
15. Why can not man through reason perceive and fulfill God's purpose?
16. Is every person aware of the presence of sin in his being?
17. What, in essence, is sin?
18. Criticize the outline of the stages of God's testing of man.
19. What would God do to man if He violated his freedom to will and to do?
20. Can you, or can you not, accept the theory that more good than evil comes ultimately to man through Adam's sin?
21. What is the great eternal purpose of God in Christ?
22. Has man ever been a success in relation to God and His purpose? Explain.
23. Does God speak to people other than His chosen people? How?
24. In what sense, or senses, is the law our schoolmaster to bring us to Christ?
25. How does each of the three divisions of the law, respectively, point to Christ?
26. Explain: the scarlet thread of Christ's atonement runs through the entire Bible.
27. Comment on prophecy as an aspect of the revelation in the Old Testament, of the purpose of God.
28. Why did not God reveal in its fullness, at the very beginning, His eternal purpose for man?
29. Are Christians bound by the teachings of the Old Testament, that is, need they give heed to them or are they free to ignore them?

CHAPTER III

The Bible and Ethics (Continued)

WHEN THE FULNESS OF THE TIME was come, God sent forth his Son, made of a woman, made under the law, to redeem them that were under the law, that we might receive the adoption of sons" (Gal. 4:4, 5). All pre-Christian history is a guiding of mankind to the Redeemer of the world. The will of God governed the history of the nations and brought about "the fulness of the time," a condition of the world suitable for the cradling of Christianity. God prepared His chosen people, Israel, beforehand through special revelation; He prepared the peoples of the world through the happenings of world events. In conceptions of government, in cultural unity and cultural attitudes, in opportunities for communication, in the condition of peace that existed in the world, in the moral degeneration that prevailed, in the yearnings of men that caused them to turn from the outward to the inward and from the present to thoughts of the hereafter, in the expectation of the peoples that deliverance would come — in all these respects the time was proper when God sent His Son.

This preparation for Christianity involved three ancient civilizations, the Greek, the Roman, and the Jewish. Each made its contribution to the fullness of the time. The content of the thought of man, including his ethical thought, has been much influenced by concepts which came from the philosophical systems of these three peoples. The Greeks, concerned mainly with man, stressed the ideal of perfection. The Romans, whose chief interest was law and government, emphasized obedience to law. The Jews, for whom ethics consisted in doing the will of God, a holy and righteous Being, laid stress on the duty of man to be righteous.

Though the philosophies of Greece and Rome have contrib-

uted to Christianity, it is Jewish thought that has exerted most
influence upon Christian ethics. The New Testament teachings of Christ and His first followers took as their point of
departure the revelation that had been made to the Jews. As
God moved in this revelation, He brought to men increasing
awareness of Christian ideals, even if these did not find expression in their practice. The Old Testament view of God
as omnipotent, holy, and righteous prevails also in the New
Testament. However, the New Testament emphasizes more
distinctly the personality of God, stressing particularly the
characteristic of love.

The ethical teaching of the Old Testament is not opposed
to that of the New Testament. Alexander points out that the
ethics of the Old Testament, being a preparatory stage in the
revelation of God's will, did not emphasize the absolute standard of New Testament morality. Judged in the light of this
absolute standard, Old Testament morality was not perfect.
Alexander says, "It was lacking in depth. There is a tendency
to dwell upon the sufficiency of external acts rather than the
necessity of inward disposition. The motives to which the Old
Testament appeals are often mercenary. Material prosperity
plays an important part as an inducement to well-doing"
(Christianity and Ethics, pp. 50, 51). Nevertheless, there is
much in the Old Testament, especially in the Psalms and the
writings of the later prophets, by way of emphasis upon inner
motive and the spiritual ideal.

The Jews in Jesus' day, particularly the leaders among them,
had lost sight of the spiritual intent and purpose of the law.
Having wandered far from God and suffered the consequences,
the Jewish people had come into a bondage of legalism. To
appease God, they multiplied regulations, setting up alongside the law as it had been given through Moses, a set of
traditions with special emphasis on forms of worship and
ceremonies without real meaning. The corrupt leaders had a
total of precepts, combined of ritualistic and ethical elements,
which they endeavored to enforce upon the people. Having no
insight into the inner meaning of the law, they were much more

concerned with legal observances than they were with the
spiritual and moral needs of human beings.

THE WORK OF JESUS CHRIST

The Old and the New Testaments merge in the announcement of the birth of him who was to be the herald of the work
of the Redeemer of mankind (Mal. 4:5,6; Luke 1:17). This
Redeemer of whom "Elijah" was the forerunner is the Eternal
God Himself. From Genesis to Malachi, the Old Testament
points forward in promise, type, and prophecy to the Incarnation of God in Jesus Christ. The supreme and perfect revelation is a revelation of the invisible God in visible human form,
a revelation in and through a perfect Man.

God Became Man that Man, Incapable of Good, Might Have Power to Achieve the Good

"There is only one morality," states Dorner. "The original
of it is in God; the copy of it is in man." To satisfy divine
justice, outraged by broken eternal law, it was absolutely necessary that expiation be made by a person whose life has infinite
value by virtue of its being divine and infinitely good. The
holy and righteous God could not ignore the broken law, He
could not forgive men by a mere decree, and it was impossible
for any human being to pay an infinite price for the redemption
of a whole fallen race. None but the incarnate Son of God,
who is the source and foundation of the eternal law, could
perfectly and completely satisfy for man's offenses. God, a
perfect Being, must require a perfect morality, and this "demands that the divine life become human in order that the
human life may become divine."

"There is none good but one, that is, God" (Mark 10:18).
"There is none righteous, no, not one: . . . there is none that
doeth good, no, not one" (Rom. 3:10-12). Yet man was
created in the image of God and must therefore be capable of
recognizing for himself that the good which is in God is also a
true part of his own nature, and that it is possible for him and
obligatory upon him to enter into full possession of it. Even
the Old Testament lays stress upon a oneness of heart and life
with God (Gen. 5:24; 6:9; 17:1; Jer. 31:34). Jesus in His

highpriestly prayer beseeches God that all Christians may be "one; as thou, Father, art in me, and I in thee" (John 17:21). Paul writes to the Corinthians about being established, or secure, "in Christ" (II Cor. 1:21). Also Paul addresses Timothy as "a man of God," implying that all Christians are men of God. And Peter writes to Christians about their being sharers "of the divine nature" (II Pet. 1:4). All this is but a commentary on the reality of God, the only source of good, in the life of man.

All good has its origin in God; therefore anything that is good is so by virtue of God being in it as a quickening power. Even the law is not really kept through obedience rendered merely as to an external standard. Any act done under constraint of will, just to escape the penalty of disobedience to law, is not truly a good act. Single acts are truly good only when done out of reverence for the spirit of the law, that is, with appreciation of, and respect for, the good which the law as a whole represents. This means that the law taken in its full signification has to do more with what a man is than with what a man does. The law is a revelation of the essential nature of God and therefore a revelation of infinite goodness. Consequently, it contains within it the image of the ideal man, the picture of the perfect man, but it brings to man no power to achieve the good presented in this ideal. In God alone lies the power to achieve good.

God became man that this power might work in us. Forsaking the splendor of heaven, the Son became as truly human as we are. The co-equal with the Creator in absoluteness became as the creature. The eternal Logos emptied Himself of divine power and took on the limitations of a human soul. The One who is love, out of love for us, gave up all to redeem us. God became man that man might become godly — that we who are utterly powerless to achieve the least good might be made partakers of the infinitely good of His nature.

Thought is insufficient to comprehend and words are inadequate to explain just how deity and humanity are united in Christ. The Incarnation has always baffled the mind of man, and it always will. The difficulty lies in the fact that both a human nature and a divine nature, with all that pertains to each, belong to one and the same Person. Thinking in terms of analogy is helpful in considering the mystery. Each of us as a person combines in himself two or more offices or functions. For example, we are both sons or daughters and students, producers and consumers, automobile drivers and pedestrians, parents and citizens, employers or employees and householders, and so on. A given person may be both a doctor and an officer in his church. Whatever is true of a doctor is true of this person and whatever is true of a church officer is also true of him. But it is evident that what is true of doctors in general is not necessarily true of church officers. Christ combines in Himself a divine nature and a human nature, that is, Christ the divine Person is both God and man. Therefore, what is true of God is true of Him and what is true of a man is also true of Him, though it does not follow that what is true of God is true of all men.

A person is a self, a personality, a being who acts. A nature is the means by which a person acts. The person who is both a doctor and a church officer acts one time by means of the nature of a doctor and another time by means of the nature of a church officer, but every doctor is a different person and every church officer is a different person. Every person is a different person, distinct from every other person in the universe; no other exactly like him ever did or ever will exist. His acts are his own; no other person in the universe could perform them.

In the Incarnation, one Person is acting in two natures, a human nature and a divine nature. The divine personality of the divine Person is present but no human personality is present, for there is no human person. The two natures are united to each other directly no more than the natures of the doctor and the church officer are united directly. However, divine nature and human nature are united in the personality of the Person of Christ, just as the doctor and the church officer are united in one person. It is the person as doctor who diagnoses diseases, prescribes medicines, and performs operations; it is the person as church officer who sits on church boards, counsels with others about church matters, and presides at church functions. It was Christ as man who hungered, who was weary, and who wept; it was Christ as God who performed miracles, forgave sins, and sent out disciples to preach the Gospel.

Humanly speaking, a person is the product of the union of body and soul. When a human being dies, the soul departs from the body, and the person no longer exists. Whatever becomes of the soul, wherever it may be, there is no person and there will be no person until after the resurrection, in which soul and body will be reunited. In the Incarnation, the Person did not result from the union of body and soul; the Person existed from eternity. When Christ died on the Cross, body and soul were separated through what happened to the human nature, but the Eternal Person lived on and ever lives.

It was God in Person who became incarnate. It was God in Person who lived and worked in the life of Jesus the Christ. It was God in Person who grew, who was tempted, who taught, who went about doing good, who suffered, who gave up the spirit. Though nature is the root of action, the responsible agent of action is not the nature of the agent but the self, the person, who acts. Because He had the nature of God, the Son did the works of God, but it was the Son, not the nature, who did the deeds. Because He had the nature of man, the Son could suffer and die, but it was the Person, not the nature, that suffered and it was the Person who said, "Father, I now commend into thy hands my spirit."

By His Death on the Cross Christ Made Expiation for Sin, the Barrier to Goodness

The Incarnation is the basis of the efficacy of the work of Christ, which He accomplished in His death, His resurrection, and His ascension. The Incarnation was for the purpose of the work of atonement on the Cross. Christ partook of flesh and blood that He might die (Heb. 2:14). He came into the world "to give His life a ransom for many" (Matt. 20:28). He assumed a nature like our own that He might offer up His life as an expiation for the sins of men. The Incarnation presupposes the work of atonement.

The death of Christ is the greatest event in the history of salvation. Jesus was not primarily a religious teacher or an ethical example; He was these, but He was much more — the Christ, the Saviour and Redeemer of men who died that we might have opportunity to become good. His death is the most prominent theme of the Old Testament (Luke 24:26, 27, 44-46; I Pet. 1:10, 11), the fundamental theme of the Gospel (I Cor. 15:1-3), and the grand theme in heaven (Luke 9:30, 31; Rev. 5:8-12). The necessity of His death arises from a twofold fact: the holiness of God that finds expression in the eternal law and the sinfulness of man incurred through violating that law. The personal relationship — the fellowship — between the holy God and His created spirit, man, is also an ethical relationship. These relationships are disordered by sin. We are morally conscious that we are guilty and that our guilt is the result of our having violated an eternal law. As God sees sin, as the Bible depicts sin, it is guilt that demands expiation and something that brings upon man wrath, condemnation, and eternal ruin.

From God's side, the death of Christ is supreme evidence of love beyond the power of the mind of man to comprehend fully. It means that He against whom the offense had been committed paid the price of an infinite ransom to deliver us who, by offending, brought upon ourselves a condition of slavery from which we are absolutely helpless to deliver ourselves (Matt. 20:28; Rom. 7:14; I Pet. 1:18, 19). "God commendeth his love toward us, in that, while we were yet sinners, Christ died for us" (Rom. 5:8), "the just for the unjust" (I Pet. 3:18). God's love is evidenced also in His taking the initiative by offering up His Son to remove the enmity between God and man, an enmity which constituted a barrier to fellowship, an enmity existing because of our sin (Rom. 5:10; II Cor. 5:18, 19; Eph. 2:16; Col. 1:20). In the second place, the death of Christ is supreme evidence of the righteousness of God. To vindicate His righteousness, God did not spare His own beloved Son but set Him forth as a propitiation for sins done by us (Rom. 3:25; 8:32; I John 2:2). Christ died in our place, bore our sins that we need not die (Isa. 53:6; I Pet. 2:24; 3:18).

God made Christ "to be sin for us, who knew no sin; that we might be made the righteousness of God in him" (II Cor. 5:21) and have imputed to us a righteousness, or goodness, which we neither have nor can obtain of ourselves.

The death of Christ takes away the sin of the world. Not a single human being, man, woman, or child, is excluded from the blessings offered in the atonement. "So precious is the shedding of Christ's blood for the unjust, that if the whole universe of captives would believe in the Redeemer, no chain of the devil could hold them." For each individual who thus believes, the death of Christ satisfies the love and the righteousness of God. The just demands of the eternal law are fully met and his past, whatever it may be, is put in order legally. In Adam we died spiritually and morally; in Christ we are made alive spiritually and morally. The sin of Adam brought death, or separation from God and all that is good in His sight; the death of Christ effected the restoration of life. Before God, the individual in whom the death of Christ becomes efficacious through faith has right standing; that is, he stands in the sight of God as if he had never sinned (John 3:18; Rom. 3:24).

By the death of Christ the believer's past is put in order legally; by the death of Christ he becomes capable of ruling his present morally. The moral principle of a new life implanted within him in divine power produces change in character and conduct. The good he once hated and refused to practice he now loves and strives to do. The evil he once loved and did, he now hates and shuns. The good he longed after and was powerless to attain because of being a captive to sin, he now finds to be a reality in his life by virtue of the power of Christ within. To the evil he hated and yet practiced he is no longer in bondage.

The Resurrection of Christ the Proof of the
Power of God against Satan and Sin

The eternal Person who dwelt in a human body for thirty-three years could, upon the death of that body, have returned to heaven, whence He had come, without a bodily resurrection. For Him to have done so would have made incomplete the work of redemption. Without bodily resurrection, there is no basis for faith. "If Christ be not risen, then is our preaching vain, and your faith is also vain . . . . And if Christ be not raised, your faith is vain; ye are yet in your sins" (I Cor. 15:14, 17). Without bodily resurrection, Christ would not have been conqueror of man's last enemy, death. If He had not risen from the dead, He would not have demonstrated the almighty power of God and the defeat of Satan. Had Christ not risen, we would not have proof that He was God, the Son, for by the resurrection from the dead He was "declared to be the Son of God with power" (Rom. 1:4).

The bodily resurrection meant the return of the Son of God to full human nature and the eternal glorification of His humanity. It showed Him to be the "last Adam, a quickening spirit" (Rom. 5:12-21; I Cor. 15:45). The resurrection of Christ assures the believer of his acceptance with God, thus giving a basis for resting in Christ for justification (Rom. 4:25). It assures him of an ever living High Priest who constantly intercedes for him (Rom. 8:34; Heb. 7:25). And it is a pledge to him of all needed power for living as a child of God and doing the will of God (Eph. 1:19-22; Phil. 3:10).

Christ Ascended, Our Intercessor and Our Advocate, to the End that We May Live in Fellowship with God

A third aspect of the work of Christ is that in which He is engaged at present as the ascended and exalted Son of God. His work of redeeming mankind was finished once and for all time by His sufferings and death, but He has a present work to do on behalf of mankind. This has various implications for the ethical life of the Christian. His intercession was alluded to in the preceding paragraph. As our Intercessor, He prays for us and strengthens us. We are told that "it behoved him to be made like unto his brethren" in the Incarnation, "that he might be a merciful and faithful high priest in things pertaining to God. . . . For in that he himself hath suffered being tempted, he is able to succour them that are tempted" (Heb. 2:17, 18). Our living Lord knows our weaknesses and our temptations, our infirmities and our failures, our limitations and our trials. He understands that there is still need for daily forgiveness. He knows the power, the wiles, and the accusations of Satan.

He knows that in ourselves we are too weak and frail to withstand the onslaughts of evil and the inducements of the flesh, the world, and the Devil. So, as He prayed for Peter that his faith would not fail, He prays for us too.

Then He is our Advocate before the throne of God. He pleads our case when we sin. He died to deliver us, not only from the penalty of sin, but also from its power. He makes provision for us that we depart from evil. He indwells us by His Spirit to empower us against sin. He renews our minds so that we may find and follow God's will. He gives us His Word to warn us against evil and to show us the good. He intercedes for us when we are tempted to forsake the good and to enter into sin. But, if and when, in spite of all, we do sin, He acts as our advocate, pleading the eternal efficacy of His own sacrifice for the remission of sin (I John 2:1,2). Wonderful is grace which gives us in the glory a Man who is our Mediator, our High Priest, our Intercessor, and our Advocate. "We are his workmanship, created in Christ Jesus unto good works, which God hath before ordained that we should walk in them" (Eph. 2:10).

Everything we need, for deliverance from evil and for realization of good in character and in conduct, is to be found in the Person of the Lord Jesus Christ, God's own Son. He is the full and the final revelation of God. It is in Him, His life and His teaching that we have the ideal and the standard of what we should be and the picture of the kind of life God intends us to live. In His death upon the Cross, our sins are at once condemned and expiated. Through His death we can be reconciled to God even though we have shamefully trespassed against Him. From Him we can receive new life and make a new beginning. In the power of the risen Christ, it is possible for us to enter into possession of the good which is in God and which is also a true part of our nature as beings who bear His image.

The Kingdom of God

Jesus came into the world as a king (John 18:36). He did not come to establish man in peace, security, and prosperity on earth (Matt. 10:34). The purpose of His coming was to show

men the love that God has for them and to win them for the
kingdom of God. This kingdom is a spiritual order; it is the
kingly rule of God in the hearts and the lives of men. This
rule is the final goal of the history of salvation. Its object is
to put men in possession, not of the things of this world but of
the things of heaven, and to bring them to their final end,
eternal union with God. As the King, it was the entire purpose of the work of Christ to proclaim, bring about, and carry
to completion this kingly rule of God.

The Origin of the Kingdom Is in Heaven and Its Nature and Principles Are Heavenly

The kingdom of God is the real theme of the Bible. Its
origin is in heaven, and its nature and principles are heavenly.
It was from the beginning, it continues through all ages, and
it will exist through all eternity. In the different periods of
God's dealing with men, He has made known His living and
powerful kingship under various forms of manifestation. The
kingdom of God is universal, including all moral beings who
voluntarily submit to the will of God, whether they be angels
or men of past, present, or future periods (Luke 13:28,29;
Heb. 12:22,23). Ultimately, "the kingdoms of this world"
will "become the kingdoms of our Lord, and of his Christ; and
he shall reign for ever and ever (Rev. 11:15).

The Gospel of the Kingdom is the basic theme of the message of Christ (Matt. 4:23; 9:35; 24:14; Mark 1:14; Luke
4:43; 8:1). There is but one rule of God, whether the message
has to do at one time with the present and at another time with
the future of the Kingdom, whether it treats of that Kingdom
in its earthly aspects or deals with the universal kingdom of
God. It is always the same kingdom, a regime where the will
of God prevails absolutely.

Two among the chief aspects of the moral content of the
message of the Kingdom proclaimed by Jesus were severity of
judgment upon those who would not do the will of God and the
necessity for unlimited obedience on the part of those who
would be subjects of the Kingdom. Men who oppose the will
of God, whatever their position or station, however they may
be looked upon by their fellows, are to be destroyed because

there is no place in the Kingdom for any who do not love God and submit to His kingly rule (Matt. 10:15; 16:25; 24:51; 25:30,41; Mark 9:43; Luke 19:27). There is to be no half-heartedness or lukewarmness in following the King who Himself poured out all in devotion to the will of God. In compliance with that will, He forsook His glory in heaven and came into a world of sin. While in this world, He esteemed the doing of the will of God more necessary than food. Never once did He falter when it was a matter of doing His own will or the will of God. When facing the unutterable agony of the Cross and of being made sin, He prayed, "Not my will, but thine, be done." Finally, He suffered death itself out of obedience to the will of God.

The King, who thus suffered, demands of those who would follow Him absolute surrender of body, soul, and spirit. Material possessions, worldly advantage, affection for earth's dearest, even life itself, must not come between them and loyalty to God. To be loyal, they must renounce all, take up the cross, and be ready to suffer. Their devotion to God will mean exclusion from participation in much that men in general do, will bring upon them ignominy and persecution, and may lead to death. In the struggle against the forces that oppose the Kingdom, its subjects must be prepared to make supreme sacrifice of self and of all that pertains to self. Only by self-denial, by dying to live, that is, by complete yielding up of all self-seeking for the sake of Christ and His kingdom, can the will of God be done.

Only a Being Made Heavenly in His Nature by the New Birth Can Enter the Kingdom

That without which no one will ever enter the Kingdom is an inward state or condition of righteousness. "Except your righteousness shall exceed the righteousness of the scribes and Pharisees, ye shall in no case enter into the kingdom of heaven" (Matt. 5:20). Righteousness is an inward matter, a state of right standing in the eyes of an all-seeing God, a state of will and character, not merely outward conduct that conforms to legal enactments. The kingdom of God is essentially a righteous order of things. "The kingdom of God is not meat and drink; but righteousness, and peace, and joy in the Holy Ghost" (Rom. 14:17). It does not consist in observance of external regulations but in a state of inward right relationship to God.

Jesus told the Pharisees that the kingdom of God does not come with visible display, but that it was then in their midst (Luke 17:20, 21). To Nicodemus He said, "Verily, verily, I say unto thee, except a man be born again, he cannot see the kingdom of God" (John 3:3). Any person who is within the kingdom of God is a special creation — the product of an unseen, but exceedingly real, process, something that nothing in the order of nature can produce, something that is a blessed reality in the experience of multiplied thousands of people. Only God can create life. Because of His great love for man, God in grace made it possible for men to pass from death in the kingdom of Satan to life in the kingdom of God. The way of grace is the Kingdom's highway. By grace, and by grace alone, does any man enter into the kingdom of God, from which all men were expelled because of sin.

The essential experience of entering the Kingdom is, then, the experience of the new birth. From the divine side, this new birth is the impartation of a new and divine life, a new creation of God in the soul (John 3:5; 5:21; II Cor. 5:17; Eph. 2:1; 4:24). It is not a change in the old nature or a reformation of the old nature or a stimulation of the old nature, but an impartation of a new nature, which after God, is created in righteousness and holiness. Henceforth the individual has two natures (Gal. 5:17). From the human side, it is the coming into the life of a new governing power by which the individual is enabled to do the will of God and to grow in likeness to Him (Ezek. 36:26, 27; II Cor. 5:17; I John 3:8, 9).

The New Birth Also the Essential for Attaining the Ethical Goal of Life Which Has to Be Achieved in the Face of Sin

This change wrought in the life of a human being is the essential also for attaining the ethical goal of life, which must be sought in the face of the fact of sin. Sin is a reality in the life of man for which natural and philosophical systems of ethics make no provision. They cannot deal with the great moral dilemma in which sin places man. Ordinarily, they ignore or deny it, but in so doing they are not true to the facts of human life. Men everywhere in all times have been conscious of moral fault or shortcoming for which they feel that reparation of some kind must be made. The sacrifices, the purifications, and the asceticisms which prevail wherever men are found testify to a deep sense of need which can be satisfied only by the making of a propitiation. Like the Athenians of Paul's day, all men make offerings to the gods, even to "the unknown God," because the soul is ever feeling after salvation and seeking a good which is not possible of attainment, except at cost to some being.

This need universally felt by mankind reaches its highest point in the sense of sin as known in Christian experience. "It is true that you cannot properly express the degree of your sinfulness; but that is because it is impossible in this life, to represent sins in all their true ugliness; nor shall we ever know them as they really are except in the light of God." The sense of sin is moral fault viewed as offense against God. The lapse, the wrongdoing, the missing of the mark, the transgression, is seen as a trespass against the law of God and lack of conformity to His will. The more deeply the soul feels the meaning of sin, the more helpless and hopeless it finds itself in respect to both past sins and present sinning.

The deeper the sense of sin, the more does one become conscious that if only his being were good, his deeds also would be good. Conduct is the outcome of what one is. "The ground upon which good character rests is the very same ground from which man's work derives its value, namely a mind wholly turned to God." One's nature determines the nature of his conduct, and the nature of one's being finds expression first of all in his mind. It is through his desires and thoughts, his feelings and beliefs, that a person's character becomes concrete in deeds. These deeds can be morally good only if the being is of God; they can be nothing but morally bad if they have their source in the unregenerated nature. Jesus told the Pharisees, "Ye are of your father the devil . . . . He that is of God heareth God's words: ye therefore hear them not, because ye are not of God" (John 8:44, 47). A man can as easily bring a clean thing out of an unclean or get sweet water from a bitter fountain as he can attain good conduct when he has only a nature that is depraved and evil.

God so loved man that, in marvelous grace, He gave His only-begotten Son that any human being who believes in Him might be born into the kingdom of God. By the sacrifice of His only Son, He made possible what man is totally and wholly unable to do. However little it is understood, whatever the difficulties of doctrinal interpretation, there is no question as to the reality of the experience of the new birth. This reality inheres in a Person and the facts of His life and death, not in a doctrine. In Christ who died, the believing soul finds a death to sin; in Christ who rose from the dead, the believing soul discovers a new life unto righteousness; in Christ ascended, the believing soul has a King with all power to make him more than conqueror. These are glorious facts to the truth of which all generations of Christian people bear witness. Through the centuries, there have been many who said as did two first-generation Christians, "We cannot but speak the things which we have seen and heard" (Acts 4:20).

Changes in Moral Attitude and in Life the Outcome of the New Birth

The experience of being born into the kingdom of God brings about two changes in moral attitudes. First, it results in a keener sense of moral values. One who has seen Christ suffering on the Cross becomes aware as never before of the awfulness of sin and moral evil. The realization of the greatness of the price that had to be paid for the moral guilt of man makes sin exceedingly sinful, causing one to set up a standard against it in all its forms. In the second place, it makes morality more than mere legalism. Appreciation of the unutterable love manifested by God in Christ elevates the soul above the realm of mere duty into the realm of reciprocating love. The love of God awakened in the soul by free forgiveness of all sin and rebellion is a dynamic force prompting to strong desire to be well pleasing in His sight. The peace bestowed by God in the forgiveness of sins awakens a new apprehension of the glory and the beauty of all goodness and a new determination to do the will of a just and kindly Father.

The Kingdom life is a life, not merely an experience of being born. The grace of God is shown in connection with the soul's spiritual activities and moral needs, not only in the beginning, but also throughout the whole of life. The love of God which leads Him to save the soul is the same divine love which prompts Him to supply continual salvation from the power of sin all the days of the earthly pilgrimage of the redeemed soul. Life in the kingdom is a life lived in fellowship and union with God, a loving Father, who seeks only the good of His child. It is a life lived in accordance with the will and the purposes of God.

The subject of the Kingdom is active in God's business, serving faithfully as a good steward who uses all his resources for the glory of the King. As one in whose heart the reign of God has been established, he lives a life in preparation for the King's fuller reign. He looks forward in the face of all discouragement and opposition to that time when Christ who now sits on His Father's throne shall sit on the throne of David in the kingdom of glory and to a later time, when He shall sit on the throne of God and of the Lamb in the eternal Kingdom. In this last of all kingdoms shall be consummated the kingdom of God as contained in the purpose which God had in creating the world — a reign of righteousness wholly in harmony with His eternal law.

THE HOLY SPIRIT AND ETHICS

The experience of being born into the kingdom of God is for the soul, then, but the introduction to a life in which a new spiritual power operates continuously. In this age, the operating power is the third person of the Trinity, the Holy Spirit. This is not to say that the work of the Holy Spirit is confined to the present age. He has ever worked and will ever continue to work a ministry to God and man. He worked in the creation (Gen. 1:2, 3; Job 26:13; 33:4; Ps. 104:30), in revelation (II Tim. 3:16; II Pet. 1:21), in previous dispensations (Num. 11:17; II Chron. 15:1; Isa. 32:15), in the Incarnation (Matt. 1:18; Luke 1:35), in the ministry of Jesus (John 1:32; Luke 4:14; Matt. 12:28), and in the resurrection of Christ

(I Pet. 3:18). The Spirit is a Person, the executive officer of the Godhead, the agent of the power of God in carrying out the eternal purposes of God.

Since the Day of Pentecost the Holy Spirit Works in the Subjects of the Kingdom to Make Actual in Their Lives the Purpose of God

To accomplish these purposes the Spirit now works as He did not work in any former period. Prior to the day of Pentecost, the kingdom of God on earth was not so real as it is now. In no previous age did the Spirit indwell the subjects of the Kingdom in the manner that He does at present. Jesus ended His teachings with the promise of the coming of the Spirit. He told His disciples that it was good for them that He go away, for without His going there could be no outpouring of the Spirit (John 16:7). His last word was an assurance of His perpetual spiritual presence and power on earth. It was the plain intention of the King that His life should be continued in spiritual grace and energy in the life of His church and in the life of each of His followers.

Consequently, after He ascended to the throne, He began His rule by sending the Spirit, thereby uniting Himself with His people. The Holy Spirit is not merely a power or an influence. He is a Person with personal attributes. He is a divine Person, co-equal with the Father and the Son. He is the Person who forever dwells in believers and works in believers to make real and actual in them the person and the work of Christ. He administers the new life implanted in us, making everything which Christ experienced our portion also.

Through the operation of the Holy Spirit, all that pertains to the purpose of God in our lives is accomplished. Christ by the Spirit gave Himself to suffer the awful penalty upon sin thus delivering us from the sentence of death. It is by the work of the Spirit that every one of us whose trust is in Christ has been brought to the place of conviction of sin, and of righteousness, and of judgment. If we are new creatures in Christ Jesus, it is by virtue of the operation of the Holy Spirit pointing us to the dying Saviour and awakening in us faith to believe in Him as the propitiation set forth by God for the remission of our sins. If we have died and risen with Christ, we have entered a new life, a life in which we walk not after the flesh but after the Spirit. If we are so walking, the Spirit is working wonders in us, accomplishing a victory over sin and evil that we are powerless to accomplish. If we are in Christ, He is in us, and we are moving forward, growing in all goodness and in likeness to Christ. Through our union with Christ, effected by the Spirit, we sit with Christ in the heavenly places (Eph. 1:20; 2:6), and at last we will ascend into heaven to be forever with Him (I Thess. 4:15-17).

It Is by the Power of the Indwelling Spirit that the Christian Is Able to Live as God Would Have Him Live

The three aspects of Christian experience are salvation, sanctification, and service. It is in connection with the second of these that the work of the Spirit has bearing on the ethical life. Jesus called the Holy Spirit the Spirit of truth and said that, when He was come, He would teach the disciples all things, guide them into all truth, and receive of Christ and declare it unto them. Undoubtedly, He was referring primarily to spiritual knowledge, insight, and the power of spiritual discernment. But it is clear that the work of the Spirit has to do also with moral truth, moral enlightenment, and ethical conduct. The experience of the first Christians is evidence of the fact that, after Pentecost, the way in which Christians should behave was to be taught to them by the Holy Spirit.

To the Christian, Christ is not an abstraction, an item of belief, an idea of the mind, a mere presence. He is a Person to whom we are united by strong ties of deep, personal feelings — feelings caused by our personal consciousness of sin, by our personal need for deliverance, by gratitude for personal forgiveness, by love which He showed to us personally. The soul thus united to the Lord through vital faith, when it experienced deliverance from bondage to the law of sin, became possessed of a realization of the righteousness of the law of God and of an earnest desire to have this righteousness fulfilled in personal experience. Having been set free, the Christian willingly makes himself the slave of Jesus Christ. When the opposition between the soul and God is removed, the result is not merely reconciliation but personal union.

This is the truth which Jesus taught in the parable of the vine and the branches and to which He gave expression when He prayed that His followers might be one in the Father and in Him. The agent who brings about this unity with Christ and the Father is the Holy Spirit who indwells the believer. That the vital union between God and man has ethical quality is well expressed in these words of Dorner: "Ethics includes chiefly the rectitude by which man is put in relation, not only with his fellows, but primarily with God, and so arrives at personality. Thus the idea of rectitude, essential to the ethical, and ever in it, preserves the distinction between God and the world; and without it love itself would not be love. An idea, therefore, of the unity of the Divine and the human, not mediated by the idea of the ethical, can of necessity be only of a physical kind, and superficial" (*History of the Doctrine of the Person of Christ*, Vol. I, p. 13).

Those who have had little teaching on the doctrine of the Holy Spirit find it difficult to understand the place that He fills in the Christian life. New Testament ethics is very much the ethics of the Holy Spirit. The first Christians fully recognized that it was from the Holy Spirit that they drew marvelous moral power. They knew that they were taught of God as to the manner in which they should behave. And this power and guidance were theirs, not as individuals, but as members of the body of Christ. It is to the many members of one body to whom the Holy Spirit comes and only to individuals as parts of the body. Always, the Holy Spirit is the governing power in the Christian life as portrayed in the New Testament. In large part, the epistles are an exposition of the operation of the Holy Spirit.

The union of God and man that took place in the Incarnation is the ground for the basic function of the Holy Spirit, namely, to unite us to Christ who entered into union with man when He took human nature. A divine Person, the Son of God, dwelt in one man, Jesus, and worked through His life the works of God; a divine Person, the Holy Spirit, dwells in the life of every believer and works through each life the works of God. God calls us to Himself for one supreme end — that we might "be partakers of his holiness" (Heb. 12:10), through meeting the requirements of His eternal law as a result of living, as those "who walk not after the flesh, but after the Spirit" (Rom. 8:4). "Ye are not under the law, but under grace." "Ye became the servants of righteousness" (Rom. 6:14, 18). Yet because of the lower nature we are entirely helpless, apart from the power of God working in us to will and to do. Christian ethics rests upon the fact, proved over and over again in human experience, that we can do nothing of ourselves. With Augustine, each of us must say, "For what am I to myself without Thee, but a guide to mine own downfall?" But, by virtue of the power of an indwelling Spirit, we can also say with Augustine, "Thy omnipotency is not far from us."

Except as the Holy Spirit indwells and works continually in him, no human being has power to live as God would have him live. Without the Holy Spirit, the ethical teachings of the Bible, which are at one and the same time requirements of the eternal law of God and of the moral law of man's own being, are wholly beyond the power of man to perform. There are those who maintain that some of these teachings are impractical. In so claiming they are entirely correct — if the Holy Spirit is not taken into consideration. From the day of Pentecost down to the present moment, it is only His supernatural power, working by love in the human heart, that enables man to keep the eternal law of God.

Absolute Obedience the Basic Requirement for the Working of the Spirit

A subject of the kingdom of God is one who submits himself absolutely to the will of God. The condition for the possession of the Spirit is obedience. He is given to all obedient souls (Acts 5:32). When we disobey, we forfeit His precious gifts. He will bear long with our mistakes, our errors of judgment, or even with our lapses into sin, but He will not remain in control of an unwilling subject. Disobedience, while it does not drive the Spirit away, grieves the Spirit and frustrates His operating. The supreme lesson we need to learn is cheerful and grateful and wholehearted yielding of self to the Spirit. In all His love, and truth, and knowledge, and wisdom, and grace, and comfort, and holiness, and life, and power, the Spirit is completely at the disposal of each and every believer who is first entirely at His disposal.

To the person who has met God in the new birth and who is sincerely and absolutely yielded to God as sovereign in his life, conscience bears witness to the law of God. The morality of such an one is not a matter of the observance of legal regulations but is the result of the working of grace. Under the influence of the Holy Spirit, he finds continual delight in lovingly doing God's will in all the duties and responsibilities of life. His is not obedience to the demands of an external law imposed by arbitrary decree. Through the operation of the Spirit within him, he has liberty and freedom to bring his members into glad conformity with the law of Christ. There is within him enabling grace and power which are in complete harmony with the will of God as revealed in His Word.

Life means problems. We meet many situations in which our duty is not immediately apparent; sometimes it is very difficult to ascertain what we ought to do. At such times, it is highly necessary to maintain toward God a right attitude and to cultivate constant dependence upon the enlightenment and the guidance of the Holy Spirit. Our business is to ascertain the will of God, then to do it at all hazards. If we are in complete harmony with God, we can rest assured that we will be guided aright. But we need to be most careful lest we follow selfish and unworthy desires. Our lower nature is exceedingly prone to seek ways of escape from the teachings of the Bible and the dictates of reason. We never escape the requirements of moral law by making and observing a number of minute regulations. The thing we must do to fulfill the moral law of our nature is to fall back on the great eternal law of which the requirements of the moral law are aspects. In times of conflict among rules, when we know not what to do, we can help ourselves by asking whether the course we consider is "the one that is most conducive to the realization of the rule of reason in the world." When we sincerely and absolutely desire nothing but the will of God, we are in a condition in which the Spirit can guide us through a clear conscience to the solution of the problem.

Even when we see what is best, our lower nature may prompt us not to choose it. In such a case, we have in the Spirit not only a guide but also one who makes us conqueror of our natural weakness. In all matters of essential importance to morality, there is one good and acceptable and perfect will of God. If our eye is single, we will not be concerned about possible safe alternatives, but it will be our aim to find this one sure way. Where the will of God is clearly and definitely revealed in His Word, it is ours to obey without evasion or hesitation, leaving with the Lord the outcome, however untoward it may seem to be. In relatively few matters does conflict arise. When it does appear, there is usually a degree of selfish interest, the elimination of which will resolve the conflict. Always, when we really desire the will of God, we can be certain that the Holy Spirit will enable us both to ascertain and to do that will.

The Holy Spirit in Relation to the Natural in Man

God does not violate the laws of man's nature. The natural is the basis of the supernatural. The Spirit operates in a soul that possesses reason and moral sense. He does not quench the natural faculties but works through and upon them, quickening, purifying, refining, and elevating their functioning. It is not the work of the Spirit to create a new ethics. There is in the ordinary life of man that which not only disposes him to strive after good but also results in a measure of compliance with moral law. The Spirit makes clear man's incapacity for attaining perfection and provides grace to help him in time of need.

That man is totally depraved spiritually and utterly incapable of doing anything at all to merit the favor of God does not mean that he is wholly incapable of any moral good. It must be remembered that though man lost the image of God through Adam's sin, he yet retains the image of God in the wider sense. On the one hand, he lost through the fall something that can be regained only through redemption. On the other hand, he is a moral being with reason, power of moral judgment, conscience, and freedom of will.

There is a common grace of the Spirit which finds expression in human lives apart from the operation of the special grace of the Spirit in redeemed lives. Every once in a while this statement is heard: "Those who are not Christians live better moral lives than Christians do." Without doubt, the statement may be true in many instances. The operation of common grace does have effect on the hearts and minds of beings created in the image of God which has never been lost. In any land where the influence of Christian teachings prevails, there is bound to be a corresponding development in the moral conduct of its people.

A world of difference exists between the morality of peoples dominated by even an imperfect conception of Christian ethics and the highest moral level of pagan life. Uplifting as many of its principles are, the teaching of pagan moral philosophers influences scarcely at all the moral practice of their people. The living and exalted Christ is yet showing man many things; the Holy Spirit takes from Him and continually sheds light on His Word, adds new facts to human experience, and discloses richer manifestations of God through His providential dealings with man and through man's personal consciousness. Christian ethics interprets and applies to human life the mind of Christ under the illumination and guidance of the Holy Spirit. The Bible is the authority, showing what Christianity is. The experience of individuals and of peoples — churches, societies, and nations — clearly demonstrates that when the teachings of the Bible are ignored, set aside, or belittled, moral degradation inevitably follows.

The Operation of the Grace of God through the Holy Spirit

The special grace of God operates, first of all, through the call of the Spirit of God to the spirit of man. In its moral aspect, this call is not the same as the invitation to accept Christ as Saviour with which it has close connection. Rather it is an awakening of the dead conscience, a convicting of the heart, and a directing of the will to respond to the invitation. This call of the Spirit is not unrelated to the ordinary processes of thought. The Spirit is not an alien power who suddenly comes into our experience. As long as we are alive, the Spirit of God is in us (Job 27:3). He is really "not far from every one of us" (Acts 17:27). No one can deny the possibility of instantaneous conversion, but it is also impossible for any one to trace in consciousness all the ramifications of the working of the Spirit in his previous history.

Unquestionably, the Spirit may bring to bear upon the soul vivid impressions through sudden impulses. However, we do violence to the teachings of the Bible to maintain that the call of the Spirit of God to the spirit of man must be in the nature of a sudden compelling conviction wholly unrelated to past experience. The Bible clearly makes appeal to the ordinary understanding, intelligence, reason, and judgment. The reading or the hearing of its truths affect to some extent the ordinary consciousness of man the same as do other experiences of similar nature. But beyond this, there is an operation of the Spirit as He speaks to the spirit of man and brings to it the message of God. No one knows whether or not the Spirit of God communicates truth directly to the spirit of man, that is, apart from the medium of the reaction of mind and thought to the written or spoken Word. It is known that He does use this medium, leading the mind to the recognition of the fact that God is speaking and to an attitude of receptivity.

But this is far from being all that there is to the ethics of the Christian life. Christian ethics is a great deal more than a glorified system of natural ethics which takes not into account the problem of man's relationship to God and the breaking of fellowship with Him through a moral collapse. From one aspect, the Bible is a book that teaches ethics. It sets before the longing human soul ideals to strive for. It teaches definite duties. It offers a highest good, even perfect righteousness and true holiness. However, wonderful as its moral teachings are, if the Bible stopped here, its message to the weak and helpless creature that is man would be nothing but a hollow mockery. The New Testament brings to us the further revelation that the Word of God is with power. It is the revelation of a wondrous act, a work of grace strange to the ordinary consciousness, whereby God makes man a new creature in Christ and thus capable of understanding the things freely given us of God. This work of grace is wrought in the soul by the Spirit as He touches our feeling, thought, and will, so that we not only desire deliverance from the bondage of guilt and evil but choose to accept Christ. The total operation, beginning with the call of the Spirit and ending with a conscious and deliberate act of faith, makes the individual a new creation but does not constitute a break in his psychological life. "The ordinary operations of understanding, feeling, and will, continue, but they are related to a different ideal, and displayed under a new control, that must inevitably secure, through the continued operation of the same Spirit, that complete conformity to the will of God which man in his natural condition neither wholly understands nor yet perfectly desires" (Hammond, *Perfect Freedom*, p. 205).

Christianity is a life, not a system of doctrine, not a creed, not a religion in the ordinary sense of the word. Apart from the principle of a life made new in Christ Jesus by the power of God, there is no real Christian ethics. The new birth does not take place without reference to the ordinary processes of moral development nor is the life of the child of God lived in separation from these same processes. Morover, the limits of moral attainment are not reached while we are in this world. For these reasons, Christians do not seem to be essentially different from other people and may, at times, the same as other people, display in conduct behavior that is far beneath the level of their ideals. Nevertheless, the fact remains that unless a person is born again, he can neither see the purposes of God nor do the will of God. The new birth takes place as the Word is heard by the ear, understood by the mind, and acted upon by the will, provided these normal and natural activities of man are accompanied by the operation of the Spirit in revealing and applying the truth of God.

The new birth wrought in the soul by the Holy Spirit, operating usually through the Word, produces change in feeling, thought, and will. This is but the beginning, for the Spirit also sustains the new life. He who is the Creator of life is also the perpetual re-Creator of life. The Spirit sustains the life by working in the heart and develops the new creation by working out through the life of the person the manifestations of the vital union of the soul with God. A newborn child is a bundle of possibilities; that is, he has numerous potentialities that will become actualities through the process of growth. Likewise, the newborn child of God is not now as he later will be. The inner dispositions created by the power of God in regeneration become, under the nurture of the Spirit, traits of Christian character. Deep within the soul, if the Spirit is given opportunity to work unhindered by self-will, He will perfect a process of conformity to divine ideals. As this process continually goes on, conscious desires emerge. Desires are the source of acts; acts become habits; habits are the basis of character.

This work of the Spirit in the inward parts involves continual enlightenment of the understanding and the putting of things in their proper relation. The eternal law of God is impressed upon the nature of man, but in his unregenerate state man does not see it aright or apply it properly. From the moment his soul first came under the blight of sin, man has had faulty moral vision. As a consequence, he has been inclined to put evil for good and wrong for right. Through the illumination of the Spirit, clear perception is possible. Along with this, the Spirit works in us to desire and to do the will of God.

The Holy Spirit Works in Connection with the Word of God and through the Experiences of Life

The internal working of the Spirit in implanting and nurturing right dispositions is the foundation for growth in holiness of life and uprightness of conduct. This growth cannot take place apart from knowledge of the Word of God. Except we live as Jesus did "by every word that proceedeth out of the mouth of God," our renewed soul cannot develop normally in sanctification of heart and life. The entrance into the heart of the light of God's Word is an absolute essential to the working of the Holy Spirit inwardly in the heart and outwardly in the life. Development toward complete apprehension of that "for which also I am apprehended of Christ Jesus" — perfection of life in righteousness and holiness — is wholly dependent upon an internal reciprocal influence of the Word of God and the operation of the Spirit of God.

In this development the experiences of life also share a part.

". . . all things work together for good to them that love God, to them who are the called according to his purpose" (Rom. 8: 28). All the experiences of daily life, whether we can see it clearly or not, have a function in the plan of God. The Holy Spirit works in and through every circumstance of our lives, the pleasant and the unpleasant, the happy and the painful, the toward and the untoward, causing all to redound to our good. Nothing we can meet, however much it may wrench our soul, will work aught but a refining, helpful influence in our life, so long as we allow God to work in us as He will what He will.

Our wills are ours. As Tennyson says, "Our wills are ours to make them thine." What we do with our wills determines our character and our destiny for time and for eternity. Character is completely fashioned will. What we are today, what we will be in the future, is the inevitable outcome of repeated acts of our will. We have abundant reason for gratitude to an omnipotent God, the Creator, the beginning and the end of all things, that we have the privilege, through the Spirit of grace, of making our wills His. From first to last the tenor of the Bible is that God alone is good, His will alone is the good will, and therefore the true end of man is to know, to accept, and to do the will of God. Eventually, every soul is going to submit to that will. It is entirely of grace that the Holy Spirit brings any of us to the realization that God is good and works in us surrender of our will to His perfect law of love.

Conscience and Reason Not Adequate for a Christian Ethic, Which Is Founded on the Eternal Law of God

We are creatures with conscience. This aims at the best but is inadequate to bring us to the goal which our nature impels us to strive to attain. We are endowed with reason. However, its working is so obscured that it shows us only parts of the way in which we should walk and gives us insufficient comprehension of these parts. Unaided by God, we have no means for restoring the image of righteousness and holiness. Even when He works by His Spirit, the restoration is relatively slow because God never thrusts Himself upon man; He always tempers His manner of working to the nature with which and in which He works. But, from beginning to end, the work is

God's work, not just a natural development of the powers of man. Man can work out only as God works within.

There is no true Christian ethic apart from the operation of the Holy Spirit. Jesus lived among men, giving us an example of how we ought to live. Jesus taught great moral ideals. But, except as the Spirit takes the things of Christ and shows them unto us, neither His teachings nor His example suffice. A living union of the life of Christ and the life of the redeemed soul is the essential to true morality. It is not enough that Jesus spake as never man spake, that He died to make it possible to impute righteousness to us, that He was resurrected to enable us to walk in newness of life. Beyond all this, it is necessary that, through the operation of the Holy Spirit, the Christ who thus spoke and died and rose again, enter into us and live His life in us and through us, bringing us into conformity with the perfect will of God. True Christian morality is not a morality plastered on to the outside of the life of a person who is called a Christian. It is conduct that springs from the depths of the soul of a person who is possessed by Christ — one of whom Christ is "his very breath, the soul of his soul, the heart of his heart, the life of his life."

Christian Moral Life the Outcome of the Working of the Holy Spirit

The union of the life of Christ and the life of His follower does not reach full perfection in this world because of the evil that remains in the spirit of man. Alongside the new man created after Christ Jesus in righteousness and true holiness, there is the old man and his deeds. Between the two natures there is continual conflict. But, as we persist in yielding to the Spirit and resisting the flesh, the union becomes more and more perfect, with corresponding progress in purification of heart and improvement in conduct. The more we recognize our dependence upon the power of the Spirit, the more we seek by faith to make real in our experience that dependence. The more real that dependence is, the stronger is our resistance to evil and wrong and the more we grow in likeness to God, both inwardly and outwardly.

Our Lord and King issues commands but, by His gracious power and infinite love, He secures our willing obedience. We gladly accept His sovereign control and acknowledge the duty of absolute obedience. The more aware we are of our own helplessness, the more fully do we rely on the power of God. Because His purpose is that we become strong, He only employs His power through our activity. Resistance to the evil of the flesh and the world must be on the basis of our own conscious determination. To arrive at a right moral determination or decision we must call into play all our normal powers of understanding, emotion, reason, and judgment. In short, we enter into the conflict only by faith in Christ and we can win in the struggle only as we put forth diligent effort.

As finite beings, we can have neither awareness of the whole moral system nor appreciation of the full worth of every moral relation. None but the infinite Author of the eternal law has such awareness and appreciation. All that we can do is humbly to seek His direction and to solve problems in dependence upon His Spirit for guidance and by means of the light we have from the teaching of His Word. In the midst of the complexities of moral interaction, it is not always easy to discover the right course.

Part of the work of the Holy Spirit is to produce in us the obedience of faith. We cannot shift our moral responsibility. Our decisions must be our own. Ours it is to do the will of God from the heart. Our actions must be our personal, individual response to the will of God as we understand it. This involves the consecration of our entire self — body, soul, and spirit — to the Lord. As we maintain with the help of the Spirit this full-fledged consecration, we grow more and more in likeness to Christ. To repeat once more, Christianity is life. Life is never static; to be alive means to be in action. Christian ethics is the life of Christ in action, expressing itself in practical, everyday conduct. It is therefore progressive. As our union with Christ becomes more perfect, we grow more sensitive even about matters which once we may have been disposed to regard lightly.

Conclusion

Ethics is a science of man, the systematic study of the principles of right and wrong in conduct. The Bible is the book of God, the record in history and prophecy of the salvation which He wrought through Christ. A certain man once made the remark, "A book is the lifeblood of its author." The salvation of God, of which the Bible is the revelation, cost the lifeblood of Jesus Christ, God's only Son. The Bible is not a treatise on ethics. The principles of conduct enunciated in it apply fundamentally and essentially to men who have been born into the kingdom of God through redemption in the blood of the Son of God. Though the Bible says ever so much about moral conduct, it was not given primarily to guide moral beings in their conduct. Its great purpose is to reveal to spiritual beings with a moral nature the way of life and to guide them in living as new creatures in Christ Jesus. Ethics is, so to speak, an adjunct to the Christian life. Ethics is not Christianity; ethics is not life. We cannot substitute conduct for Christ, rectitude for repentance, legal observance for life, ideals for imputed righteousness, goodness for godliness, optimism for obedience, self-determination for sanctification, standards for sincerity of heart, happiness for holiness, morality for mastery, ease for earnestness of effort in the fear of God.

The Bible does not pretend to be a treatise on moral guidance. Its teachings must be interpreted and unified to form a system of ethics. To the sincere follower of Christ who lives in vital union with Him, the Bible is an authority for the guidance of conduct. However, it is more than a mere external authority which imposes regulations in a mechanical or a legalistic way. Ethics as deduced from the Bible is not a harsh code of rules prescribed by God which man must blindly and slavishly obey. The eternal God has too much respect for the personality and the dignity of man to force upon him unwilling servitude. He lets every man as free to exercise his own personal choices as He let Adam and Eve in the Garden of Eden.

Instead, the Bible is an inward authority to which the Christian is bound because it is the expressed will of God whom he loves. This does not mean that he lives in ignorance of, and heedless of, the commands of the written Word. On the contrary, he accepts these as the definition of the will of

Him whom he loves and seeks earnestly to reduce them to practice in his life. Jesus expressed love for the Father, but the will and the law of God were written in His heart and were manifest in His every step and decision. Likewise the Christian in whom Christ dwells has one supreme motive: to learn how he "ought to walk and to please God" so that he "would abound more and more" (I Thess. 4:1).

In the Bible the Christian finds Christ who is his life because faith, born of the Word and the Spirit, unites his life with the life of the Saviour to whom both point him. Faith is never a finished thing in this world. Once it exists, it continues only as it is nourished, that is, by constant renewal through the Word and the Spirit, the agents which brought it into being. It is unfinished also in the sense that it is yet imperfect and in need of growth which can take place only through the Word. Whatever purports to be a principle of Christian ethics must be in harmony with the written Word. Christian ethics being progressive, we shall never, so long as we live, be able to grasp all the ethical content of the Bible or reach in our attainment the limits of what it teaches. Always and ever we shall be obliged to express the same ethical truth in constantly higher forms than those in which we had previously expressed it.

QUESTIONS

1. What influences have been wrought upon Christian ethics by Greek, Roman, and Jewish civilizations, respectively?
2. How do you account for the seeming discrepancy between Old Testament practices and New Testament ethical teachings?
3. Show from the standpoint of morality the necessity of the Incarnation.
4. In what sense, or senses, is God the only source of good in the life of man?
5. What is the distinction between "a nature" and "a person"?
6. Can you give illustrations other than that of a doctor who is a church officer which help to understanding of the union of the human and the divine in Jesus Christ?
7. Did Jesus teach ethics? Explain your answer.
8. In what sense is a Christian made alive morally in Christ?
9. What state would we be in morally had Christ returned to heaven without a bodily resurrection?

10. List the implications that the work of the risen Christ has for the ethical life of the Christian.
11. Need any Christian do wrong morally?
12. What is your conception of the nature of the Kingdom of God?
13. How long has this Kingdom been in existence? How long will it continue?
14. Describe a subject of the Kingdom.
15. What is the one thing of which natural and philosophical ethics take no account?
16. What is the implication for ethics of the fact that one's nature determines the nature of his conduct?
17. Was the work of the Holy Spirit in the realm of ethics prior to the day of Pentecost? After the day of Pentecost?
18. In what sense does the vital union between God and man have ethical quality?
19. Do you attach any significance to the fact that early Christians were taught as members of the church, not as individuals, how to behave?
20. Explain: "Christian ethics rests upon the fact, proved over and over again in human experience, that we can do nothing of ourselves."
21. Is the above fact ever given expression in general ethics? Explain.
22. Show the place of, and the necessity for, absolute obedience as a condition for the working of the Holy Spirit.
23. Can a Christian be moral in any part of his life if he is not wholly obedient to God in everything?
24. Outline a procedure which is safe for a Christian to follow in dealing with moral problems.
25. Discuss: the Holy Spirit works through and upon the natural faculties of man.
26. Distinguish, from the standpoint of ethics, between common grace and the special grace of God.
27. Does the Holy Spirit ever speak to the spirit of man entirely apart from his past experiences?
28. Do you agree that, apart from a life made new in Christ Jesus, there is no real Christian ethics? Why, or why not?
29. Explain the relationship between the eternal law of God and the work of the Spirit.
30. How are the Word of God and the operation of the Spirit related?
31. Show the inadequacy of conscience and of reason as a basis for conduct.
32. What is the one and only source of true Christian morality?
33. Can we be too much aware of our own helplessness? Explain your answer.

34. What place has faith in the perfecting of Christian conduct?
35. What does it mean to say that "Christian ethics is the life of Christ in action?
36. Do you agree that the Bible is not a book of ethics? Why?
37. Why shall we always be obliged to give constantly new expression to the same ethical truth?

CHAPTER IV

The Place of Ethics in the Christian Life

WE STUDY ETHICS FOR THE SAME REASON that we study a physical science — to gain the knowledge we need for effective control and direction of action. In the case of a physical science, it is physical objects and conditions that we seek to learn to control; in the case of ethics, it is factors of the moral life that we would understand and know how to direct. The principles of any physical science are the basis for rules or directions for dealing appropriately with the objects and conditions peculiar to that specific science. The principles of ethics are the foundation for proper guidance of the conduct of a moral being. Every true moral principle or rule exists for a particular purpose. All such rules or principles function together to keep us going as we ought to go. There are two ways in which we may go wrong: we may function wrong within ourselves, and we may disturb the well-being of persons around us. We are like members of an orchestra: each of us must play well his own part, and we must play in unison and in harmony with each of the players, as all play together under the direction of the leader.

Ethics, then, has to do with three things: first, with the individual and what he must do in order to fulfill his part; second, with cooperative and harmonious activity between individuals; third, with the purpose of life as a whole, with what man was made for, with the accomplishment of the end that the Director of life has set. General ethics deals almost entirely with the second of these, quite commonly ignoring or, at least, stressing little the other two. Consequently, though there is much that is worthy of note in the various systems of general ethics, all of them are inadequate, lacking in basic principles affecting character and its issue in conduct.

91

It is natural to begin with relations among individuals, for man cannot live his life without giving some attention to the way in which he should behave in relation to his fellows. He must observe certain rules and submit to at least a few restrictions in any social group of which he is a member. Every civilization has had an ordered expression of a moral code, or rule of life. Anthropology shows that even among savage peoples, conduct is controlled by many customs and observances. Without some kind of ethical teaching in the form of either laws or customs, social life is impossible.

Through the ages, many of the greatest minds have engaged in the scientific or philosophical study of human conduct and its ends. The outcome is a large body of literature constituting no insignificant contribution to the intellectual heritage of mankind. Yet there is no agreement among these students of the subject upon any one theory of morals. They have not given us a scientific system of ethics which we can accept without question. They are united concerning the main rules which must be followed in the ordinary activities of life. Almost all accept the fact that practices like lying, stealing, adultery, and murder are to be condemned as immoral and unsocial. But there is no agreement among these thinkers as to the fundamental principles basic to such rules and practices.

Thinking about morality counts for little if we center our thoughts upon social relations alone. No number of books on ethics will cause men to function properly in living with their fellows if their inner purposes are not right. All the rules for social behavior drawn up by the most brilliant group of thinkers will be to no avail so long as the individual to whom they are meant to apply is filled with pride, selfish ambition, lust, greed, envy, hatred, ill temper, and self-conceit. Men are not made good by rules, and without good men, there can be no good society. As a free moral agent, as a being who can think and will, man is able to set before himself certain ends and to act with a view to attaining them. He always is, therefore, in some measure, the arbiter of his own acts. Moreover, as a being responsible to another Being who created him for His own purposes, man has obligations and duties which he would not have if he had only his fellows to consider.

So to control and direct our actions as to have them issue in right conduct, we must be able to meet life appropriately in terms of all three of our relationships: to ourselves, to others, and to our Creator. We have an inborn sense that some things are right and others are wrong. We know this intuitively, that is, without study and reasoning. It is probable that this moral intuition is connected with the innate knowledge possessed by every man that there is a God. Our moral intuition may be developed through observation, reflection, and study, but it is not derived from observation, reflection, and study. No amount of study "could ever impart the idea of a difference between right and wrong to one who had it not."

Deep within us is the conviction that there is a good which we should do, and that there is a right way and a wrong way to act. Also we have a deep-seated feeling that we are responsible somehow for the choices we make. This is true even when our concern is solely with the effects upon ourselves of our decisions. Every day — almost every hour of every day — we ask ourselves questions such as, "What ought I to do?", "Which is the right course for me to follow?", "How can I discharge my obligation?", "What is my duty in this situation?" We devote far more thought to daily matters of conduct than we do to theological doctrines or other theoretical considerations. This is not to say that we should give no heed to doctrine. It is but to emphasize the fact that most people, Christians and non-Christians, are concerned much more with practical problems of conduct than they are with those of belief and reflective reason.

GENERAL ETHICS AND CHRISTIAN LIVING

In the last section of the preceding chapter, it was said that the ethical teachings of the Bible apply primarily to Christians. While this is true, it is not to be assumed that Christian ethics has to do with ethical content that is binding upon Christians only. Rather it is such a moral rule as is required by the Christian system. There is no double standard of morality, one for non-Christians and another for Christians, the former developed by general or philosophical ethics and the latter by Christian ethics. God, the Creator of all men, is the source of the eternal law which is binding on all men equally, regardless of class, relationship, or any other distinction. It is this eternal law which is written into the very being of every man and is known to every man through moral intuition.

Every Christian owes to himself, to others, and to God the duty of becoming thoroughly familiar with, and convinced about, principles which should govern his conduct. We meet many kinds of ethical problems. We need, therefore, to be able to interpret accurately the nature of each situation, to understand clearly and definitely our ethical responsibility, and to decide wisely what ways and means we should use to accomplish that which we ought to do. Vague talk about the power of Christianity to solve all moral problems is worthless. Paul says we walk by faith, implying that faith is a way of walking, not of mere talking. No one can solve a problem except as he understands it and its implications and knows exactly what difficulties must be overcome and the best manner for dealing effectively with them.

Men's Troubles Caused by Moral Factors

The causes of the troubles men have are moral rather than economic, social, political, or military. "Current political and economic dislocations culminating in the military threat of world conquest are in large part the effects of world-wide intellectual confusion and spiritual and moral deterioration. This deterioration of standards of thought and action affected society in its most sensitive aspects." These are words from a statement of the Third Annual Conference on Science, Philosophy, and Religion. What is needed is a return to the universal morals of personal and social conduct. Professor Albert Einstein has said, "The political and economic complexities of the last few decades have brought before our eyes dangers that even the darkest pessimists of the last century did not dream of. The injunctions of the Bible concerning human conduct were then accepted by infidel and believer alike as self-evident demands for individuals and society. . . . Yet today we must recognize with horror that these pillars of civilized human existence have lost their firmness."

One of the greatest tragedies of our day is the way in which theories are being equated with facts, and mere hypotheses are being accepted as truths, under the influence of modern scientific teaching. Dogmatic assertions of scientists are widely received as solid facts though they are nothing but theory. No scientist can prove the non-existence of God, that Jesus was not His Son, that there is no life after death. Scientists can say they do not believe such facts, but disbelief is not demonstration. Yet men and women accept their theories as facts and confuse hypotheses with truth, to the destruction of belief in the supernatural. And the immediate result of loss of spiritual faith is revolt against the moral teachings of the Bible and the degradation of moral life.

Need for Familiarity with Various Systems of General Ethics and with Moral Values

It is of the utmost importance that we, as Christians, not only "be ready always to give an answer to every man that asketh you a reason of the hope" we have (I Pet. 3:15), but also be familiar with the claims of the different systems of general ethics. No one of these can compare with Christian ethics in the actual outcome of its teachings. In our Lord, His teachings, and His work, we have the principles of an incomparably superior system. No philosopher is at all like Him; no ethics presents the challenge that Christian ethics does. None lived as He lived. Never was there a philosopher who so lived that it could be said of him, "What he was, all men ought to become." None taught as He taught. Of no philosopher can it be said that to follow him and to learn of him is to find in the highest duty the most perfect rest. Of Christ alone can it be said, "To have His mind is to be perfect even as the Father in heaven is perfect."

It is this same Lord who establishes the kingdom of God in the hearts of those who receive Him. If we are of this number, we are subject to the laws of that kingdom. We are citizens of a heavenly kingdom and should conduct ourselves as such

(Phil. 3:20). Like all the heroes of faith, we aspire to "a better country," "a heavenly one." We are destined to live in a city which God has prepared for us. Therefore, we should strive with all that is in us to live in accord with the standards of a heavenly commonwealth, whatever other people may do. To this end, we need to learn all we can from every possible source so that we can distinguish clearly between human and divine standards and measure up more perfectly to the latter.

It is impossible for us to divorce ourselves from our own past and from the past of the world of men in which we live. We are victims of a dangerous delusion if we assume that being born into the kingdom of God is the inevitable and only essential for the living of an ethical life. Little do we realize how great is our debt to those who have gone on before us. If any individual were obliged to begin at the beginning of the task of ascertaining and estimating moral values, he would have an immense and a most complex undertaking. Ever since man began his course, he has been engaged in this task. Through all the generations of past time, the work of studying and formulating principles of moral conduct has gone on. These principles come to be expressed in the teachings which parents receive from their parents and, in turn, pass on to their children, and which society emphasizes in the ever-continuing process of education. Each of us is born into a social group which has already defined right and wrong. Each of us learns to respect what this social group accepts as right; each of us undergoes punishment when we do what this social group considers wrong. Because of this control, we come to think of moral principles derived from many sources as something inherent in our world. The fact is that, in our own thought, we are debtors to many men in many places and to men of all stations of life. It is the accumulated experience of all preceding generations that enters into the moral content of our own living.

General Ethics Are Different from but Also Like Christian Ethics

The fundamental distinction between ethics as developed by man apart from special revelation and Christian ethics lies in the fact that man, through reason, can neither know God as He is nor understand aright His moral requirements. This distinction is the cause of a wide gap between Christian ethics and general ethics. They move in quite different realms. The latter begins in a study of human nature, conduct, and experience and is completed in a process of reasoning through which the results of the study are formulated in ethical principles. The former is founded upon a special revelation of final and absolute truth made by God to man. Morality is basically theological, and ethical duties are such because they are the will of God. Christian ethics does not deny that there is much truth in general ethics, but it sets before the Christian a higher standard for ethical life as well as a new motive for ethical living and a power, not of man, for attaining the standard.

General ethics and Christian ethics deal with the same material — man, a being with an inborn sense that some things are right and others are wrong, a being who, deep within himself, realizes that wrong and evil are foreign to the nature he had in the beginning. Because all ethical systems have this common material, they are alike in many things, however much they may differ in other ways. Since it is impossible for us to separate ourselves from this body of general ethical knowledge, we do well to familiarize ourselves as thoroughly as we can with it.

Even the grace of God operates through natural channels and human influences. The transformation wrought by the operation of God which is fundamental in Christian ethics is less the destruction of the past than it is a taking up of the past into a new life and transfiguring it with a new value. James Stalker, writing of Paul, says, "His character presented a wonderful combination of the natural and the spiritual. . . . In no saved man's character is it possible to separate nicely what is due to nature from what is due to grace; for nature and grace blend sweetly in the redeemed life." If the natural man were without susceptibility to the appeal of moral ideals, if there were nothing in him to cause him to be dissatisfied with the evil and to reach out for the good, he would be without basis for the redemptive call of God. The fact that the power of sin entered into the first creation does not mean that the natural man has no true moral perception. In us who are the children of God through the redemption that is in Christ, natural knowledge of morality and the Christian knowledge of morality combine into one.

The Place of Reason in Ethics

The reason of man is the source of our natural knowledge of morality which finds expression in natural goodness. Every one of us has to say to the Lord with the psalmist, "my goodness extendeth not to thee" (Ps. 16:2), but there is in man, as seen by man, a relative goodness. No man ever gets so low that there is nothing at all of good in him. Undeniably, natural goodness when taken by itself has more value than badness.

Nevertheless, we must be most careful in respect to the findings of human reason, which general ethics represents. Reason makes its appeal, calling men back to the good and the right. As moral beings, we know the essential distinction between right and wrong. Therefore, we cannot reject flatly any call of reason. To do so would do violence to our nature, for we are creatures of reason. However, we must remember that our reason is under the blight of what happened to human nature in the fall of Adam. Theologically speaking, we are totally depraved beings, with a nature that is tainted in every part. The powers given us by God in creation remain and function in their natural order, but they function under the limitations of a total disability. Reason, the same as all our other powers, shares in this disability. Through reason, therefore, man cannot develop full and clear conceptions of ethical truth.

As was said earlier, men have always reflected upon ethical matters. Ethical truth, as we possess it today, is the result of two lines of influence, that of reason or thought, particularly of the Greeks, and that of revelation, coming through the Hebrews. The reason of man, beginning in and much influenced by classical thought, has had so large a part in the fashioning of our present-day conceptions that it is impossible to understand ethical matters except as we know something of the outcomes of this thought. An understanding of what man through his reason has developed helps us to place in proper perspective the ethical truths that come to us through revelation. To acquire anything like fullness of understanding, one must devote himself to the study of a history of ethics. Yet the brief sketch that follows may be an aid to understanding.

The Early Development through Reason of General Ethics

General ethics may be said to have commenced with the Sophists, who were the first philosophers to make the nature of man their subject of study. Protagoras, the best known of the Sophists, held that "man is the measure of all things." Man's business is to satisfy himself; moral precepts have no general validity; truth is for a man just what he believes to be true. After the Sophists, Socrates taught that "virtue is knowledge," meaning that if a man has a full appreciation of his acts and their consequences, he cannot fail to act virtuously. Reason is the key to the good life. The "wise man" by patient endeavor develops moral insight into the universal standard and science of good conduct. This moral insight is the means for right living and the greatest thing in the world. Next was Plato who interpreted and systematized the ethical theory of Socrates. To Plato, ultimate reality consists in ideas; perceptions of the senses are poor copies of reality. There is the sphere of relative knowledge, or opinion, derived from perception, and the sphere of absolute knowledge, developed from reasoning. "Reasoning is the only road to truth." Plato's highest idea was the idea of Good, to which he applied the name of deity. However, his Good was not a personal, or even a spiritual, being but a purely ethical end. The absolute good is realized in the State, the fullest expression of the unity which belongs to virtue. In the State unity is achieved by adjusting the lives of many individuals to each other. In this process of adjustment, the cardinal virtues, wisdom, courage, and temperance are developed. Justice, the application of wisdom to the whole of society, is the bond which unites the three into an ordered whole.

Aristotle, even more than Plato, emphasized reason. He taught that reason is the guide, for virtue is achieved when a thing acts according to its highest function; and for man, reason is this highest function. Because of his emphasis on reason, Aristotelianism rather than Platonism, came to be synonymous with rationalism. Virtues are developed through discipline, that is, the repeated choice of the good which becomes habitual. Reason is the source of happiness because it leads to right conduct through the avoidance of all extremes — the doctrine of the "golden mean." Aristotle's reality is active and dynamic as opposed to Plato's Idea, which is static and unchangeable. Virtue is a matter of *doing* rather than of knowing. The final or moving cause is God who, to Aristotle, is pure reason, an objective and universal reality.

Both Plato and Aristotle stressed "happiness" or "well-being" as the inner response of the soul, or mind. It was not, therefore, an experience of mere pleasure. The Epicureans based all truth upon sensation and sought happiness in a life of feeling. Pleasure is the only ultimate good and pain the only evil. This doctrine degenerated into the theory that the purpose of life is pure sense enjoyment and indulgence of appetite. In contrast to the Epicureans, the Stoics, among whom are Zeno, Seneca, Epictetus, and Marcus Aurelius, sought happiness, not in outward things but in indifference to all passions and desired changes. Reason is to be in control; virtue and right reason are synonymous. If pleasure and right reason come into conflict, pleasure must be sacrificed. The purpose of life and conduct is the perfection of the individual, which must be attained through rigid conformity to unchanging law.

In the later part of the Greek period there developed a feeling of dissatisfaction with the dogmatic assumptions of man's reasoning and a sense of need for authority in morals. One expression of this dissatisfaction was Skepticism. The Skeptics doubted the validity of human reason and declared a disbelief in the possibility of true knowledge. They maintained that man knows only appearances, that he can never actually know anything, and that only by giving up concern for both good and evil can he ever attain happiness. To meet the demand for supernatural authority, attempt was made to synthesize the chief elements of the Old Testament revelation and the views of Plato. Philo of Alexandria was the first to try to expand the ancient Hebrew Scriptures in the light of Plato. He endeavored to show that, after all, Greek thought was identical in principle with the teachings of God. This attempt — the forerunner of many later fruitless attempts to find a middle ground between the wisdom of God and the reasoning of man — turned out to be a strange mixture of intellectualism and mysticism that was profitable for nothing.

Philo wrote about the time of the birth of Jesus. For two or three centuries before Christ an inner conviction had been growing stronger that the reason of man is insufficient. As this skepticism increased, belief in the authority of the supernatural superseded belief in the authority of reason. Along with the growth of this inward tendency, there was an external effect upon men from the many eastern religions that were being introduced into the western world. The demand for supernatural authority found expression in various and curious ways. Following the work of Philo and continuing over into the early centuries of the Christian era, there was a revival of Platonism.

The Coming of Christianity and Its Influence on the Reasoning of Man

Into the midst of the philosophic gropings and the religious yearnings of men, Christianity was given to the world. It is God's own answer to the eternal riddle that is man and to the urgent yearning of his soul. It is God's offer of truth to man, giving God's answer to the problems that man cannot solve for himself. During the first century of the Christian era, the New Testament appeared. It was the completion of the revelation of God to show man the scope of His whole purpose, the foreshadowings of which had been given in the Old Testament. For the first two centuries, Christians were content to live in simple faith, devoting their energies to missionary activity. Only later did they manifest much interest in doctrinal matters and philosophic conceptions.

Thus, out of the longings and the unrest of man at the beginning of the Christian era, there emerged two distinct currents of thought that extended down into the Middle Ages. These were: (1), the religious philosophies of the still persistent Hellenic civilization; and (2), the newborn Christian religion, which was to exert potent influence on the thought of men. Both currents finally merge in Augustine.

The unwillingness of Greek philosophy to give up its long hold on the thoughts of men and to accept the revelation of God in Christ manifested itself in what was called Neo-Platonism. This movement centered in Plotinus who was bitterly opposed to Christianity. The goal of all true well-being, he maintained, is the absorption of human reason into a mystical union with the Supreme Being, a supra-conscious, pantheistic sort of God. Man's ethical task is to turn away from the material world, not only in its abnormalities but in every way. Another attempt of man to weaken or to supplant the force of the revelation of God was a movement called Gnosticism. Following Philo, the Gnostics sought to reconstruct Christian doctrine by harmonizing the New Testament with the ideas of Greek philosophy. Also they brought in elements from the religions of India and Persia to make an even more fantastic cult than Neo-Platonism was. They transformed every ethical problem into a cosmological problem. They considered the dualism of good and evil to be the same as that between spirit and matter. For the Christian redemption of man from sin, they substituted the redemption of the philosopher from the limitations of matter and the material.

All history demonstrates the truth that is exemplified in these two movements: the innate persistence of man's unwillingness to accept authority other than his own reason. These two systems sought to substitute pagan philosophy for Christian doctrine; the early church fathers, entrusted with the responsibility of shepherding churches in a hostile world and having the obligation to interpret the teachings of Christianity in the face of attacks by philosophy, undertook a zealous defense of the faith. Trained in classic philosophy, the church fathers sought to appeal to the rational man, "to represent the Christian doctrine as in accord with reason." Thus they started a movement which led to the union of Christian truth and Greek philosophy. They asserted the pre-eminence of Christianity because it is a perfect revelation of God through Jesus Christ. It is the only true philosophy; it alone is the source of correct knowledge and true holiness in this world and the world to come. Man can become rational only by being saved, and he can be saved only through a perfect revelation. God has always been revealing the truth; He has revealed it through the reason of man. However, revelation apart from Christ is not complete; the Logos of God has especially appeared in Jesus Christ, in order to redeem men from their sin and establish the kingdom of God.

The writings of the church fathers, especially those of Augustine, are founded upon Pauline theology but show the influence of Plato. Augustine emphasized the personal relations between God and man. Though man cannot attain to full knowledge of God in this life, all morality consists in love for God. "Thou hast formed us for Thyself, and our souls are restless till they find rest in Thee." God's sovereign love to man and man's response to that love is the chief good. "The happy life is this, — to rejoice unto Thee, in Thee, and for Thee; this it is, and there is no other." In our being is the eternal law untouched by the limitations under which we live. "Theft is punished by thy law, O Lord, and by the law written in men's hearts, which iniquity itself cannot blot out." By faith and love God calls man back to Himself and the soul acquires what God requires. "When I shall cleave unto Thee with all my being, then shall I in nothing have pain and labour; and my life shall be a real life being wholly full of Thee."

As Augustine, who built into church dogma the synthesis between Christian truth and Greek philosophy, was influenced by Plato, so Thomas Aquinas, took Aristotle for his standard. It was Aristotle's metaphysics and ethics which gave him the trend of his system. From them he obtained the purely rational framework for his thought. Then he filled this in with the doctrines of the church which were founded upon revelation. To Aquinas, revelation and reason are distinct, but they are not opposed to each other. Reason alone is not sufficient to guide men; they need revelation. Faith transcends reason and is the clue to difficulties which reason cannot solve. The world is determined by goodness, and man's will is determined by the same goodness. Sin results when sense conquers the morally determined will. Therefore, the senses, not the will, are the causes of moral evil.

Attempts to Support Revelation by Reason

A chief weakness in the life of the Middle Ages, including its ethical life, was man's attempt to support revelation by reason. As Smyth says, "A moral ideal which was not co-extensive with the whole spiritual nature of man was taken by the schoolmen from the Aristotelian ethics, and then the so-called religious virtues were more or less cumbrously and precariously built upon it. Supernaturalism in morals was added to the classic naturalism as a divine appendix to ethics. But Christianity cannot consent to be regarded as an appendix to nature, nor is divine grace an afterthought of the Creator" (*Christian Ethics*, p. 133). No system, or product of man's thought and work, that is founded upon a double standard of truth, can long endure. The attempt to defend the infallible and revealed by the fallible and secular involves calling into question the infallible. Two realms of truth, each with its own standard, means that man must build upon the one or the other. The medieval age began as an age of faith in divine revelation. When reason became separated from revelation and got the support of empirical investigation, the medieval order founded upon faith was at an end.

The Renaissance, the introductory period of the modern age, was marked by a reaction against the Catholic church and an extreme emphasis upon the powers of the natural man. Men in large numbers who, when they turned away from the Church, might have accepted the authority of the original Word of God, forsook instead all revelation because, to them, revelation meant the pronouncements of an institution in which they no longer had confidence. At that time, there was only one place they could go to find secular truth to replace the wisdom of what stood to them as revelation. This one place was the classical writings of ancient Greece and Rome — writings which exalted the powers of the natural man. Aristotle, "the prophet of the natural man," strongly influenced these writings.

This extreme humanism, like church dogma, proved insufficient to meet the need of men. As they had tried all else, it was now time for a call to come back to the first principles of Christian truth, which had long been lost sight of, in the midst of ecclesiasticism. This call came in the form of the Protestant Reformation, the key phrase of which was, "The just shall live by faith." In essence, this meant that God Himself, through His Word, will, by the enablement of the Spirit, make known to each individual, independent of priest or church and with no guide other than the Holy Spirit and his own enlightened conscience, what God's purposes are and how he may fulfill those purposes.

Reason Set against Revelation

But, once again, reason set itself against revelation. Erasmus, the most brilliant exponent of humanism, even before the Reformation itself began, made the Bible and the classics coequal, thus destroying respect for revealed truth. Luther was much influenced by Erasmus, as well as by humanistic studies in general. Social humanists like Melancthon, on whom Luther leaned heavily, and the educator, Sturm, helped along the union of humanism and Protestantism. The Reformation leaders sought in the ancient classics, light on theological matters. "Plato and Aristotle were rescued from the oblivion of centuries and again studied." Luther studied classical literature and philosophy, advocated the mastery of the Greek and Latin classics, and, even after he had rejected scholastic Aristotelianism, his associate, Melancthon, made humanistic Aristotelianism the philosophy of Protestantism. Zwingli devoted much time to the study of humanistic writings and maintained harmonious relations with humanists. Calvin's background was strongly humanistic. Even after his conversion, he published writings which indicated definite sympathy with humanists. He was on intimate terms with Melancthon. When he reorganized the school system of Geneva, he gave large place to the humanities in the curriculum.

Official Protestantism failed, therefore, from its beginning, in spite of the spiritual heights it both achieved and made possible, to adhere solely to the truth of revelation. Instead, it poured into the current of human thought worldly intellectual elements of paganism. Soon after the death of the Reformation leaders, secular philosophy openly disavowed dependence upon revelation and insisted upon "the acceptance, in the name of Christianity itself, of general moral reason as the supreme guide." The Catholic church, in the Counter Reformation, likewise put itself under humanistic influences. Thus the products of human reason took the place of the doctrines of both churches in the thought of man.

This development did not occur, however, without skeptical reaction. Montaigne pointed out that if man does not rest upon faith in revealed truth but brings in reason to support faith, he must trust his senses, which are subject to illusion, or his subjective powers, which are dependent on the data of observation that are doubtful. If we reject faith, Montaigne said, we can do nothing more than to keep our thinking as scientific as we can and thereby gain as perfect knowledge as is possible.

In spite of skepticism, the early scientific movement followed and emerged eventually into a philosophic point of view called scientific realism. This realism was the beginning of the reign of rationalistic philosophy, which depends wholly on reason, denying the authority of revelation. This philosophy found expression in two directions, that of rationalistic materialism, an echo of Aristotle, as typified by Francis Bacon, and that of rationalistic idealism, an echo of Plato, as introduced by Descartes.

Bacon stressed the power of man to find all answers in *nature*. Beginning with doubt, man attains to knowledge, and "knowledge is power." Bacon held that, by experimenting and inventing with a mind free from all "idols," or presuppositions, man can gain control of things. Hobbes carried these materialistic ideas still further. The first cause, he claimed, is unknowable. Matter is the one substance; motions of atoms act upon the senses and cause reactions in man. Thought does not exist apart from sensation. Mind, or spirit, is only brain in action. Every act of man is determined by mechanical laws; behavior and all moral action is the product of natural laws. Man is guided by the desire to achieve the good, or agreeable, and to avoid the bad, or unpleasant. Good and evil are relative to the individual.

Descartes, like Bacon, started with doubt. His aim was to find principles that could be defended with mathematical certainty. He built up a philosophy of doubt, maintaining that the fact of doubt proves the existence of God. Put no dependence on the senses, he said, and trust to reason with its distinct and clear ideas. In spite of his idealism, the emphasis of Descartes served later as a foundation for a rationalistic philosophy which was materialistic. Spinoza denied revelation and the personality of God. An Eternal Substance is for him the core and explanation of all being. God as impersonal neither loves, hates, nor purposes; there is no design in nature, and all is subject to mechanical laws. Concepts of good and evil, of human responsibility or freedom, must disappear in the Eternal Substance. Inherent in the reason of man is the necessity to develop a moral code in relation to his actions; this is an inner urge to self-realization.

Many Systems of Ethics Developed out of Man's Reason
Make for Much Confusion

Thus has man, beginning in a series of diverse speculations in Grecian times and continuing in ever increasing number and diversity to present times, cast aside all help but his own reason. There are today many systems of general ethics, making for numerous complexities and no little confusion. In the midst of these complexities and this confusion, one fact stands out clearly and definitely: man is incurably inclined to try to solve the problems of life and conduct in human wisdom, whether this wisdom be creative or imitative. This brief survey demonstrates that he has borrowed much from the past, particularly from Aristotle. The influence on medieval theology of human reason, especially as represented in the philosophy of Aristotle, was immense. Thomas Aquinas, whose *Summa Theologica* became the foundation of Catholic doctrine, found in Aristotle his ideal estimate of things, and he followed Aristotle unconditionally. Doughton exclaims, "What a strange prank of history that the pagan Aristotle, who died more than three hundred years before Christ was born, should have become the dominant master of mind in the Christian church!"

Though Aristotle expressed ideas that influenced Christian theology and ethics, we need to remember that an ethics which is solely the outcome of human reasoning can be nothing but a human ethics, a morality for this world only. Through the bearing that his teachings had on theology as well as philosophy, Aristotle has influenced most profoundly a great many of the conceptions of Christian ethics. In part this influence has been for the good, but it has also led to the acceptance of non-biblical ideas and conclusions. "Where is the wise? where is the scribe? where is the disputer of this world? hath not God made foolish the wisdom of this world?" (I Cor. 1:20) If man were able by his wisdom and reason to solve the problems of life and conduct, God would never have made a revelation of Himself and His salvation. That revelation is far from being an appendix to, and an emphasis upon, ideas discovered by the reason of man.

Always, puny man whose life is "a vapour, that appeareth for a little time, and then vanisheth away" (Jas. 4:14), who is helpless in the grip of forces without and of a corrupt nature within, has overweening confidence in his own powers. The early Greeks were strangely modern in their chief emphases. They were essentially like men typically are in all times in that they had boundless confidence in the ultimate efficacy of human reason. On the strength of this confidence, the Greeks built a philosophical structure that has been the admiration of all ages since. Socrates said that reason is the key to the good life; Plato taught that reason is the only road to truth; and Aristotle made reason not only the guide to all happiness but also the crowning achievement of man. Ever since their day, men have been enamored with their teachings, imitated them, enlarged upon them, increased the number and the variety of speculations, and had the same confidence in the power of natural reason.

The Message Men Need for Right Living Is the Revelation God Made in His Son, a Message That Does Not Do Away with Reason

The revelation of God came to the world, not as another philosophy, not as a program of ethics, not as a system of institutions, not as a set of rigid rules or of mere definitions, not even as a "way of life" for us to live. It came as a *life*, the life of God's own Son. The message men must have as a basis for right living is not the message of man's wisdom, developed through man's reason; it is the message of the Cross of Christ. "For after that in the wisdom of God the world by wisdom knew not God, it pleased God by the foolishness of preaching to save them that believe. For the Jews require a sign, and the Greeks seek after wisdom: But we preach Christ crucified, unto the Jews a stumblingblock, and unto the Greeks foolishness; But unto them which are called, both Jews and Greeks, Christ the power of God, and the wisdom of God. Because the foolishness of God is wiser than men; and the weakness of God is stronger than men" (I Cor. 1:21-25).

Smyth says, "In the ethical view we are forces among forces; our life is a question of moral forces; earth and heaven, light and darkness, this world and the powers of the world to come, meet and contend for mastery, act and are acted upon, for good and evil, in the will and character, the life and the destiny of each living soul, and in the history likewise of the great social whole of humanity" (*Christian Ethics*, pp. 479, 480). Does Christian ethics hold that the Christian should not use his reason in this struggle? Far from so doing, it demands that reason be employed. Christianity offers us a solid rational basis for morality. It tells us that God is the source of the moral order, that He is our Creator, that He has absolute right over us, that we owe everything to Him, that we can do nothing apart from Him. Moreover, it tells us why we should avoid evil and why we should do good.

God's call is, "Come now, and let us reason together." This is not a call to use our faulty reason to judge the truth of God's Word or the measure in which its teachings are compatible with man's reason. It is a call to a reasonable consideration of facts as they are, made to the end that we may, through faith, be delivered from the moral consequences of our wrongdoing and thus become able to perceive clearly our moral duty so that we can live a truly moral life. In other words, we come to the knowledge of the truth of revelation through faith for the exercise of which God gives us reasonable grounds. Once we have this knowledge, reason, in union with faith, serves to develop us in moral understanding and moral conceptions. Accompanying the process of development is the operation of the Holy Spirit who gives us personal guidance and knowledge, without which we could not rightly understand the revelation. Reason acts upon the natural moral knowledge which we possess as well as upon the knowledge which comes to us through revelation. We are to be capable of proving the will of God and of discerning between good and evil (Rom. 12:2; Heb. 5:14). From the standpoint of Christian ethics, a truly moral act is an act willed as that which is good because it is seen and understood to be the will of God. We are not to be as dumb animals which are without understanding because they have no power to reason.

The realization of the ethical ends of Christian living demands the employment of all the powers of our being in the service of God. A moral life does not just happen; it is the outcome of painstaking and discriminative judgment. Living morally is synonymous with living thoughtfully and involves intelligent and sincere effort. God expects us to use, in humble dependence on Him, the powers of reason and moral judgment with which He has endowed us. Peter tells us that God has given us precious and glorious promises "that by these ye might be partakers of the divine nature, having escaped the corruption that is in the world through lust. And beside this, giving all diligence, add to your faith virtue; and to virtue knowledge; And to knowledge temperance, and to temperance patience; and to patience godliness; And to godliness brotherly kindness; and to brotherly kindness charity" (II Pet. 1:4-7).

We could not, if we would, keep the mysteries of faith out of the hands of reason. The very necessities of belief and of a Christian walk combine to bring reason to bear upon faith. Far from being opposed, faith and reason are necessary to each other. Were it not for reason, there would be no doctrine and no creed, nor would we have a well-grounded faith or a science of Christian conduct. Without the exercise of reason, we would never have had those treatises on the great teachings of the Bible which have kept faith living and Christianity a reality. Through the rational faculties we apprehend moral truth and apply it to life. No Christian can despise or distrust reason so long as it functions in complete reliance on, and in absolute subjection to, Him who is the Author not only of faith but also of reason.

CHRISTIAN ETHICS IN ACTION

This means that we will accept as true no ethical teaching which we recognize as contrary to the revealed Word and the known will of God. Always, the written Word is the criterion by which we evaluate whatever purports to be true. In many systems of ethics, especially those largely influenced by the content of the Christian revelation, there is a lofty idealism against which we need be on our guard lest we make compromise with the revealed truth of God. General ethics can deal with man only as he is; it is limited by the things that man can do for himself. Apart from the influence upon it of Christianity, it finds its end in man. Even when it makes reason dominant, it defines the end as man's highest good, ignoring the truth that God is the supreme good.

Inadequacies in General Ethics

The chief defect in general ethics is that it does not take God into account. Consequently, it is characterized typically by these four inadequacies: (1) it fails to set up the only perfect standard for character and conduct; (2) it ignores the actual moral standing and condition of man; (3) it rejects the only means for the realization of the true ideal; (4) it disregards, or applies imperfectly, the sanctions suitable to the adoption of this ideal and these means. The only perfect standard is the character and the will of God revealed in Jesus Christ. The actual moral standing of man is that of a guilty sinner, and his condition is that of a being enslaved by a carnal nature. The only effective means for the attainment of the true ideal are the atoning death, the bodily resurrection, and the continuing advocacy of Christ, coupled with the regenerating, sanctifying, enlightening, and enabling work of the Holy Spirit by the Word of God. The proper sanctions are the reverential fear of God, the love of God, charitable regard for our fellow men, and the rewards which are the portion of one who is in complete accord with the purpose and the will of God.

The Adequacy of Christian Ethics

Christian ethics rests upon the teaching of the Bible concerning the moral goal of man. The first step is the restoration of man to fellowship with God. In love, God provides an atonement which removes the obstacles of sin and guilt and makes it possible for us to become His children. Then, in the person of His Holy Spirit, He takes up His abode within us. The Holy Spirit, dwelling in the new nature, both initiates and continues to bring about goodness of heart and of life. Through the Spirit, our Lord continues His work of teaching and presenting truth to mind, making known ever new aspects of truth and goodness, giving power to meet the growing needs of the developing life, and revealing new aspects of Himself and His own sufficiency.

Anything in our conscious experience constituting the basis for an act of will lies within the scope of moral conduct. Involuntary acts are not moral acts, but anything in which we exercise a choice is moral. By the enablement of the indwelling Spirit, we bring forth the fruits of the Spirit in all the moral connections of life. We meet moral problems everywhere and in every relationship we have with objects, with self, with other people, and with God. The motive power to moral action is the love of God. In relation to others, Christian love first finds expression in the Church, the company of those who are born of God. It is manifest also in all the natural relations of life, including those of the family, economic and industrial life, community activity, political connections, civic matters, and religious life. The Spirit always acts through the Word, never contrary to the Word. Moreover, all the moral conduct of the Christian is inseparably bound up with the person of Christ.

Our task is not to discover moral truth but to practice it. In matters of Christian faith and Christian conduct, it is not true that "every man is entitled to his own opinion." Christian truth is revealed truth; it is "from heaven" and not "of men." The content of ethics for a Christian is the outcome of an impartation from above. It is the result of the coming into a human being's life of the Spirit of God as a living, dynamic Person (I John 3:4-10). This makes for a sharp demarcation between the things of God and the things of Satan, between good and evil, between right and wrong, between righteousness and unrighteousness.

The Christian has within himself a source of ethical knowledge in harmony with the teachings of the Word of God. His renewed mind, enlightened by the Spirit, standing in accord with the Bible and regulating itself by the Bible, is able to prove what is good, well-pleasing to God, and perfect. Just as the earthly life of Jesus was determined by His union with God the Father, so the life of the Christian is Christ, now operating as the Holy Spirit in his soul. This Person dwelling within is the source of a new life, of enlightenment, and of progressive sanctification, or the separating of the life from a sinful world and dedicating it continually more and more unto God. The Spirit dwells in every true believer, from the lowest and least gifted to the highest and most talented. Under His guidance, every believer must apply the principles of the teachings of the Bible to his particular circumstances. The Spirit can and will teach each sincere and humble child of God many spiritual and moral truths as he is able to receive them. It is not by gifts of intellect, strength and power of mind, level of education, economic status, esteem in which we are held by men, cultural level, position, or possessions that our place in the kingdom of God is determined. What counts there is our heart relation to God.

Christian ethics is not intended to be a system of rules for conduct. It is not concerned fundamentally with presenting solutions to moral problems or with dictating in detail the moral behavior appropriate in particular circumstances. Instead, it sets forth the principles which must be kept in mind by those who meet such problems and to which conduct must conform in this or that set of circumstances. Character — Christian or non-Christian — cannot be compelled. Acts done merely because of external force — law, rules, social pressure, custom, or fear of consequences — are not truly moral. Christian ethics is an ethics of the spirit of man controlled by the Spirit of God; it is inner and free, not dominated by legalism, authoritarianism, or any form of externalism.

Christian Ethics in Relation to Law

To be of value and usable by all persons, ethical goals and principles must be general rather than specific. Life is a process of continual adjustment to changed and changing circumstances. Morality is founded on eternal law which is unchanging; in principle, what is wrong at one time is wrong at all other times. Yet morality is not a set of rigid rules applicable to all times and to every condition. Moral ideals cast definitely into a particular code tend to become static. Circumstances differ from time to time, from place to place, and from person to person. In the midst of change, the original reason for sanctioning a way of behaving may be entirely forgotten and the code may come to be considered an end in itself. The Bible does not give us a code of ethics with definite rules. Christian ethics does not give instructions in detail. It is the work of the Holy Spirit to guide the believer in the details of his life and conduct. However, it is incumbent upon every Christian to study diligently the life of our Lord and the teachings of the Word of God so that he may know the right as it is expressed in the example and the law of Christ.

The true Christian neither is, nor desires to be, without law. Yet he has no servile spirit of bondage to law. He is as the man who "looketh into the perfect law of liberty" and he acts like people "that shall be judged by the law of liberty" (Jas. 1:25; 2:12). Birth into the kingdom puts the Christian under a new rule and a new covenant — a covenant under which the law of God is written in the heart. The spirit of the Christian is not the servile spirit of an unwilling slave but the free spirit of a beloved child who delights to do its father's will. Accordingly, the Christian is bound to obey the Father's faintest wish, the least intimation of His will. He rejoices to yield obedience to

God's law because God is his Father and has upon him a claim he does not dispute. To him, the word "law" has lost those elements of severity, bondage, and terror which legalism gives it.

As Christians, "we are debtors, not to the flesh, to live after the flesh," but by the Spirit we "mortify the deeds of the body" (Rom. 8:12, 13). "God sending his own Son in the likeness of sinful flesh, and for sin, condemned sin in the flesh: that the righteousness of the law might be fulfilled in us, who walk not after the flesh, but after the Spirit" (Rom. 8:3, 4). That is to say, Christ fulfills God's law by taking us into fellowship with Himself, placing His image and His Spirit in us and making them our personal possession. That is, we have the inner law of the life of Christ. Every one who is born of God has immanent within him, as an end and as an impulse, the activity of the kingdom of God; he is under the rule of the law of love.

The apostle Paul, writing to the Galatians, corrects an error in two forms, both of which cling most tenaciously to the thought of man. One form of this error is that works have a part in the sinner's justification; the other is that the justified believer attains perfection through deeds of good in obedience to law. Paul refutes the first by showing very clearly that "a man is not justified by the works of the law, but by the faith of Jesus Christ" (Gal. 2:16). He met the second and more subtle form of error by pointing out that it is union with Christ Jesus which counts and that "faith which worketh by love" is the foundation for moral living and the bearing of fruit to the Spirit.

Paul's admonition is, "Walk in the Spirit, and ye shall not fulfill the lust of the flesh" (Gal. 5:16). And in the next verse he says that "the flesh lusteth against the Spirit, and the Spirit against the flesh: and these are contrary the one to the other." Then he lists the practices of the lower nature: "Adultery, fornication, uncleanness, lasciviousness, idolatry, witchcraft, hatred, variance, emulations, wrath, strife, seditions, heresies, envyings, murders, drunkenness, revellings, and such like." Finally, he shows that Christian character, whence issues Christian conduct, is produced by the Holy Spirit, not by human effort. That is to say, Christian character, far from being a matter of legal or moral correctness, is the possession and the manifestation of nine qualities wrought in the believer by the operation of the Holy Spirit. These outcomes of the Spirit's working are love, joy, and peace — character as a state of the heart; patience, kindness, and goodness — character as expressed in contacts with fellow men; faithfulness, gentleness, and self-control — character directed Godward. All of them together are a moral portrait of Christ.

Christ the Standard for Moral Living

The supreme virtue of Christianity is that it presents as a standard for moral life a character that is concrete and living. "Christ is the standard of personal conduct." In Him we have the demonstration of a life lived as we should live. His is the divine character manifested in the human sphere, in true subjection to the will of God. He exemplifies the supreme standard of goodness in relation to the ordinary life of man. In Him we find at their highest all the great moral qualities which we unceasingly long for and continually strive to perfect in ourselves. In the person of Jesus is presented to us the Incarnation of the Ideal. The union of the divine and the human in Him is a demonstration to the struggling children of men that human nature is adapted for perfect morality.

Seeing Jesus as He lived among men, "in all points tempted like as we are, yet without sin," constitutes a powerful incentive to us to make our conduct right, even as His was. Yet the view would be only a hollow mockery, if we had nothing beyond this incentive. If we were obliged to strive after His example without being united with His Person, all our striving would be losing. Only in the living union between us and our Lord, mediated by the Holy Spirit, can the ideal become actual. By virtue of this union we shall eventually attain "unto a perfect man, unto the measure of the stature of the fulness of Christ" (Eph. 4:13). ". . . We shall be like him; for we shall see him as he is. And every man that hath this hope in him purifieth himself, even as he is pure" (I John 3:2, 3).

"We are . . . created in Christ Jesus unto good works" (Eph. 2:10). ". . . . Abhor that which is evil; cleave to that which is good" (Rom. 12:9). "Whosoever abideth in him sinneth not: whosoever sinneth hath not seen him neither known him" (I John 3:6). "Whosoever is born of God doth not commit sin; for his seed remaineth in him: and he cannot sin, because he is born of God" (I John 3:9). Goodness is a condition of heart, not mere outward conformity with rules or law. It works from within outward, not from without inward. It begins in the heart, but it does not stop there. If we have the nature and not merely the name of a Christian, good works flow out inevitably; if there are no fruits in the life, we are not children of God, whatever we may think we are, however we may be regarded by our fellows. Profession counts for nothing; adherence to a creed is worthless. Fervently saying "Lord! Lord!" is to no avail if we be not planted in Christ and if we have not in us the root of sincere allegiance to Him whence grows the plant of godliness.

We were not made for easy things; we were made for hard things — things too hard for us except as God works in us and through us. It is not difficult to understand the moral requirements of Christianity, but it is infinitely hard to reduce them to practice in daily living. The living of a Christian life calls for the best that is in us, plus the grace of God. It means unswerving loyalty to our Lord, and it requires unremitting attention to social and ethical situations in order that we may discern the moral implications of ever changing circumstances. In a sense, Christian living is a simple matter of loyalty to Christ and to duty. In another sense, it is a most difficult undertaking, involving adherence to high standards and individual struggle. The servant is not above his Lord. "Though he were a Son, yet learned he obedience by the things which he suffered" (Heb. 5:8).

Though our Lord said that the yoke He offered is easy to wear and His burden is light, the moral requirements of the Christian life are most exacting. Love, it is true, makes all duties easy, and the rest which He gives is blessed in comparison with the tortures of an accusing conscience and the inner conflict of a divided allegiance. But the way of no true Christian is a flowery path of ease. There are battles to fight and

victories to gain at the cost of everlasting vigilance and the expenditure of much energy. He who would live righteously must
contend against foes within and enemies without. In morality,
as in every department of conscious life, man attains perfection
in practice by dint of long and disciplined effort. There is no
magic about morality; the presence of the grace of God
does not mean that there shall be an immediate and compulsory
moralization of the individual's life.

Spirituality and Morality

The Christian life is like a tapestry woven of two chief
fibers, spirituality and morality. The former has to do with our
relation to, and our fellowship with, God. The latter means that
this spiritual relationship must be characterized by truth, uprightness, goodness, honesty, purity. Jesus said we must worship
God "in spirit and in truth" (John 4:24). "In spirit" means
to be spiritually minded, to be in vital touch with God. "In
truth" means to be thoroughly sincere and honest, that is,
ethical. There is, then, an essential connection between spirituality and morality. Whatever our profession, we do not
live on a very high level of spirituality when we are lax in
moral life. The fact remains that morality belongs to spirituality, if spirituality be real. If spirituality be not conformed to
morality, there is a defect in spirituality itself. Morality likewise can be neither perfect nor pure unless it include in the
sincere love of goodness true love for the Author of goodness —
in other words, unless it become spirituality.

We are what we are by our old evil nature which we shall
have so long as we are in this life. God is a God of exactness, in-
sisting upon things being done in order. Without the least bit
of hesitation, we acknowledge the necessity for order in the
physical world. Why should we not accept it in God's dealings
with us? The new wine of a life hid with Christ in God cannot be kept in an old bottle of a depraved nature and an immoral
life. There is no harmony between the light of a new life and
the darkness of an evil heart which issues in wrong moral practices, however much it is painted up and made to appear as it
is not. The two are wholly and irrevocably incompatible. We
must subject everything in us to God in Christ — our thoughts,

our feelings, our imaginations, our every faculty and power, our every deed. Being is fundamental, then comes doing; never do the two occur in the reverse order in the kingdom of God. Until we have a full and correct conception of the estimate which God places upon being, we will never be moral in the way He designed we should be.

True spirituality does not consist in a fancied security, arising from the recollection of a past experience. Where a real spiritual life exists, there is constant activity, unceasing striving against sin and evil, repeated humiliation before God, increasing dependence upon the Holy Spirit, and patient continuance in well doing — the last as well as, and just as much as, the others.

Bryant said that those who make compromise with evil enslave their children's children. When we Christians make compromise with sin, when we violate moral principles, when we are careless or negligent in living, when we quench the Spirit in His promptings to duty, we bring a blight upon our spirituality, dim our vision of God, weaken our moral character, discredit the Gospel, and dishonor the holy name of Him whose we profess to be. Moral living is not a pleasant kind of day dreaming. Whatever God in grace has done for us, however rich our spiritual experience, we do not and we cannot dream ourselves into a Christian moral character. There is one, and only one, way to fashion a moral character and that is to hammer and to shape it into being on the hard anvil of daily living. It is not enough to have noble aspirations and good intentions; it is not enough that we mean well; it is not enough to have exalted feelings; it is not enough that we be held in high esteem by our fellows. We must also have adequate knowledge of the conditions of moral living, good sense, and, above all, we must be willing to spend and to be spent in the unremitting effort to do all the will of God in every avenue of daily living.

QUESTIONS

1. Why study ethics?
2. With what does ethics have to do?
3. Give illustrations to show that a man cannot live right if he himself is not right.

4. Give from personal experience or from investigation of books on human conduct, examples of lack of agreement as to fundamental principles of right living.
5. Have we inborn sense that some things are right and others are wrong? Discuss pro and con.
6. Examine your thinking of a day to ascertain what proportion of it was devoted to consideration of practical problems of conduct.
7. Is there a higher moral standard for Christians than for non-Christians? Give reasons for your answer.
8. What proportion of the troubles of mankind do you estimate would disappear if men lived right in every phase of life?
9. Give examples of present-day acceptance of theories as facts.
10. What values do you see in being familiar with the different systems of general ethics?
11. Stress the importance of a Christian's having his conduct right. Can it be stressed too much?
12. Wherein is general ethics different from Christian ethics? Wherein are the two alike?
13. To what extent does one's past remain the same after he becomes a Christian?
14. Why can we not "reject flatly any call of reason?" Does God expect us to reason?
15. What is wrong with the statement, "Reasoning is the only road to truth"?
16. Wherein are the conclusions of Plato and Aristotle right? Wherein are they wrong?
17. Why did Skepticism rise?
18. Criticize the teachings of Plotinus.
19. What do you think of the effort of the Church fathers to unite Christian truth and Greek philosophy?
20. Discuss the fundamental positions of Augustine and Thomas Aquinas.
21. Can revelation be supported by reason?
22. Why does humanism fail to meet the need of man?
23. With the teachings of which of the Reformation leaders do you find yourself most in sympathy? Why?
24. Wherein was Montaigne right?
25. Do you favor Bacon or Descartes in your thinking?
26. What is the one fact that stands out clearly in the midst of the complexities and the confusion that are the outcome of man's reasoning?
27. Wherein has human reasoning failed?
28. How does revelation meet the need of man for a rational basis for morality?
29. What place has reason in connection with revelation?

30. What is the danger we confront when we study the various systems of general ethics?
31. Criticize the listing of the inadequacies of general ethics. Would you add to the list?
32. Show in respect to each inadequacy of general ethics how Christian ethics is adequate.
33. What is the parallel between the earthly life of Jesus and the life of the Christian?
34. How are Christian ethics and law related?
35. Comment on the two errors that cling tenaciously to the thought of man.
36. Can we live as Jesus lived? Are we supposed to so live? What proof can you give?
37. Just what is goodness?
38. Is it easy to live as a Christian should?
39. Is morality the fruit of spirituality? Does a person become spiritual from being morally upright?
40. Is the picture of what we do when we violate moral principles overdrawn? Give reasons for your answer.

CHAPTER V

The Goal of Life

THE FIRST CHAPTER OF THIS BOOK was an introduction to the treatment of the subject of Christian ethics. The aim of the next two chapters was to show the relation between the teachings of the Bible and the practice of right conduct. The fourth chapter was devoted to a consideration of the place that ethical principles have had in the thought of men in general and the part they play in the life of the Christian in particular. In the present chapter and the four chapters following, the five main problems of ethics that were mentioned in the first chapter will be discussed briefly.

GOALS IN GENERAL ETHICS

General ethics does not regard humanity as a collection of isolated individuals. Each of us is a tiny part of a great moral process that was going on before we were born and that will continue after we have departed from this earthly scene. General ethics finds in the progress of the individual the progress of all mankind. We cannot act or think, or even live, except as we use what is given us. Every moment of every day, we take advantage of resources not within ourselves. This is true when we perform the little, supposedly insignificant acts and when we do deeds deemed to be of great import. Each of us is a part of all we have met in experience, and we are heirs of the experience of those who have gone before. In turn, each of us has a share in determining what men in the future will experience. To the on-going moral process, every individual contributes, "some with massive deeds and great, some with ornaments of rhyme." In the total, "nothing useless is or low," and "what seems but idle show" may be most necessary.

Life Is Action Dominated by Some Purpose

We live in a universe where life and energy are in constant action. To be alive means to be in action. The activities of life go on in ways and by interactions which have reference to the needs of life as a whole and thus take on intellectual quality and moral quality. Human action is by no means identical with that of inanimate objects or with that of animals. In human beings, behavior is so organized as to issue in what we call civilization and culture, that is, in language, law, morals, science, institutions, and the arts. In other words, human behavior is endued with purpose and meaning. Man has an impulse to be, to act, to know. All his activities have as their source and energy some perception of an end to be attained. "Nothing walks with aimless feet."

Some over-all purpose dominates the common, daily activities of the life of every one of us. These are not bits of unrelated, involuntary behavior. A man gets out of bed in the morning; he prepares for the day; he goes to the station; he buys a ticket; he boards a train; he rides to the city; he makes his way to his office; he performs the duties of his business or profession. These are the activities of eight or more hours of one day. They are part of a series of acts leading to an end result — the making of a living, the massing of a fortune, the gaining of renown, the achieving of an ambition, or the attaining of something else chosen as the goal of life. What one has for a goal determines what he does step by step and day by day.

Desire and Values

The driving force back of action is desire. We seek nothing unless a desire to secure it has arisen. Our natural life is "nothing else in itself but an extremity of want continually desiring, and an extremity of desire continually wanting." Values in some form are the only things we can desire. First unconsciously, soon consciously, we evaluate the things we desire and the experiences we have. With the reaching of a judgment of value, the sense of obligation arises. Obligation is a moral term, referring not to what we must do by reason of the presence of some external force but to what we ought to do. The only force a moral obligation can have without destroying its own nature is the inner consciousness of moral value.

The right is based on the good; the good is that which has value for a person — a being conscious of distinction between right and wrong with freedom to choose the one and to reject the other, one who is responsible for his acts and who is capable of feeling a sense of innocence or of guilt. Not all evaluations are correct. When we pass judgment upon what our desires indicate to be good or bad, we often find it necessary later to reverse the decision we first reached. As we learn more about ourselves, our fellows, and things in general, we are likely to find that what we first judged to be good is, in the end or in a larger context, bad, and, conversely, what seemed bad is something we ought to do.

Values of some kind are essential to the living of a life that is at all worth-while. The particular values any person desires depend upon his individual temperament and training and upon the circumstances of the situation in which he lives. The deeper a person's moral insight is, the more sound is his judgment of values, that is, the better is he able to say what is good in the longest run and the largest context. The stronger a person's moral character, the more ready he is to act upon the outcomes of his insight, even when these are unpleasantly or even painfully opposed to his first, spontaneous evaluation.

In actual practice, moral insight is seldom, if ever, strictly a personal matter. We all move in a system we inherit; we come into a group which has moral standards based on what previous generations learned through experience to regard as good. Some of us are incapable of doing our own thinking; the majority of us are too lazy to think for ourselves to the extent that we are able to do so. Moreover, life is too short and too much taken up with necessary problems to regard every question as open for consideration each day. From the earliest times, men have found it necessary for the welfare of the group to accept certain general principles and practices and to require adherence from the members of the group. The particular views held by any one of us rest in part upon the authoritative standards of our group and in part upon the rational reflective process working upon our own experience. Parents, associates, teachers, and all our relations with the world supply us with a sum total of knowledge, opinions, prejudices, and rules of conduct. Consequently, most of the members of any given social group let themselves be guided as a matter of course by the generally accepted standards; those who reject these are few in number. Still fewer in number are those who choose to live in accordance with higher standards.

When we come face to face with life as it is lived and see the evil, the lust, the vice, the greed, the wickedness in high places and in low places, the graft, the corruption of men, we do not find it easy to subscribe to the abstract idea that there is in man's nature a law which inclines him to seek the good. Yet, if there were not in his nature that which prompts him to want the good, the world would be in a far sorrier state than it now is. Men are often mistaken in their judgments as to what is really good. Many moral judgments are passed on the basis of hasty generalizations. That which makes an immediate appeal to the senses may seem to be a supreme good but bring evil consequences. It is necessary, therefore, to judge every act not only in the light of its immediate appeal but also in terms of its consequences. In seeking the good, we are led to make comparisons, to balance present satisfactions against ultimate outcomes, to try to estimate the relative values of opposing situations, and to make comparisons between our own views and those of other people. In thus pondering, we attempt to find an answer to two age-old related questions of general ethics: What is the ultimate nature of the good? and, What is the true purpose and the last end of human life?

What Is the Good Which We Seek?

It is impossible to live without acting. Whenever we act, we are obliged to make choices between the right and the wrong, the good and the bad. All along the line we make decision after decision, — insignificant ones and tremendously important ones. Some acts are almost universally disapproved among men; other acts are widely approved. Between these two classes are many others upon which there is much discussion and no small amount of disagreement. Hence the necessity of the effort to ascertain what the good is which we should seek.

Obviously, there are "goods" which are not "the good." We are continually seeking "good" things and avoiding "bad" things in life. We do our best to secure "good" food, "good" clothes, "good" houses, "good" positions, "good" schools, "good" communities, "good" government, "good" conditions for living. In spite of our lack of clear conceptions of what goodness actually is, we do not refrain from the practice of seeking good instead of its opposite in the numerous avenues of daily living. One mark of goodness which is a help in determining the good in the case of conflicting interests is the probable permanency of the good chosen, that is, will we always be satisfied with what we have selected?

Moral good is something men feel impelled to seek even in the face of impulses that urge to the contrary. There is a law of nature as known by man and enforced by man upon himself. Any action that is against nature is an evil action; we cannot go against our nature and thereby do good. Of course, not every man yields to the law of his nature, but when any man does as his highest nature indicates he should do, he does good. To go with the best in human nature is good; the good is what makes a man fully a man. This means that moral behavior is often different from that which at the moment is the "natural" way to act. Also, it is most easy to assume something is good when it is not actually so. Therefore, we must be in constant quest for the highest good.

The Answers of General Ethics to the Question

This brings up the second of the two related questions, What is the true purpose and last end of life? or, What is the highest good for man's attainment? This is the primary question of theoretical ethics, the oldest and perhaps the most fundamental ethical problem. Whatever man possesses in his nature, however closely he adheres to the eternal law, he is never without awareness of having come short; he is always conscious of not being as he should be; he always has the realization that there is a better state of being than the actual, that some condition of life higher than the one attained lies ahead of

him. The entire history of ethical thought is a commentary on
the necessity of man's having some conception of an ultimate
good, the *summum bonum* of his existence, the highest for
which he should live.

This problem of the highest good is considered in every
system of ethics. It has always been a source of perplexity to
ethical thinkers, and to it they have given various solutions.
Socrates made knowledge the source of all virtue. Plato emphasized likeness to God, though he does not seem to have a
clear idea of a personal God. To Aristotle, happiness, or well-
being based on rational or virtuous activity, is the final end of
man. The end or goal for Hedonism is happiness in the form
of physical pleasure or sensuous enjoyment and, so far as possible, freedom from pain and misery. There are two types of
Hedonism; the type that considers happiness for one's self
the end of rational living, and the type that considers the
greatest happiness of the greatest number of people the goal of
ethical striving. The first is known as Egoistic Hedonism and
the second as Universalistic Hedonism, or Utilitarianism. Eudaemonism makes human well-being, or the development of
human personality in all its potentialities, the supreme good.
Altruistic Eudaemonism, or Altruism, is the pure seeking of the
happiness and good of others, regardless of one's own interests.
Evolutionary Naturalism stresses adaptation to environment as
the goal of life. It holds that evolutionary progress, which is
moral as well as physical, leads to self-realization, or the highest
possible development of the individual.

To Intuitionism, duty or "obedience, pure and simple, to the
objective moral law" is the highest good. Kant is the outstanding
exponent of this system. He maintains that we act under "a
categorical imperative," an unconditional law of duty which
impels to obedience whatever the consequences may be. Implicit obedience to this categorical imperative is the highest and
only ultimate good. The guiding principle of action is the
will. The laws of nature are the laws of reason; when our
will is governed by reason and not by inclination or desire, it
is the moral law that legislates within us. Kant says, "Nothing
in the world is good except the good will." We are responsible

for directing our will aright. To correct the tendency to exercise our wills in a mistaken and wrong way, we are to take for a guide the maxim: "Act only on that principle which you can, at the same time, will to become a universal law." A second maxim for guidance is, "Act so as to use humanity, whether in your own person or in the person of another, always as an end, never as merely a means."

Inadequacy of the Answers

Thus have the originators of systems of general ethics chosen some one "good" as the supreme good and made it the standard for judging the goodness of all "goods." Each system stresses the supremacy of its chosen "good." In every case, the "good" emphasized has value for life. None of the goals presented is false, yet none of them is adequate. Each "good" is desirable, but the very fact that such is the case proves that it is insufficient in itself to be the goal of life. In other words, there is a good higher than any of the highest goods offered us by general ethics.

The Goal in Christian Ethics

The concern of ethics is with the needs, the ideals, and the aspirations of man as he lives his life here and now. Any ethics which ignores these is out of perspective and can be harmful. It is with the processes of the lives of persons, or beings capable of distinguishing moral values and reacting to them, that ethics is largely concerned and in connection with which moral issues are settled. The operation of God in the life of man, without which there would be no Christian ethics, is definitely related to the same processes of living that ethics in general has for its concern. There is bound to be, therefore, some identity of content between Christian ethics and every system of general ethics.

The Goal of General Ethics Suffices for a Superficial View of Man and a Superficial Belief

From the standpoint of general ethics, the best life for man is the moral life. By this is meant a rich and free life filled with all that contributes to the worth of human living. It signifies the fulfilling and the enlarging of the best powers of man and the eliminating of any capacities of his nature which, if developed and expressed, would diminish in any way the worth of living. In that morality has to do with the living of the best possible life, it must always stress those values that enrich life in any way. A value, whatever it may be, has moral significance when, and to the extent that, it contributes worth to human living. Morality is not an adjunct to life, nor is it merely a part of life. It is a way of living; it is the ordering of the activities of life so as to increase as much as possible the worth of living for one's self and for one's fellows. To live well, we must be capable of wise discrimination of the relative worth of the needs, the interests, and the possibilities of men and of intelligent organization of our activities so as to secure the best combination of values. Moral regulations and moral prohibitions are not morality; they can be no more than a means for guiding conduct to the end that moral values may be realized. They constitute a guide for living, but they are neither the end nor the way to the end of living.

All this is very well as far as it goes, and it may go far enough, at least temporarily, for anyone who, in his thought, is satisfied to regard man as less than he actually is. Interpretations of man which make him a mere animal, a part of a mere mechanical process, nothing but a physiological being, a mere creature of the world of time and sense, or similar half-truths, need not go deeply into problems of morality. Of course, it is not the province of ethics to formulate answers to questions concerning the nature of the universe, the purpose and the meaning of things, and the nature of man. But the answers given such questions by any individual in the depth of his being have everything to do with his ethical theories and his moral practices. It is not possible to keep apart permanently questions of morality and questions concerning the nature of man and of the universe in which he lives. What man ought to be and to do depends upon what man is and upon his place in the totality of things. An ethics founded upon the assumption that man is the measure of all things and which denies his kinship with any being higher than himself can do nothing better than to consider man's highest welfare. Such an ethics is bound to conceive that the good sought by man ends with what man can make of himself.

From nothing, nothing comes. No stream rises higher than its source. "Man is made by his belief. As he believes, so he is." The belief that makes any man what he is in worthy moral life is not the belief that he says he has, or the belief he holds to in a general sort of way, or the belief he acquires incidentally through his contacts and his relations with his environment. A belief held to even lightly does affect one's life, but it does not produce that character which is the source of true moral life. Superficial belief spells superficial character and finds expression in superficial living. Belief founded upon sincere and deep conviction of the truth of what is believed is the only kind of belief that can make for depth in moral living. It is the truth which grips one in his inward parts that molds one's character solidly and determines truly moral conduct.

The Goal of Life for Christian Ethics Is Inseparable from Christian Doctrines

There is no Christian ethics apart from a Christian view of life as revealed to man in Christ. The practical question of Christian ethics is, How ought a Christian to live? It is therefore a system of morals founded upon Christian faith, and its content is the nature, the meaning, and the principles of moral living revealed to man in the person and the teaching of Jesus Christ. He for whom Christian morality is a reality is a person in whose experience Christ has become a reality through vital faith. Such an one does not subscribe to Christianity as one system among many, all of which make equally genuine appeal to thought and experience. Instead, with living and actual faith in Christ as the Son of God who redeemed mankind, he vigorously proclaims that Christianity is a system of doctrine and of practice with definite bearing on the whole range of the moral experience of all men. As such it demands universal allegiance.

It is impossible to discard the doctrines of theology, because they enter directly and definitely into a system of Christian ethics. The knowledge of anyone into whose heart God has shone to give "the light of the knowledge of God's glory, reflected on the face of Christ," is, primarily, knowledge of God and, consequently, doctrinal in character. But it is also knowledge of an ethical God and therefore the source of true moral knowledge, which is the subject of Christian ethics. The point of departure for Christian ethics is a holy and righteous God — an ethical Being — as He is made known to faith by the facts of revelation.

The fundamental doctrine of Christianity is the Incarnation, a union of God and man in a Person who so manifested the nature and the will of God as to be the exemplification in human life of the good that man should seek. The fundamental fact in Christian experience is the new birth, in which divine life unites with human life. Christ who lived, died, arose from the dead, and ascended into heaven, in the person of the Holy Spirit takes up His abode in the heart. The regenerating power of God creates in man "the new self" which, as is the case with all life, embarks upon the process of growth, and "is renewed in knowledge after the image of him that created him" (Col. 3:10). The result is that the knowledge attained becomes more and more perfect. For the natural man, to know is not always to do. Often we know and approve the good, yet in self-will refuse to do it. In human weakness, we frequently find ourselves powerless to do the good we approve and would do. The new self inclines us to such things as are right; the Holy Spirit inspires us to seek after Christ, enlightens us concerning right and duty, and enables us to perform the good thus made known to us.

This means, of course, that Christian morality has a source higher than human reason. The new birth is the entrance into another life and the reaching of another manhood. There follows fuller understanding of our own life, the life of our fellow human beings, and of God. It is human to be more concerned with doing than with being; God is more concerned that we should be creatures of a certain kind or quality than He is with what we do. The nature of our being determines the nature of our actions. "From within, out of the heart of man" proceeds all that makes him good or bad. When our being is good, our actions shine forth brightly. If we are right with God, we will be fundamentally right in the outward relationships of life.

For Christian Ethics the Highest Good Is Being in Harmony with the Will of God

This is equivalent to saying that man's highest good consists in being in harmony with the will of God, who is the source of all good. Jesus came into the world to do the will of God before men and for men. He lived so that men might see the will of God in action and He died so that men might have that life which makes it possible for them to do the will of God. "This is the will of him that sent me, that every one which seeth the Son, and believeth on him, may have everlasting life" (John 6:40). "I am come that they might have life" (John 10:10). Life, the life that is found in Christ, the life that makes man a new creation, is the *summum bonum*. Its standard is the character and will of God revealed in Jesus Christ. The difference between the living of a good life and the living of a bad life does not lie in the fact that one person wills that which is good and the other does not, but solely in this, that the one is in harmony with the life and will of God within him, and the other is not. Acts centered in God are morally good; acts centered in self are morally bad. Our moral character is what we are before God; it is in our character that we are good or evil. The Bible tells us plainly that we can be guilty of the grossest evils when we are blameless in outward action.

Though Christian ethics is founded on something higher than human reason, it does not ignore human reason. The appeal of Christianity is not an unreasonable appeal, inviting men to follow blindly that which is incomprehensible to their minds. On the contrary, Christian ethics appeals continually, not only to our natural sense of right and wrong, but also to the conceptions developed through the power of thought. Christianity teaches us that we have the ability to reason by virtue of the fact that we are made in the image of God and thus raised above the brute creation. It gives us the ideal of a reason which, freed from the blight and darkness of self-will and sin, can function perfectly in connection with the operation of the Holy Spirit. Faith neither obliges us to believe anything against right reason

nor leaves our reason unassisted in our never-ending search for
the good and in our unceasing striving to make the good actual
in our lives.

The highest good is not, then, merely an end worthy of
man's pursuit. For us there is a goal — the completion, the
perfection, the complete fulfillment of the purpose for which
God gave us being. "Man's chief end is to glorify God, and to
enjoy Him forever." God, the reality which endures forever,
not a passing thing or something merely human, is the true end
of life and the highest good. He is the source of all goodness;
other goodness is a limited representation of the limitless goodness of God. We were made for God, and in God our nature
finds completion. Our destiny or end is a matter of both nature and grace. We are in nature what we are, in order that
we may be what our nature makes it possible for us to be and
that we may be fully that which we may be. Through the
grace of God in Christ we are raised to a new life and a new
destiny, even fellowship with God and participation in eternal
life. Herein lies our well-being and the realization of that fullness of life for which we were created.

Happiness for us lies in this participation in the life of
God. Never do we attain happiness by pursuing it as an end in
itself. Happiness is within and not without. There is no real
happiness save in the union of the soul with God, and this is in
no wise dependent on outward circumstances. True happiness,
eternal happiness, is the consequence, the by-product, of being
in right relation with God. No created thing, not man himself,
not all the things of the world and the glory of them, can ever
really satisfy for a single moment a single human being. All
the "goods" of life lack the complete perfection of which man is
capable and for which his whole being yearns. Man must find
satisfaction in something higher than man. He can find satisfaction only in perfect good, and perfect good exists only in God.
In God man finds his rest. Possessing God, he has perfect good;
possessing perfect good, he has perfect happiness — happiness
that has no ending, for it, like God, is eternal.

We cannot get into right relation with God until we learn —
really learn for ourselves in personal experience — the fact that

man as he now is has a corrupt nature which makes it impossible
for him to do the good he sees, knows, and approves. The gate
of entrance into the way of true well-being and real happiness is
complete realization of our own bankruptcy and the loss of all
confidence in the flesh, leading to our placing of ourselves wholly
in God's hands and putting all our trust in Christ. From this
gate "there runs a royal road laid by God, wending its way
from earth to heaven. A way of sorrows passing through a vale
of tears; a way of thorns that turn to roses; a way of peace that
passes understanding; a way of faith foreseeing the unseen; a
way of hope piercing death's dread portals; a way of love losing
itself in Love Eternal; a way of unearthly beauty illumined by
the dawn-light of eternity; a way of happiness undimmed by
any shadow of ending, entering the heart of the Everlasting.
It is called the way of grace" (Dudley, *Will Men Be Gods*,
pp. 57, 58).

The Goal of Life Is God Himself

What is the highest good? The highest good is God Himself.
The eternal, personal, perfect Creator and the perpetual re-
Creator of all finite beings, who is holy and righteous in His
nature and has been so from eternity, is the source of all goodness. God is not a great eternal power to whom we must submit
because He is stronger than we are and of whose goodness we
partake by virtue of His enforcing upon us obedience to His
will. God is the one who "giveth to all life, and breath, and
all things." In every one of us God is more intimately present
than we are to ourselves, "for in him we live, and move, and
have our being" (Acts 17:28).

This is a truth of which we need to remind ourselves over
and over again. We misunderstand what we are and what God
is when we conceive of the relation between man and God as
being like that of a subject and a sovereign in the human sense.
Unquestionably, the will of God is to be done, but, since He
has created us after His image, His will is our will. Were it
not for sin, we would naturally follow the will of God, and the
goodness that is in Him would be continually evident in our
conduct. In the new birth, the new self becomes a part of the
highest good, or rather, it is an offshoot of the highest good.

In that it is born of God, it partakes of the nature of God and is in its very essence absolutely pure and good.

What is the highest good for man's attainment? There can be only this answer: likeness to God. A child born with the nature of its parents, through identification with them and obedience to them, becomes like them in its behavior and conduct. The Christian born with the nature of God, through expressing in action his inner life and yielding obedience to the indwelling Spirit, grows in likeness to God in spite of the deformities still remaining through sin. The basis of Christian ethics is obedience to the will of God as made known to the individual by the ever-abiding Spirit. The written Word of God has regulative worth, supplying a criterion for the discerning of spirits and serving as a base of operations for the Spirit.

To the Christian every man is an image of God. Therefore, in devotion to the Lord who commands his unquestioning and unhesitating allegiance, he treats each of his fellows as one who is eternally precious in the sight of God. By the law of love, which means that we are members one of another, he seeks the good of each and thereby promotes the welfare of all. Thus are conceit and selfishness eliminated. With a view to becoming perfect even as our Father in heaven is perfect, he always places the better above the good and puts the best in place of the better. Thus he lives on a higher plane than that of seeking happiness, his own or another's.

God is the original and the sole perfect exemplification of perfect love and perfect goodness. In obeying His will and in becoming like Him in character, we attain a good which includes every good — "pleasures for evermore," happiness that is complete and unending, the highest development of individual character, the most perfect well-being, fullest scope for the use of all of our powers for doing good, unselfish treatment of all our fellow beings and of the things of the natural world, satisfying sense of having done our duty, loving and joyous fellowship with God, and gratifying service to Him. No higher good than this is possible even to the thought of man. Human life can have no higher goal.

QUESTIONS

1. Does all mankind progress when an individual progresses?
2. Is anything we do without a purpose, even though we be not conscious of that purpose?
3. What connection is there between desire and value?
4. Can we live without values?
5. Give illustrations to show that moral insight is essentially an impersonal matter.
6. What are the advantages of its not being strictly personal?
7. Should we ever judge an act morally only in terms of the appeal it makes to us?
8. Why is it necessary to ascertain what we should seek as the good?
9. Wherein is moral behavior different from the "natural" way of acting?
10. If an individual always did only that which the best in his human nature prompted him to do, would he be perfect in moral life?
11. What relation exists between the purpose, or end, of life and the question of the highest good?
12. Take each answer of the different systems of ethics one after the other and show wherein it has value and wherein it is not adequate.
13. Why is there some identity of content between Christian ethics and every system of general ethics?
14. Discuss: morality is a way of living.
15. What is the connection between questions of morality and questions about the nature of man and of the universe?
16. How many ways of believing are there?
17. What kind of believing makes a person what he is?
18. Why can there be no Christian morality apart from vital faith?
19. In what sense does Christian morality have a higher source than human reason?
20. Illustrate the difference between the view of man and the view of God on doing and being.
21. Do you know anyone who sought happiness as an end in itself? What was the result?
22. Do you agree that the way of entrance to true happiness is complete realization of our own utter insufficiency? Why?
23. Why need we remind ourselves continually of the truth that we live in God?
24. Do you accept or reject in your thinking the line of reasoning in this chapter leading to the conclusion that likeness to God is the highest good? If you reject it, wherein is it wrong?
25. What are the implications of the fact that every man is an image of God?
26. Show the superiority of likeness to God as the good of life over each of the goals of the various systems of ethics.

CHAPTER VI

The Knowledge of Good and Evil

THE SECOND MAIN ETHICAL PROBLEM perpetually before the thought of men is that of determination of what is good and right. The leading question for consideration not only from the theoretical point of view but from the practical standpoint as well is, What is right? There is no short and easy way to decide in numerous situations what the right course of action is. True, there are principles by which human conduct has been governed ever since man had a beginning. However, our relationships with the world and with people are so complex that we must constantly be asking questions such as, What is the good and right thing to do? Is this the best course to follow? What principle fits this situation? How is a particular principle to be applied in a given case? The living of a good life necessitates ceaseless inquiry about, as well as constant obedience to, moral principles. We need additional information on many issues of long-standing import, and we must analyze new issues as they arise.

In general, we know very little though what we do not know is immense in its extent. Moreover, as someone has well said, "All the knowledge that we mortals can acquire is not knowledge positive, but knowledge comparative, and subject to the errors and passions of humanity." In no field of human activity is the realization of the limited, relative, emotionalized character of our knowledge more disturbing and more baffling than in the field of ethics.

The nature of man is a mysterious thing in itself, being a fusion of the material and the spiritual. Our knowledge, too, is a most mysterious thing, originating in the physical world, reaching to heights far above this earth, and taking on spiritual

137

characteristics. From the highest level of sense knowledge, intellectual knowledge comes. The transition from sense to intellect is not simple. On the contrary, it presents difficulties that have challenged the thinking of many a philosopher.

A chief characteristic of man is thought, and thought is a reality which cannot be explained in terms of the physical. Though our thoughts are valid for things, they are not things. Kant said that there are three ideas of the reason — the soul, the world, and God. The soul stands for the finite knower, the world for the things of objective existence, and God is both the presupposition and the bond uniting the two. The world of things is something altogether independent of us; the finite thinker can in no way be identified with the objective system of things. The finite knower and the world of things must find their common ground and their union in God. Both human minds and cosmic things have their source in the creative thought and will of God. Behind all volition there must be a rational being with freedom to will in terms of purpose fixed and determined by the notion of good. Intellectually speaking, we have but little insight into the nature and the meaning of that purpose or into its relations to the supreme good. Yet, recognition of purpose is essential to a rational conception of knowledge. Every theory of knowledge must posit the existence of God, whose will is in control of the energy of the universe.

God's real creation is spirit, and we could not conceive of His creating anything for motives other than good. As His created spirits, we are more than beings who can be explained by theories of knowledge; we are not summed up in the category of intellect. We are doers of deeds with specific qualities which are judged by ourselves and by those among whom we live. Such judging implies three things: freedom to choose and to act; the presence within us of faculties or standards which qualify us to use our freedom; and the feeling or sense of obligation to use them. In other words, we carry within ourselves the moral law which we must obey. Conviction of the correctness of our moral actions must come from within, and the guarantee of that correctness is not given in theoretical knowledge but as a moral judgment.

Thus intellectual knowledge and ethical knowledge are closely connected. Some things we know are based partly on sensuous experience and partly not so based. Such knowledge may be called composite knowledge; it contains in itself both *a priori* and empirical elements. There must be *a priori* elements of the understanding to make knowledge possible; in human nature there must be *a priori* moral elements for the genesis of our moral actions and the understanding of our moral judgments. Both our intellectual ideas and our moral ideas and judgments are creatures of experience. However, there is a difference between the process of knowledge and the development of morals. Knowledge results from the action of things through sense upon what we call mind. Moral ideas are acquired not so much directly from things in the material world as indirectly through the action of man upon man, that is, the interactions of the individual in the varied relationships of living.

This means that ethics is both an historic and an experimental science in which the essential element is the study of the experience of men. We live under a sense of obligation to seek our ideal. It is impossible for us to know the content of this ideal *a priori*; it is always the outcome of the experience of men — the experience of those who preceded us, of those among whom we live, and our own. The moral law with its sense of moral obligation is categorically final; we cannot escape it, however much we may attempt to mold the world to our way of thinking. As for the content of moral experience, our finite knowledge is capable of only a relative approach to truth. Therefore, a primary moral obligation is to put thoughtful content into our moral ideals. The conduct of a non-thinking man cannot be highly moral. In some phases of life, poorly grounded views may not do much harm, but they can be most damaging in their moral effects. Ethically speaking, we can be destroyed for lack of knowledge.

Three Answers to the Question

How do we know what is good or evil? How can we distinguish between right and wrong? A good deed is not made good nor is a bad deed made bad by the fact that a person or a group of persons judges it good or bad. Fact, not opinion, is what determines the moral quality of a deed. The purpose of considering this moral problem is to bring our opinions into line with facts. The solutions are varied and rather mixed, depending on different points of view concerning the origin, the nature, and the limits of knowledge. However, it is possible to distinguish three main answers: the empirical, the rational, and the intuitional.

The Empirical Answers to the Question

Empiricism stresses chiefly the actual experience of mankind. As man's knowledge of himself and of the world grows and increases, he gains empirical knowledge of the world and of the nature of man, learns the laws of their harmonious operation, and thus becomes acquainted with the conditions of moral life. The knowledge he thus derives from personal experience is increased through the authority and the teachings of others such as parents, other relatives, associates, and teachers, who have had different, and perhaps wider, experience. Also, there is a handing down of the experience of previous generations, especially in the form of laws, customs, and sources of moral knowledge such as epigrams, proverbs, and maxims. Thus is built up through generation after generation a large stock of moral ideas from the varied spheres of life.

The materials of moral knowledge thus collected contain many contradictions and may be the source of considerable confusion with regard to moral ideas. The things which are permitted at one time or place may be prohibited at another time or place. The empiricist tries to obtain a general standard of conduct by a careful comparison and the separating out of the relevant facts to discover the general principles which should govern the whole moral life of man.

Because of the difficulties involved in this task, the great danger faced by empiricism is relativism, or the denial of a universal, objective, moral standard. Relativism holds that there are no absolute standards; it says that there is no ultimate and objective distinction between right and wrong. Morality is all a matter of tastes and opinions. Different people have different ideas, all of which are equally right or equally wrong because there is no real distinction. A person's ethical principles are a matter of how he feels about things, and the way he feels depends chiefly on how he was brought up. The number of different codes of morality is the same as the number of the different societies and cultures in which the codes originated. Each code, far from representing anything definite and permanent, is nothing but a convenient pattern of behavior.

Relativism is a very agreeable position for anyone to take. It automatically eases tensions and makes life pleasant. One need not take a stand on anything; he is free to do what he likes. It is a human trick to make the world conform to our way of thinking rather than to mold our thought in harmony with the hard realities of truth. There is that in us which finds satisfaction in release from moral considerations and in being permitted to get what we want. In all of us is a strong tendency to believe our own opinions and to affirm that they are true while those of other people are false.

The Rational Answer to the Question

Rationalism makes reason the dominant factor in determining what is good or evil, right or wrong. Socrates, with his theory that all virtue is knowledge, is a representative of ethical rationalism, as also are Plato, Aristotle, Spinoza, and Hegel. Kant emphasizes reason but is better placed when he is classified among the Intuitionists. He believed in two realms of reason — the pure and the practical. To have real validity, the laws of ethics must be derived from reason and be applicable to experience everywhere. Reason, in the form of knowledge, or pure reason, is restricted to experience. Reason, in the form of will, or practical reason, is not restricted to experience. To Kant, will does not mean the individual will expressed in a particular act of choice but the underlying impulse which, like reason, is expressed in the individual choice but is itself universal. It is our responsibility to direct our will by reasoning rightly on particular issues.

Reason is often appealed to as something fixed and everywhere the same. Actually, it is variable. Its demand is for consistency in thinking and living. Logical consistency is conformity to the established principles of thought. Factual consistency requires recognition of the nature of the world in which we live. This makes reason subject to history and to growth. Only on the basis of a reflective evaluation of principles and a careful examination of facts in the light of such evaluation can we formulate moral judgments through reason.

Ethics is not a matter simply of cold intellectual judgments as is mathematical reasoning. For ethical living, there must be a scale of values. It involves, therefore, affective reactions somewhat like those of esthetic appreciation. Unquestionably, emotional reactions are interwoven with and have effect on moral judgments. So essential a part of moral life are they that some philosophers have maintained that moral judging is necessarily a matter of feeling. The emotions often motivate right actions and counteract distorting biases. Yet emotion judges nothing and has no part at all in judgment as such. Even when emotion strongly and beneficially influences moral judgment, it is yet emotion, not judgment. A good emotional state can prepare the way for sound moral judgments, but a good reason must do the actual judging. Emotions cannot be denied a place, but judgments must be kept as free as possible from the effects of emotional reactions. Reason, not emotion, should rule.

The Intuitional Answer to the Question

Intuitionism claims that moral values are intuitive or self-evident. Some intuitionists maintain that there is a law ultimate and absolute in the nature of man — ultimate in that it neither asks nor gives a reason for its dictates, but simply commands; absolute in that it speaks in the individual in tones of perfect and universal authority. This law is immediate; nothing comes between it and the individual. It enforces duty and allows nothing to qualify or repeal its authority.

Kant, in his emphasis upon the categorical imperative, is one exponent of this type of intuitionism. In this oft quoted sentence, he pointed out the immanence of moral truth: "Two things fill the mind with ever new and increasing admiration and awe, the oftener and the longer we reflect upon them: the starry heavens above and the moral law within." The world of morality is absolute reality; the world of knowledge is only relative. The only unqualified good thing is the good will. That will is good which acts from duty, not simply from inclination. Duty is respect for, and obedience to, law. It is a categorical imperative expressed in an unconditional "thou shalt." One of several of Kant's formulations of the categorical imperative is, "Act only on that maxim whereby thou canst at the same time will that it should become a universal law." The conscience may be said to be the expression in the individual of the categorical imperative. Kant maintained that conscience is not an acquisition, but every man has it originally in himself. Of the conscience he said, "An erring conscience is a chimera."

Butler is another ethical thinker who views ultimate moral truth as something inherent in the nature of man. However, he works out the principle in a way different from that of Kant. Butler argued that men ought to live according to nature, which is not doing as we please but as we ought, in obedience to conscience. It is the whole business of our lives, as moral agents, to conform ourselves to conscience. It is the very nature of conscience to be superior to other faculties of man. It makes distinctions among both internal principles and external actions. It pronounces judgment upon the individual, his principles, and his actions. "You cannot form a notion of this faculty, conscience, without taking in judgment, direction, superintendency. This is the constituent part of the idea, that is, of the faculty itself; and to preside and govern, from the very economy and constitution of man, belongs to it. Had it strength, as it has right, had it power as it has manifest authority, it would absolutely govern the world." Conscience is over all men because it is in all, therefore it regulates all of human life and defines its end.

Other intuitionists hold that instead of intuitive knowledge of ultimate moral law, we have such knowledge of the moral character of certain general types of conduct. Still others deem that we have intuitive knowledge of the moral value of separate acts, either in an absolute sense or in relation to other acts. Intuitionists differ among themselves not only concerning the object of intuition but also in their conception of the nature of the intuitive process. Esthetic intuitionists stress the sense of the fitness of things, maintaining that moral knowledge is a kind of feeling, similar to that of esthetic appreciation, which indicates to us what is right or wrong. Then there are ethicists who claim that the intuitive process is a kind of perception, that we have a "moral sense" which functions to inform us what is right, somewhat as our physical senses function to give us knowledge of things. Still others consider that the intuitive process is a function of reason. Kant is an intuitionist who stresses reason in conjunction with intuitive knowledge.

Intuitional ethics, the same as empirical ethics, can end in ethical relativism. Most prone are we to become a prey to our own capricious fancies; even more prone are we to deceive ourselves by rationalization. We delight to substitute subjective opinion for objective fact. It is not easy for us to be honest with ourselves. On the other hand, it is most easy for us to hoodwink ourselves into believing that what we want to accept as moral truth is given us in intuitive knowledge. Beyond all these factors which make for insincere or deluded judging, it is definitely possible for different individuals to judge differently. When Pope said, "Our consciences are like our watches. None go just alike, yet each believes his own," he uttered a truth which probably applies to all ethical intuitions, including conscience.

THE ANSWER OF CHRISTIAN ETHICS
God's Will Is What Is Right

Christianity is essentially a revelation of the nature of God. The supreme manifestation of that revelation is Jesus Christ who not only demonstrated but also taught what God is like. Jesus showed that God is the fixed point of reference for all that occurs in nature and in man. He brings our moral life into relation with God at every point. However, He offers no system of ethics. His way was to present the truths of God and allow them to commend themselves to the minds and the hearts of men through their own intrinsic quality. He knew that man can discern moral truth when it is presented to him. The central element in His teaching, completely reduced to practice in His living, is the absolute claim that God has on our obedience. We are God's creatures, with no existence in our own right. We should, therefore, be and do what God desires. We possess nothing absolutely, not even our own bodies; all that we are and all that we have is of God, who is Creator of all things. Consequently, we are bound to use everything in subjection to the will of God. Jesus said, speaking of our heavenly Father, "Seek ye first the kingdom of God, and his righteousness" (Matt. 6:33).

There is one perfect and acceptable will of God in each situation, and it is plain in all the great matters of conduct. Where God's will is clearly known, there is no question as to what is right. However, there are cases in which we must choose between two rights that seem to be in conflict. Or, we may be obliged to decide which is the lesser evil of two courses of action, neither of which we deem can be called good. In our imperfect world, with our complex interrelationships, many questions not easy to answer arise. When we make the will of God our guide for living, we must do as Jesus instructed — "seek first the kingdom of God and his righteousness."

Means Used by Christian Ethics to Find What Is According to God's Will

Christian ethics makes use of all available means for determining what is right and what is wrong. Influences from the past — the results of the experience of men through the ages made concrete in customs, laws, legends, maxims, sayings, traditions, beliefs — help to make clear the distinction between good and evil. Few of the things we see, hear, and read are without content for the moral instruction of a thoughtful mind. The lives and the acts of men, past and present, teach lessons, some showing us what we should be and do, some indicating what we should not be or do. Our personal experiences, even from early childhood, furnish no small amount of content for moral edification.

Intelligence and Reason

In connection with these two classes of experiences, our intelligence and our reason function to declare what is good and right in character and conduct. Christianity places no premium on our ignorance. The admonition of the apostle Paul is, "Wherefore be ye not unwise, but understanding what the will of the Lord is" (Eph. 5:17). In the same context he says, "See that ye walk circumspectly, not as fools, but as wise." We are to use the mind and the powers which God has given us. Never in this life will we be able to comprehend the mystery of godliness, but we need not this understanding in order to know the will of God. To discern His will, it is not required that we have either "the wisdom of the wise" or "the learning of the learned." We do not have to know the nature of the sun in order to utilize its light and heat. Not even the most learned scientists can tell us what electricity is, yet we need not possess gifts of intellect to make electricity serve us. Likewise, any one of us is capable of heeding the injunction to live with sensible, careful, thoughtful consideration of the will of God for his life.

Reason, however, is no infallible guide to what is right and wrong. Were we perfect, as God made man in the beginning, we would naturally follow the will of God. All our desires, impulses, urges, and tendencies would work in complete harmony with our reason. There would be no problem of right and wrong; our moral conduct would be automatically perfect. Sin has brought complexity into the life of man, twisted and perverted our acts, turned faculties and powers intended to be our servants into our masters, and so obscured our reason as to make it fallible and susceptible to error. There is that in our nature which demands good, but human reason is both limited and darkened in its perception of what good is. This we must admit on the grounds of both the experience of mankind in general and of our own experience. Adam's sin made for a defect in human nature, giving every one of his descendants a proclivity toward evil and contaminating not only will but also reason. By our own sins, the wounds to this nature are increased so that "reason is obscured, especially in practical matters, the will is made obdurate to evil, good actions become more difficult and concupiscence more impetuous." Therefore, while the Christian does not decry reason but demands it and though he glories in the possession of reason rather than deprecates reason, he is aware that he cannot place full confidence in reason.

Unquestionably, one of the elements which make up the moral self is the power of reason. Man refers his actions to himself and carries out a process of self-examination. As an intelligent being, he must have consistency in his thinking and living. Consistency means living according to principles. An essential to morality is the forming of moral judgments on the basis of a reflective evaluation of principles and a careful examination of facts in their bearing upon action and conduct. But morality is more than a matter of reason and intelligence. The statement, "knowledge is power," does not apply to the moral life. Knowledge alone, at least in the ordinary sense of the word, is not enough; it does not of necessity make any man a moral being. One can know ever so much and be not at all morally good. Intelligence and knowledge, while essential components of morality, are not the only ingredients thereof.

The foundation of morality is the eternal law of God. "Law is the rock on which ethics rests, and it reaches down to the lowest depths." Paul tells us in Romans 1:19 that what can be known of God is clear to the inner moral sense. In the nature of man, the created being, is implanted the moral law which is but a reflection, as it were, of the eternal law of the nature of God, the Creator. Therefore, man knows intuitively, that is, apart from experience and reasoning, that some things are right and others wrong. This knowledge is developed *through* experience, observation, and reflection but is not derived *from* experience, observation, and reflection.

Conscience

In the determination of the right and the wrong, the moral reason acknowledges the law, and the conscience urges compliance with that law and judges our states and acts on the basis of that law. In Romans 2:14, 15, Paul distinguishes between the conscience and the law by which it judges in particular cases: "When the Gentiles, which have not the law, do by nature the things contained in the law, these, having not the law, are a law unto themselves: which shew the work of the law written in their hearts, their conscience also bearing witness, and their thoughts the mean while accusing or else excusing one another." Altogether independent of moral feeling, moral sense, and conscience, there exists the objective eternal law of God. Further than this, the consciousness of morality is independent of the knowledge and even of the being of man. The ultimate source of morality is God. The objective eternal law is what finds expression in the nature of man. It is God who implants the principle of morality in the spirit of man. Created in His image, we bear the imprint of the law of His nature.

How do we learn from this principle what particular things are right and what are wrong? We learn through our experiences of utility, through the exercise of our intelligence and our reason, from the influences of society and tradition, and through positive divine revelation. The law's demands are written on our hearts as a possibility, not as the actuality of the good or the evil. The potentialities become actualities through the experiences of living and learning. However, because our moral reason is depraved by sin, our view of the eternal law is darkened, limited, and distorted. Consequently, the conscience has an imperfect standard or law by which to judge. Paul says that although men once "knew God, they glorified him not as God, neither were thankful; but became vain in their imaginations, and their foolish heart was darkened" (Rom. 1:21). Only as God shines in the heart to open our eyes and to turn us from darkness to light, only by having the eyes of our hearts enlightened (Acts 26:18; II Cor. 4:6; Eph. 1:18), can we perceive the true standard of God's eternal law. Only when this is the standard is it possible for the conscience to render an infallible judgment.

In its derivation the term *conscience* means "accompanying knowledge." Conscience is, therefore, a knowing of our moral states and acts in connection with the moral standard or law. It is not the ground of the moral law but the perception thereof. As a result of the functioning of conscience, we perceive and sense the right and wrong. Perception precedes feeling; the mind must perceive a thing before it can have any feeling about that thing. Remembering this, we may define conscience as "the feeling of obligation or duty toward what through training, experience, and honest reflection one comes to consider right and wrong, and the feeling of obligation toward the right and opposition toward the wrong, and the feeling of approval or disapproval of conduct when one does or fails to do what he is convinced is right." The outstanding fact about conscience is the judgment of ourselves, our words, and our acts. Conscience is a judge within us, freeing us or condemning us in our conduct. When we go ahead in our thoughts, words, or deeds without taking time to consider moral values, it passes judgment after we have acted. If we pause to weigh matters before engaging in any conduct, conscience gives warning judgment beforehand of the moral implications of the act contemplated.

Right is the standard of the good; it is the end expressed in the idea of law. In us is implanted the idea of a supreme standard which embodies the good. One meaning of *right* is law denoting a rule of moral action, obliging us to do what is good. This moral law originates neither in divine, nor in human, arbitrary choice but is the expression in man of the eternal law of the nature of God. Its end is the realization of the divine image. "Be ye holy, for I am holy." "Be ye therefore perfect, even as your Father which is in heaven is perfect" (Matt. 5:48). Its source is God's spiritual essence (Rom. 7:14). Therefore, it is eternal and not subject to change by human will. The question, What is good? is, therefore, the question of what is the will of God as He has revealed it to man.

Paul clearly shows in Romans 2:14, 15 that moral ideas and moral practices arise among people apart from special divine revelation. From the beginning of human life, the objective eternal law has been operative in man. God created man for moral ends and bestowed on him whom he created in His own image all the powers essential to the realization of his moral destination. Also, God arranged these powers to work harmoniously with reference to that destination so man cannot fulfill his nature, except as he lives morally. To this end, God did not give man a ready-made conscience, that is, He did not furnish man from the first with complete moral knowledge adequate for all circumstances. Instead, He endowed man with a conscience that grows as man passes through the different stages of life and meets the varied circumstances of living, with the different duties these circumstances impose. In other words, God made it necessary for us to acquire moral knowledge in a manner specific to moral life. Conscience as He gave it to us must undergo a process of self-culture, dependent completely upon the activity of reflection. "As your first duty keep on looking for His standard of doing right, and for His will." It is not implied that the knowledge which we acquire through reflection should displace conscience.

The more the content of experience and the results of reflection are interwoven with the developing conscience, that is, the more the conscience is developed, the better does it portray the objective eternal law of God. Potentially, the conscience covers every duty of man — the whole of the eternal law of God. The revelation of the law that God makes to man provides the basis for the growth of conscience. Through the Holy Spirit, God is ever speaking within us, illuminating our minds and showing us His will. The complete development of conscience is an outcome of revelations, both general and personal, so to speak.

Conscience really witnesses to One who is higher than man. Hammond says, "It is the recognition of the divine demand. But the recognition is met by a corresponding revelation. God addresses Himself to man. Conscience hears His voice and seeks to relate His demands to the actual circumstances of the moment. The measure of authority is regulated by the measure of apprehension. Always there is 'the categorical imperative,' the demand to conform to an objective standard, which has been also subjectively realized. But always there is the possibility of clearer apprehension as the voice of God becomes distinguished in its moral imperatives from customs, conventions and man's unaided struggle after the best. God may be to some men a very vague concept, in certain circumstances nothing more than the recognition of an immediate 'ought.' This is the best available to the individual in such circumstances, and if he acts against his conscience, violating his sense of 'right,' he acts wrongly. Thus it is said somewhat paradoxically, 'If you follow your conscience you may not be right, but if you do not follow it you are certainly wrong.' But to the man to whom the revelation of God has come in clearness, and who recognizes His sovereignty, conscience bears witness to the law of God. Day by day, under the influence of the Holy Spirit, there is an indication given of the application of God's will in the serious duties and responsibilities of life" (*Perfect Freedom*, p. 61).

Thus, in the words of Dorner, "The Christian as such has a personal knowledge of his own concerning objective good, allied with inward certainty; he carries in himself a higher than the merely subjective form of moral consciousness (I Cor. 4:3ff.), something higher than the current opinion of the world; he has the spirit of wisdom. This comes from *faith* in so far as the latter, formally regarded, is certainty of a divine yet human kind, and in so far as the contents of this certainty are derived from the moral archetype and principles of the kingdom of God given us in Christ (Eph. 5:14). United to Christ we are united to God, and therefore the Christian conscience is always in the presence of God and is manifest to Him (II Cor. 5:10; 1:12; Titus 1:15; I Pet. 2:19; 3:21)" (*System of Christian Ethics*, pp. 247, 248).

Smyth writes as follows concerning the effects on conscience of faith in Christ: "Faith by which conscience becomes Christian produces two marked effects in the moral consciousness: it greatly intensifies the sense of personal responsibility, and it lights up conscientiousness with a sense of freedom. The touch of the Spirit awakens conscience to a sense of the whole obligation of a human life before unrealized. The effect of conversion on the natural conscience is to raise it to a higher power. In so far as the conscience feels and responds to the influence of Christ, it is clarified in its moral judgments and rendered more efficient in its moral action, though men of naturally fine moral discernment who are not professedly Christians may have finer consciences than men of naturally low moral development who have become Christians.

"Faith imparts freedom to the Christian conscience. It is distinctive of the Christian life, that while it grows more conscientious, it also grows less and less a task of duty and more and more a service of delight. The Christian faith renders life throughout a fulfilment of a trust. By faith the love of love is transformed into the love of law. And almost in proportion as the law is loved, it ceases to be felt as law. Hence Christian conscientiousness ceases to be a hard, punctilious moral accounting and becomes an eager and glad fulfilment of the commandments. The love of God masters the Christian man, and the mastery of Love is found to be perfect liberty. The man who looks into the perfect law of liberty is blessed in his doing (James 1:25). Fear is cast out by perfect love (I John 4:18).

"Love is itself a power of knowing, and science without love fails of insight into the heart of nature. Love is likewise a principle of moral discernment; love abounds in good judgment. There is no clearer light for the determination of what is duty than this; let your love abound in your practical judgments. The largest, surest common sense is that in which love abounds. Selfishness never shows the best judgment. On the whole, and in the larger issues of things, love always proves to have been the happier discernment. We may be distrustful of any position which we hold, and of any course we are pursuing, if we find that our love does not grow in it. The unfailing light of the divine wisdom is love. Infinite love can make no mistakes. And the surest ways are the ways wherein there is most love: the clearest parts of our conduct, amid these perplexities of things, are the Christlike parts of our lives" (*Christian Ethics,* pp. 293-295).

As was previously suggested, conscience, like reason, is fallible because we are human beings existing in flesh with a nature blighted by sin and with powers limited by infirmity. When man has no specific, concrete directions, he is in danger of taking wrong for right and right for wrong, of getting confused, and of becoming a victim to his own fancies. He is prone to imagine that strong desires are divine impulses and thus to make his practices the outcome of mere natural inclinations. The New Testament teaches that conscience can be distorted and debased. Being a free agent, man can disobey his conscience, with injurious consequences to his life and character. Conscience may be weak in that its standard of judgment is yet imperfect (Rom. 14:15; I Cor. 8:12). Conscience may be contaminated or polluted in its very texture through violation of its dictates (I Cor. 8:7). A seared conscience (I Tim. 4:2) is one that has become insensible through repeated disobedience to all feeling of good. A defiled conscience (Titus 1:15) is one whose verdicts are no longer clearly perceived. The evil conscience (Heb. 10:22) is tortured with a sense of guilt. Conscience can become so perverted that the light within becomes darkness, resulting in the individual's calling evil good and good evil. Despite these ways in which the conscience may become imperfect, the Bible gives no indication that it can be destroyed.

The Word of God and the Holy Spirit

Above all else, the Christian has, for determining what is right or wrong, a source of information and guidance in the Word of God and the indwelling Holy Spirit. With Augustine, he realizes that to himself he is nothing but a guide to his own downfall, so he continually takes refuge in the divine promise, "I will guide thee with mine eye." The inner guidance of the Spirit in the form of a clear perception of what is right to do, in harmony with the teaching of the Word of God, is essential in numerous connections. Through persevering, prevailing prayer, every Christian can have such guidance; apart from prayerful reliance upon God, no Christian can properly perceive the path of ethical duty.

In all matters giving rise to question concerning what is right or wrong, the guiding principles of the written Word are basically sufficient as indications of the general lines we ought to follow in determining our course. The Holy Spirit illuminates the Word, quickens the conscience, and gives definite guidance when further need exists. Jesus said of the Holy Spirit, He "shall teach you all things" (John 14:26), and "he will guide you into all truth" (John 16:13). The Holy Spirit, under whose inspiration the Word was written, never leads us contrary to the Word. When we have a commandment of the Word which clearly applies to a given situation or circumstance, we need nothing more. Further, we are not justified in accepting as a revelation of the Spirit anything tending to supersede what is plainly taught in the Word.

The Solemn Duty of the Christian Is to Be Careful in Respect to Morality

"Be ye not unwise, but understanding what the will of the Lord is." "See then that ye walk circumspectly, not as fools, but as wise." It is our solemn duty to be alert to moral issues and to take moral problems seriously. That "everybody does it," that "it has always been done," that "it does no harm," that "this one time won't matter," that "I was taught this way," and all like statements that keep us from facing facts thoughtfully, are insufficient reasons for engaging in any conduct. In matters of moral implication, there is no place for excuses, thoughtlessness, mere prejudice, bigoted opinion, shallow belief, narrow-minded views, selfish whims, or capricious fancies. Upon every one of us rests the definite obligation, not only "to have a conscience that is clear before God and men" but also to use every means at our disposal to be as certain as we can that our conduct is right. Desperately difficult as it is to be honest with ourselves, we need to be completely honest with ourselves before God.

In case of serious doubt or unrest about the rightness of an act, it is our responsibility to make inquiry. Our first duty is to put forth sincere and genuine effort to ascertain God's standard of doing right and His will. We are without excuse when we do what we know to be wrong, or suspect may be wrong, just because other people do it. Of course, we are not to be unduly concerned over trifles, but we are to give careful thought to every moral problem in terms of the degree of importance of the issue involved. Right conduct is unequivocally right. Our decisions must be made according to the standards of God's eternal law. Even if we judge mistakenly, our judgment must be that we are following the will of God as we sincerely conceive it to apply in the given circumstances.

There are several specific and practical things we can do when we are seeking to determine what is right. We can search our hearts and try our ways to make certain that we are in God's order. If our hearts and purposes are not right before His all-seeing eyes, our hope for being set right in conduct are slim. We can pray to God for enlightenment and wisdom. We can ask Him to protect us against ourselves, our own foolishness, our selfishness, our bias and prejudice, our passion and desire, our rationalizations, our evil tendencies, and the corruption of our lower nature. We can search the Scriptures to find whatever light they may shed on our problem. We can use our reason to try to ascertain what is right. We can recall past experiences that give promise of being helpful in the present situation. We can read books other than the Bible which might give information. We can seek the advice of other people, especially of those with wider experience than we have had.

QUESTIONS

1. Cite from personal experience illustrations of the difficulty of determining the right course of action.
2. In what ways have you been baffled by the mystery of knowledge?
3. Can any thinking person be an atheist? Explain.
4. What is meant by the statement, "we carry within ourselves the moral law which we ought to obey?"
5. Why must there be *a priori* bases for both knowledge and moral actions and moral understanding?
6. Why can the conduct of one who does no thinking not be highly moral?
7. What are some of the implications of the fact that a deed is not made good or bad by the judging of a group of persons?
8. State clearly what you understand empiricism to be.
9. Define relativism in your own words and illustrate it.
10. Trace as best you can the source from which you have derived three of four of your moral concepts.
11. Give from observation, experience, or reading some examples of the baleful effect of relativism in morals.
12. Wherein is reason variable instead of fixed?
13. Why can ethics not be a matter only of cold intellectual judging?
14. Is feeling a sound basis for moral judging? Why do you answer as you do?
15. What is your understanding of the term, "categorical imperative?"
16. Contrast Kant's and Butler's views, and criticize each set.
17. What is the chief danger of the intuitional position?
18. Which of the three answers—empirical, rational, and intuitional— do you favor and why do you favor it?
19. Why did Jesus not set up a system of ethics?
20. Can you accept as true the statement, "There is one perfect and acceptable will of God in each situation?" If not, why not?

21. Why should Christian ethics not take only the Bible as the means for determining what is right and what is wrong?
22. What is the place of reason in Christian moral living?
23. How are eternal law and the nature of man related to each other?
24. Can conscience ever render an infallible judgment as to what is right or wrong? Discuss.
25. Criticize the quoted definition of conscience given in this section.
26. Does any knowledge we may acquire displace conscience?
27. What is the difference between the conscience of the unregenerated person and that of the regenerated person?
28. In what respect is love a principle of moral discernment?
29. Give illustrations of perverted conscience.
30. Make a list of the means available to the Christian for determining what is right and what is wrong.
31. Can a Christian exercise too much care in determining what is right and what is wrong?
32. What can you add to the several "specific and practical things" given in the last paragraph of the chapter?

CHAPTER VII

The Standard of Conduct

By way of emphasis, let it be said once more that man is a being who thinks. Through, and because of, his thinking he comes to know. He is also a being who acts. He is a doer of deeds as well as a thinker and a knower. His actions have specific qualities which are judged with approval or with disapproval by himself and by others. This approval or disapproval is dependent on belief in the ability of the individual to will freely; anything done under compulsion is recognized as the act of the power that compels, rather than the act of him who is compelled. This capability to will freely — to choose to do or to refuse to do — and the passing of judgment implies that there is a standard which ought to govern man's conduct whether or not it is allowed to do so.

The life of any person is complex, and it is lived in complex interrelationships with the lives of other people. He belongs to a family whose members are in contact with each other as well as with people in a wider society. The family is judged in the same way as the individual; its character and collective conduct are considered good or bad, right or wrong. The family is within the larger society of a city, or other groups, and the city and these other groups belong to the still wider society of the state. Law, written or unwritten, governs the actions and the relations of these persons and groups — the conduct of the members of the family, and of the family as a whole in relation to the city, to other social groups, or to the state, and also the acts and relations of the city, other groups, or the state to both individuals and family. The standard by which the individual judges is called "moral"; the standard by which the state judges is termed "civil" or "criminal" law. But in all cases, the standard is rooted in moral ideas which affect or condition the judgment pronounced. That is to say, judgment of the acts of men and communities means approval or disapproval according as the qualities are deemed to be good or bad.

Furthermore, individuals, societies, and states exist in almost every condition, from the lowest savage to the most highly civilized. Yet, in spite of wide and varied differences in cultural level, their moral judgments are essentially alike in kind. This signifies the existence of a pattern of general behavior, a code of things to do and not to do, founded on nature itself, being present simply because man is man. True it is, anthropologists have shown that scarcely none of the generally accepted moral teachings has not at some time in some place been denied. In different societies the most immoral practices have been practiced and even commended. In our own generation we have been astounded at the moral code of Naziism and Communism which inculcate lying and cruelty as virtues.

These facts are used by some as an argument in favor of relativism and against the idea of a moral code inherent in the nature of man. However, no reason can be advanced to make conformable to nature and morally good anything that is intrinsically against nature. There is that in man which judges acts according to their true quality, in spite of the perversity of human reason. In no society does public law uphold the lie, approve theft, or condone cruelty. It is entirely correct to say that universal law, universal custom, and universal language witness that when man, individually or collectively, judges actions, either those of an individual or a group, he does so according to a standard which must be characterized as moral.

Man a Being with a Free Moral Nature

Man is a being who chooses his acts and directs his conduct. He has a moral and free nature which makes him responsible for his own acts. There is a standard according to which he uses his freedom. Moreover, he has a sense of obligation, or "oughtness" that impels him to seek to bring his conduct into conformity with the standard. This freedom, standard of right, and sense of obligation are not creations of experience, either individual or collective; they are inherent elements of human nature, involved in its very idea and developed in their forms of expression through experience. The very fact that they exist now is proof that they have always existed. Never does something come into being from nothing.

In so far as man is man, he is not driven by mere physical necessity; he is not mere mechanism subject only to physical laws. Man is in part a physico-chemical system, and there are things in relation to him which can be described in terms of mechanical law. He is in part an animal organism or a physical system; he has characteristics that are common to animals. However, these mechanisms and these animal characteristics are not distinctive of man as a person. He has also characteristics and powers which place him far above the mechanical and the physical. He has self-consciousness, the power of reflective thinking, or reason, and the ability to distinguish between right and wrong. He has sense of responsibility for his acts and is capable of feeling innocent or guilty. He is his own director. He is a person with a moral nature endowed with the power of choosing its paths to the goal of living.

The Field of General Ethics

The thought of man is much concerned with the goal of living. Philosophy, which has been defined as "the attempt by reasoning to know what is ultimately real," is the study of the truth or principles underlying all knowledge. General ethics is the branch of philosophy that seeks an answer to man's question as to the ultimate purpose of his existence and how to achieve this purpose. It is the study of the "ideal" in human conduct. The "ideal" is conduct which conforms to the ultimate standard. Ethics is concerned with wholesome living; it has no direct interest in anything artificial or shallow, in forms of public opinion, in mechanical necessity, in mere emotion, and, least of all, in the denial of life and its ends. It seeks to know the authority for making the choices of life. One of its basic questions is, What is the final, the ultimate, authority for what is right and what is wrong?

Though a branch of philosophy and, therefore, dependent upon the philosophical sciences, ethics has its own distinct content and scope. Its subject of inquiry is the end of life for which man should live, with all the implications thereof. Its concern is not merely with what a man is or actually does but more specifically with what he should be and do. The moral impulsion — the mystery of the claims of the "ought" of life — is the purpose, the law, and the reason of conduct. The task of ethics is to discover and to enforce the ideal in human conduct. Ethics deals, therefore, with man's "highest good," or the ultimate end for which he ought to live, with the standard which is finally binding on all men and by which all aspects of conduct are to be tested, with the applications of this standard to the everyday circumstances of moral living, and with the psychological problems of desire, motive, and will connected with the individual's carrying out of ethical principles.

In other words, the special field of general ethics is that of human relationships. Its task is to find the most rational relation of the individual to himself, to his family, to other social groups, and to society at large. It is a search for a satisfactory way of living in association with people. The primary concern of morality is relationships among people. It involves the discovery by the individual of how his actions can contribute to the total value of life for himself and for his fellow men. For general ethics, that is moral which is most in accord with man's true nature, which results in the fullest development of the personality of the individual, and which makes life as a whole more worth living for human beings.

Ethics and the Individual

For general ethics, the basic problem is not that of determining the goodness or the badness of specific actions taken separately. It emphasizes the fact that circumstances have definite bearing on the determination of the goodness or the badness of most actions and things. It recognizes that rigid rules can blind us to the real moral meaning of our conduct. It holds that the best combination of many values, rather than emphasis upon one particular value, makes for the best living. General ethics does not tell the individual exactly what is the best combination for him; this he must determine by the use of his own intelligence and reason. For the guidance of his thought, ethics suggests basic principles through the application of which the individual can bring his conduct into conformity with the moral standard.

The organization of the diverse values of life into a harmonious and workable whole must be undertaken by each individual for himself. Nothing in the power of man enables any one of us to know for another person. The great wonder of knowledge "that a mind, without pattern or copy, upon occasion of nervous changes, of which, moreover, it knows directly nothing and commonly knows nothing whatever, should develop out of itself the vision and knowledge of the world" has its parallel in the wonder of the acts that are moral. This led Kant to say, "There is, however, one thing in our soul which we cannot cease to regard with the highest astonishment, and in regard to which admiration is right or even elevating, and that is the original moral capacity in us generally."

The latter is just as individual and personal as the former. Moral values exist in the relationships between the individual and the objects and experiences of living. Because of differences in temperament, powers, and tendencies, these relationships and these values are not the same for all. Each of us must make for himself what, for him, is the best organization. The elements for moral action, as for knowledge, are present in the world and in ourselves but their effective organization is dependent upon a careful observation of experience and a wise use of all of our capabilities. The moral standard is universal; the moral life that is the outcome of the application of the standard is personal and individual.

THEORIES CONCERNING THE STANDARD

The fixed point in ethics is the universal recognition of the existence of a standard of distinction between good and evil, between right and wrong. With this point as a center, there are various circles enclosing areas of human conduct of diverse nature. Each type of civilization and each great religious system has its own form of ethical teaching or characteristic morality. Everyone knows that things regarded as moral at one time or place are frequently condemned at another. However, the more such differences are examined, the clearer does it become that there is a single unifying idea in moral judgments, even when they seem superficially to be diverse. The lie which is held to be better than truth is the lie that is not found out; the stealing that is praised is that which is so cleverly done as not to be discovered. In short, the approving judgment depends on taking the thing for its opposite; if found out, it is judged according to its actual quality.

However much ethical systems may differ, they must have a fixed center for moral experience and moral teaching. Without this, human society cannot exist. Except as its members have confidence in one another, any society would eventually disintegrate. This confidence has for a foundation the individual's exercise of a reasonable amount of self-control in restraining his own desires so as to promote the interests of others and the welfare of the whole group. There must be among any people a measure of honesty and truthfulness, of purity and self-control, to keep their society from going to pieces. Only when the primary virtues of wisdom, courage, temperance, and justice are present in some form or degree in the practice of its members can any society continue to exist. Moral character in individual life is the rock upon which the family, the social group, and the state are built. That is to say, while the ethical conceptions and practices of men may vary widely, they yet witness to the presence of a universal moral standard.

Among men as individuals and as groups, there are diverse views concerning the nature of this moral standard. Some conceive it to be an ultimate and absolute law incorporated in the very nature of man. This law makes man to be man; through its functioning he becomes human; by obeying it his potentialities become actualities. Others consider the standard as fixed and immutable objective law, that is, external to the nature of man, having its source in God or in "the nature of things." Then there are those who contend that the moral standard is a matter of evolution, a movement of progress towards the "ideal congruity," which is the life of "the completely adapted man in the completely evolved society." For the individual, the standard is self-realization — the highest development possible to him during the little period of time in which he is an active part of the total evolutionary process by which the race is approaching the ideal. Finally, there are those for whom the highest good is so worthy in itself that their answer to the question of a moral sanction is that the *summum bonum* is its own standard and its own authority.

The Theory of Law Incorporated in the Nature of Man

The view that makes the standard of authority a law which man carries within himself sees the whole essence of morality as man's approach toward or his drawing away from his goal. Human life is directed motion, always carried on in reference to a goal. The work of law is direction of the motion which is life. It is not law as it is filed away for reference in statute books, nor law in the form of rigid edicts, nor law that gives impersonal information. It is a friend to man, giving him helpful direction with the one and only purpose of keeping us on the right road. In doing this, it must use severity when there is danger of our going wrong. It is a command; it is a rule of action.

Law as a rule of human action is a thing of reason. Actions are human in the measure that they are reasonable. Laws made by men, if they are really laws, if they are expressions of reason, are made with a goal in mind. The goal of all law is "the common good," the attainment of the end for which a society exists. Only as a society moves in the direction of that end does it truly belong to the social order. In its application to the state, for example, the common good could be summed up in the word "peace" or in the phrase "the preservation of unity." Essentially, it means the guaranteeing to all the subjects the right of following the law of reason to individual perfection. This implies opportunity to live so as to make steady progress to the goal for which the individual was made, the opportunity to realize to the full the possibilities of his nature.

Law is necessary to the completeness of man but it is no less necessary to the completeness of the universe. What is in him does not exist independently of what is without him. The inner repeats and reflects the outer. It operates in active relations with what is above and around him, just as his organism operates in and through its environment, taking into itself therefrom what is needful to growth and development. Law holds in the ethical realm as in the physical and in the intellectual realms. There can be a personal conscience only as there is the expression of a universal law. Moral freedom exists only where a supreme ethical will is in control. Except as man's nature corresponds with the constitution of the universe in which he lives, moral life would not be possible to him.

The universe does not run itself. It is governed by law, regulated for the common good by the dictate of the reason of its Creator. The detailed plan of that government exists in the mind of God. The universal principles of the plan, like everything in the mind of God, are eternal. These principles, through which God executes His providential direction of all things, constitute the eternal law. The same law as it functions in creatures is called the natural law. Natural law is simply a participation of the eternal law by creatures. This participation may be passive — natural inclinations to suitable goals such as are common to all creatures. It may be passive in another sense in men only — intuitive knowledge of fundamental principles. It may be active — the natural dictate of reason by which man exerts control over his own life and actions.

God, having established all of nature, governs or directs each thing according to its nature. Man, like every other object of creation, is governed according to his nature: wherein he is physical only, natural physical law applies to him; wherein he is a mechanical structure, natural mechanical law operates. But wherein his nature is moral or free nature, causing him to be responsible for his own acts, he is under the direction of natural moral law.

Eternal law is the universal principle. However, universal principles do not suffice in themselves; they must be clarified and applied. Accordingly, men find it necessary to make human laws to set forth the universal principles of natural moral law. These laws neither abrogate nor change natural moral law but supplement it by more definite determinations. Any human law is really a law only in so far as it is in harmony with the natural moral law.

The natural moral law is a completely intrinsic law, not a law imposed upon man from without. Moral legislation is wholly autonomous. The command of the law is imposed upon us from the depths within, instead of from the heights above. Law is a thing of reason; its obligation is established by reason.

Its necessity is the necessity of an act in relation to a necessary end. This relation of act to end determines how the will must function in order to attain the end but does not destroy the liberty of the will to function. There is no more compulsion in the natural moral law than there is in a mathematical law or a physical law. We are free to defy moral law just as we are free to defy the law of gravity. However, if we would attain our goal, we are obliged, in either case, to act rationally. Human action, according to Kant, is distinguished from animal behavior by the fact that men act in harmony with principles. "Everything in nature," he says, "works in accordance with laws. Only a rational being has the power to act in accordance with his idea of laws, that is, in accord with principles."

It is not necessary that man know God in order to fulfill the obligation of the natural moral law. As Paul says, heathen people may do what the law demands, thus showing that the requirements of the law are inherent in their nature. The natural moral law is a part of nature, and obligation is an essential element of the notion of law or command. Being primarily a rule of order, law includes in its very essence the concept of obligation.

That the effectiveness of the natural moral law is not dependent upon man's knowing God does not imply that God is unnecessary in the moral order. We do not need to know God to plant a garden, but without God there would be neither a garden nor a planter. That natural law is effective does not exclude dependence on God. The natural moral law carries obligation in the order of things as understood by natural reason and as reacted to by the free will of man, but the supreme and first cause of this obligation is the eternal law, whose author is God. A sense of dependence upon God is not the source of morality inculcated by the natural moral law. Such a sense of dependence adds much to the motives and the authority of the morality established by the natural moral law, but this law in its own right does establish morality.

The Theory of Law Eternal to the Nature of Man

There are various views of the concept of law as a standard external to the nature of man. The theocratic view makes the will of God the law of the moral life. From God the law derives its authority. Christians, of course, do not question divine authority. However, general ethics is not disposed to accept divine law as the only source — in some cases not even as a source — of authority in morals. Instead of the personal authority of God, some ethicists find the authority for universal moral law in "the nature of things." The Stoics taught men to live "according to nature," holding that there is a "universal reason" whose dictates men ought to obey. Some of the weaknesses in such a claim are these: neither the meaning of "nature" nor the end to which nature is tending is clear; it is difficult to determine which aspects of nature should be stressed and which should be ignored or repressed; following nature does not solve the problem of sin and evil in man's being.

The Esthetic school of philosophers takes the fitness of things to be the standard of moral conduct. They teach that certain principles are basic to observed differences and relations, and these principles determine what is fit or unfit in the circumstances. In criticism it can be said that "taste" is an insufficient standard for conduct. Feeling is essentially always obscure. A "feeling of fitness" is an undefined base for moral conduct, with a tendency to degenerate into unreasoning routine.

The Moral Sense philosophers emphasize the presence in man of a faculty, a "moral sense" corresponding to the feeling of "oughtness," which tells him what is right. This view does represent an improvement on "the sense of fitness in things." Yet it still involves feeling, which is intangible and not sound as a basis for authority in morals. Moreover, the theory is weak in that it takes habits which are the source of morality to be an instinctive moral sense, that is, it gives to what is built up in man through habit the appellation "moral sense."

Butler sought to make conscience, instead of the moral sense, the authority. He taught that men ought to live according to nature, which means not acting as we please but doing as we ought in obedience to our sovereign, the conscience. The whole business of our lives as moral agents is to conform ourselves to conscience. But though conscience gives us mandates, the native impulses of our lower nature frequently still its voice. Moreover, conscience is individual in character. Butler himself recognized that there must be a universal standard to which each individual's conscience ought to conform.

The Theory of the Evolution of the Moral Standard

Herbert Spencer undertook the task of applying the principles of evolution to the moral life. The essence of his argument is as follows: Life is a continuous process of adaptation to environment. Therefore, the conduct which promotes this adjustment is good, and the more it promotes it the better the conduct becomes. Thus moral progress is movement towards the "ideal congruity" or the individual completely adapted in a society that has reached its highest point of development. The process of struggle toward this end results in the origin of the moral sense. "Experiences of utility, organized and consolidated during all past generations of the human race, have been producing nervous modifications" which "by continued transmission and accumulation," have become in us instincts or intuitions which discern the fit action and are the source of the feeling of obligation.

By way of comment on this conception of authority in morals, it may be observed, first of all, that there is no scientific proof of the actuality of a process of evolution. From many points of view the theory is irrational: it cannot account at all for its own existence or for progress in intelligent and teleological directions. Moreover, the hypothesis that acquired characteristics or qualities are transmitted by heredity is a dubious one. Even if such transmission is a reality, it is certain that most acquired characteristics will perish. Often, the very things most needed, individuals must receive, not by inheritance but just as their ancestors did — through bitter experience. Apart from these considerations, it must be remembered that evolution is a cosmic process. Between it and the ethical process, as Thomas Huxley pointed out, there is definite opposition. Two of his statements are relevant in this connection: "The ethical progress of society depends not on imitating the cosmic process, still less in running away from it, but in combating it"; "The ethical process is in opposition to the principle of the cosmic process, and tends to the suppression of the qualities best fitted for success in that struggle."

Ethics involves the voluntary decisions of free agents who are conscious of a moral end. This is what gives moral content to an action. The obligation of moral beings is not to adjust themselves to their environment, but to adjust their environment to the higher ideal they have. This ideal is native to us and dwells inseparably in us. It compels us to seek the common welfare as well as the improvement of self. Thus it aims at the adjustment of the two, not simply to each other, but to a more absolute law. Consequently, evolutionary doctrine leaves us with an end which does not explain the beginning. The mystery of the moral ideal and moral obligation is inherent in the nature of man, not in his environment.

Moreover, man's origins are obscure and a slow, gradual progression of the human race is not an established fact. Some races have developed; others with the same capacities, have failed to progress. Even if progress were inevitable, the theory of evolution gives no indication as to what the highest point of development is. Were this known theoretically, there would yet be the problem of making it concrete enough to provide man with a practical standard for the guidance of his daily conduct. Unquestionably, anything that shows now the moral value of an earlier experience is helpful to human progress. However, an appeal to man to adjust himself to better conditions means nothing unless it points the way to an ultimate worthy end of still greater value. This final end evolution does not define.

Conditions in our world today are not encouraging to the thought that we are beneficiaries of moral progress. Present political developments certainly do not display wholesomeness of moral conduct. There is a wide gulf between scientific advancement and moral attainment. Likewise, the gap between knowledge and practice is immeasurably great. If knowledge could make for better conduct, we should be superior moral beings in comparison with those who preceded us. Much as we would like the contrary to be true, it must be acknowledged that man today is fundamentally as low down morally as he ever was. There can be no reasonable question about the fact of evolution in connection with morals if we mean that there can be change for the better in the life of an individual or that of a given group. However, it is necessary to go against evidence to assume that the moral standard is the product of the working of a law of continuity making for evolutionary perfection in the race.

The Theory of Well-Being as Its Own Standard

One theory is that law is the universal standard. Another is that the ultimate authority is an ideal developed through the ages by the process of evolution. The third view is that pleasure, happiness, or well-being should be taken as the authority for conduct. Hedonism makes pleasure the ultimate aim, holding that all men ought to seek pleasure and avoid pain. Man's chief interest is the pursuit of his happiness or well-being. This he attains when he does what gives him pleasure and fails to realize when he does what brings him pain. Some Hedonists are satisfied with low ideals of what constitutes pleasure, but many of them distinguish between transient pleasures and permanent pleasures, between pleasurable experience for self and pleasure at the expense of other people, between pleasure of a higher and a lower quality.

By way of criticism, it need be said that to have pleasure, or happiness, either high or low, as the end of conduct impairs the quality of the standard of morality by making the motive selfish and grasping. Morality is a chief end of life, not something to be measured in terms of present satisfaction. Goodness, like beauty, "is its own excuse for being." Happiness is the outcome of upright living; we do not become upright merely because we seek happiness. Again, pleasure is a secondary experience in that it results from the satisfying of a particular urge; it is not reasonable to make a secondary experience primary. Desire, not pleasure, is the primary spring of action. Further, there is a conflict among pleasures, even in the life of the individual. Also, the individual's pleasures conflict with the pleasures of others. These conflicts demand that there be some principle by which to determine choice of pleasures. Moreover, the fact that Hedonists find it necessary to distinguish among pleasures, higher and lower, proves the insuf-

ficiency of pleasure as a standard of action. If some pleasures
are nobler in quality, then moral quality must be the standard
by which the pleasures themselves are judged. It seems then as
if pleasure is an impracticable standard of the right.

Universalistic Hedonism, or Utilitarianism, seeks to overcome some of the difficulties met in setting up individual happiness as the standard for moral action. Utilitarianism takes as
its standard, "the greatest possible well-being of the greatest
possible number." The principle is expressed thus in the pre-
cise and definite words of John Stuart Mill: "The creed which
accepts as the foundation of morals, Utility, or the 'greatest
happiness' principle holds that actions are right in proportion
as they tend to promote happiness, wrong as they tend to produce the reverse of happiness. By happiness is intended pleasure, and the absence of pain; by unhappiness, pain and the
privation of pleasure."

Essentially the same objections can be levelled against this
form of Hedonism as were mentioned above. Giving the system
a universal character does not change its fundamental nature.
Pleasure is individual and the use of terms like "good" and
"happiness" does not alter this fact. We are concerned to know
what happiness is, what kind of happiness is to be sought, and
whose happiness is to be promoted. Happiness is infinite in
nature and intangible in form. No man can set forth its many
varieties or distinguish its numerous forms. As the sorts of happiness are innumerable, so the persons who may be happy or
unhappy represent all degrees of capacity. We cannot deal with
happiness satisfactorily without qualifying it or without bringing
in a standard by which to measure it. As soon as we introduce
a standard by which to measure it, we have something different
from what it measures — something that is deemed higher.
Therefore, happiness being something which is itself determined, cannot be the standard of the quality of moral action.

Even if we were able to test the quality of happiness in a
satisfactory manner and to differentiate appropriately among the
many kinds of happiness, we would yet be faced with the
question of whose happiness we ought to promote. So closely
connected with the welfare of the group is the welfare of the

individual, so far-reaching in their effects are his actions, so complex are social relations, that the standard of pleasure, or happiness, fails as a means for ascertaining what is for the universal good. What is the measure of the greatest happiness of the greatest number? Who shall estimate the number? Who is to say what classes of people belong to the number whose happiness is to be sought? Who is to indicate the sort and the extent of their happiness? Is the greatest number to do this for themselves, or is it the duty of the individual to decide the kind and the amount of happiness they shall have? How is the individual to determine the acts that fulfill their idea of what their happiness is or his notion of what it consists in? In short, the standard of happiness always is in something outside of happiness. Search must be made elsewhere for the sanction of morality.

The Moral Standard of the Universe

Obviously, the moral law whose existence is universally recognized and the authority of which is generally acknowledged, could not have originated itself. A law connotes a lawgiver and an executor — a person to frame it and to carry out its provisions. A law is simply a rule of action, enunciating the principles which direct movement toward an end set by the person who formulates the law. The thought of man cannot be satisfied with superficialities; in its quest for the real, it does not rest until it has gone back as far as it can. When man's reason is given as the source of good and the right, the inevitable question is, "From where did man's reason come?" If it is assumed that right is founded on some objective law, we are impelled to ask, "Who framed the law?" To be told that good is a matter of utility causes us to inquire, "Why is good beneficial and why is evil harmful?" Thinking ends only in the conclusion that all things have their origin in one Being who is absolute and eternal, the self-existent moral Person.

"It is God's perfect nature and holy will which form the norm of character and duty for man." The moral standard of the universe is the character and will of God who creates and preserves all things. He did not speak the word which brought worlds into existence, then withdraw and let His created things go for themselves. Physical things are not God's chief creation; His real creation is spirit. That in the universe in which He is most deeply interested is man whom He made like Himself, endowing him with rational and moral qualities so that He might have personal and moral fellowship with him. God does take care of His great universe, but He maintains positive and moral relations with men, His created spirits, though He may be totally unperceived by them. The Person, who flung worlds into space, unlimited in power, perfect and complete in personality, holy in character, having moral qualities in the supreme measure we finite beings long for, strive after, and never attain, is really "not far from every one of us: For in him we live, and move, and have our being" (Acts 17:27, 28). Our life has its roots in God, and we can reach out and draw into ourselves from the inexhaustible goodness of His perfect nature. It is His will that we do so. The standard of perfection given us by Jesus is to be "perfect, even as your Father which is in heaven is perfect."

Though we are usually not aware of it, a process of intercommunication of God with man and man with God is continually in operation. This means that the perfections and the excellencies of His infinitely perfect nature are in never-ceasing activity toward us. Goodness beyond the power of man's mind to conceive is the characteristic of His personality. Holiness is the fundamental attribute of God. The only ends that could satisfy Him must, to be worthy of Him, be found in Himself. If He is moved to activity by an end which may be described, on the divine side, as His own glory, this end will be, on the human side, the highest good of His created beings. Perfect, as He is, He could have no other end.

If God can act only for motives that are good, still less could He be unstable and change from the purpose He had when He began His activity. God never changes; as He was in the beginning, so He is now, and so He will be forever. With Him, there is no change or shadow of alteration. In personality, character, and purpose, He is eternally the same. However, unchangeability does not mean immovability. In modes of action, God is as varied as the multifarious needs of changeful created beings. Nothing done by man, nothing man could do, would ever cause any change in the principles which determine God's ends. However, what man does may cause Him to change in the things He chooses to do and in His way of doing them. Through the ages of time man has lived and may live, as well as through the life of each of us, "one increasing purpose runs." The unchangeable God is ever working, fitting His modes of action, not to what the creature deserves but to its needs, capacities, and responses, seeking to bring mankind and each one of us as individuals, to an end predetermined from the beginning in His own purposes. What He said to the Jews in Jeremiah's day He is saying to men of any time and of all time: "For I know the thoughts that I think toward you, saith the Lord, thoughts of peace, and not of evil, to give you an expected end" (Jer. 29:11).

The Eternal Nature of the Ethical

The ethical, then, is not the result of chance, not the outcome of development, nor the end of a process of evolution. In God the ethical has existed from eternity. He is without beginning of days, and He has always been as He is now. There never was a time when He was not holy in nature and in character. The ethical is grounded in the very nature of God, not only in His will. He is, as He has been from eternity, holy in essence. It is not simply His will that makes actions right or decides that actions are wrong. There is nothing arbitrary about morality. Yet, as a moral Being, God is free to choose the right. Morality can no more be determined by necessity than by arbitrary choice; it exists only where there is freedom. God wills the right because it is right, and it is right because He wills it. In God, the perfect moral Person, what is ethically necessary and ethically free are found together in perfect harmony.

The standard of morality is, therefore, the character and will of God. Since holiness is the fundamental attribute of God, we must recognize the holiness that is His as the ultimate test of character and conduct. As was stated in a previous chapter, there are not two standards, one for the Christian and another for the non-Christian. For any man, for all men, a thing that is in conformity with the holy character and will of God is right, and a thing that is contrary to the divine character and will is wrong. Alexander says, "To realize the perfect life as it is revealed in the character and will of God is the supreme aim of man, and it embraces all that is conceivably highest for the individual and for humanity as a whole." The ultimate standard of moral goodness is God Himself.

This establishes the absoluteness of the good. It makes goodness fixed and unchangeable, not conformity with an arbitrary law dependent upon the caprice of the lawgiver. It is a standard that is not subject to the limitations of finite knowledge, human insight, finite understanding, and human ways of interpreting reality. It makes goodness that which is in harmony with the ultimate standard of all perfection. Goodness finds its justification in the very nature of things — the nature of the eternal God.

Man Originates in God and Can Therefore Become Like God

Moreover, this standard uplifts and ennobles man. It is impossible to conceive of anything higher for man than that he should realize within himself a goodness that is of God, that he should be like God in character and conduct. So high is the standard that the question arises as to the possibility — rather the impossibility — of man's ever being able to attain it. If man were a mere animal, he could never become like God. However, he was created in the image of God with a spiritual and moral nature that constitutes kinship with God. We are His offspring, endowed in creation with a nature like unto God's nature. We carry within ourselves, therefore, capacities and a personality linking us with the divine; we have endless potentialities, which reach out and seek their fulfillment and their completion in His infinite Being.

Our kinship with God, then, involves the possibility of our becoming like God in character, at least in some degree. Here lies the necessary condition for the first and greatest commandment, as well as for the second, which is like unto it. We cannot love in a true sense that which has no capacity for spiritual and moral response. It would be impossible for us to love God if we could discern in Him nothing that could respond to our

love. As we find in Him a nature of infinite love, our love
goes out to Him in supreme devotion. As we discern in our
fellows their kinship with our common Father and capacity for
spiritual and moral response, such as we ourselves possess, we
can love them as we do ourselves.

In the nature of man exists the consciousness that the qualities and the traits which he seeks to possess are already present
and fulfilled in God. The Christian conception of God is that
of a superlatively high moral Being. There is a moral as well
as an intellectual demand for belief in God. Man is not content to think of God as "away off somewhere," nor separated
from the universe keeping watch over it, nor in a state of rest
and quiet blessedness. He must think of God as present in the
very structure of the universe. He cannot conceive of Him
as not entering into the religious and moral life now being lived
by men.

The end for which man was created is unbroken fellowship
with God. This is an experience which it is possible to have in
a measure even in this life. Certainly, such an experience with
the highest moral Being is dependent on living in accord with
the law He established, and the outcome is increase in personal
holiness. It is not "experiences" of any particular kind that
count but being in right relation with Him and having a right
attitude toward Him. This relationship and this attitude are
possible through Christ, the revelation of God. He that has
seen Christ has seen the Father. ". . . The Father sent the
Son to be the Saviour of the world. Whosoever shall confess
that Jesus is the Son of God, God dwelleth in him, and he in
God" (I John 4:14, 15). "Experiences" in themselves mean
nothing; it is the fact of relationship that is all-important. "If we
say that we have fellowship with him, and walk in darkness, we
lie, and do not the truth: But if we walk in the light, as he is
in the light, we have fellowship one with another, and the
blood of Jesus Christ his Son cleanseth us from all sin"
(I John 1:6, 7).

Laws That Work in Relation to the Standard

In the preceding section, mention was made of three laws:
eternal law, natural moral law, and human law. These three

laws are not enough to guide man to his end. The eternal law and the natural moral law, clarified and interpreted by sound human laws, are sufficient for the guidance of man's natural life. However, man is more than a natural being; he lives a supernatural, or spiritual and eternal, life. He must, therefore, have a law to govern him in his supernatural living. This God provided when He gave a divine positive law through Moses.

Yet the writer to the Hebrew Christians says that "the law made nothing perfect" (Heb. 7:19). It takes more than laws, whatever they be, however well-written, however much justified, to make men and nations responsible. Men cannot be made law-abiding by law alone. If laws were enough, the people of Israel would have had a glorious history instead of the one they did have. If laws made men virtuous, we in the United States would be models for right living, because never has there been a nation with so many rules and regulations, which are steadily increasing in number.

Law exists to guide men to the right goal — the realization of complete likeness unto God through the sharing of fellowship with Him. Eternal law, natural moral law, divine positive law, all aim at this goal of human life; all three of them come directly from God, who is the goal of life. Human laws rightly rest upon a higher law, a native endowment divinely set in man's nature. In so far as they are truly law, they give to men peace and opportunity to work their individual way to the supreme goal of human life.

The same verse in Hebrews which states that the law made nothing perfect says also "the bringing in of a better hope did; by the which we draw nigh unto God." The goal of human life is an impossible goal if we must depend upon the powers of our fallen nature. The good that we know we cannot do because of the law of sin in us. Likeness unto God is a mockery, except for the help by which the power of God Himself is made available to us. This help is grace, or everything for nothing to those who deserve nothing. In grace God bridged the gap between the supernatural and the natural, thereby making it possible for us to be born again of Him and then to grow in likeness to Himself. What was lost by sin is restored in Christ who fulfilled the law in His own Person. Right standing with God is "for us also, to whom it shall be imputed, if we believe on him that raised up Jesus our Lord from the dead; who was delivered for our offences, and was raised again for our justification" (Rom. 4:24, 25). That is, the active and passive obedience of Christ, whereby He perfectly fulfilled the law and propitiated the justice of God, is imputed, or put to the account, of us who receive Christ by faith; our sins are pardoned, and we are created anew "in Christ Jesus unto good works, which God hath before ordained that we should walk in them" (Eph. 2:10).

In our fallen state, the will is not totally subject to God nor is the heart firmly fixed on God. Action is always determined by that upon which the heart is centered. Apart from grace, we are powerless to keep actually and absolutely any law — eternal, natural moral, human, or divine positive. Unaided by God, we can do nothing good, nothing godlike. In turning from the will of God, man destroyed his own glory, perverted the order of nature, sold himself to evil, and put himself under the just condemnation of a holy God. Without grace, he cannot know supernatural truth, desire supernatural things, aim at them, or do supernatural works. All his attempts at self-improvement, all his exercise of will power, all his education, all his scientific research, all his legislative action, are to no avail. Only by the grace of God can he be restored; only by grace can he turn back to the goal of life. Only God whom he offended and who judges the secret motives of men can do anything to remove the consequences of man's sin.

Laws are not enough! Law is the eternal will of God, but this law is something deeper than moral, ceremonial, civil, and judicial laws, which are concerned with the external man. Beyond these laws, men need a change of nature; they must have life of a sort that gives rise to desire to keep the law because it is right, right as David believed it to be right when he said, "I delight to do thy will, O my God: yea, thy law is within my heart" (Ps. 40:8). Through the divine life, through Christ in us, ethics belongs to the supernatural, or the eternal or spiritual, world. Moral conduct is the outward or visible sign of faith

and love directed to God, who is holy in His nature. Thus is
morality founded upon absolute truth and goodness, even the
will and character of God.

Christian Ethics an Inner Compulsion

Ethics is, therefore, an inner compulsion. Man is free from
all merely external law in so far as he is in vital relation with
God. The acts the Christian does are acts of perfect freedom.
Love is the Christian's real law. There is a constant appeal from
all outward authority to the inward voice as final. The inner
longing of the soul is in harmony with the outward doing of
what is right. This, as was said above, is the universal moral
standard, for all men are under the moral obligation to do the
will of God. What He wills is, first of all, that they believe in
His Son as Saviour and Lord. The basis for true ethics is represented in these words of the Psalmist: "The law of his God
is in his heart; none of his steps shall slide" (Ps. 37:31).

In Christ the old law was fulfilled by a new law. "Christ
is the end of the law for righteousness to every one that believeth" (Rom. 10:4). This new law is not merely a written
law but a law implanted in the hearts of the children of God.
Instruction by spoken and by written word is necessary to ac-
quaint men concerning the things they are to believe and the
things they are to do, but over and above this instruction is the
grace of God working by the Holy Spirit in the hearts of the
followers of Christ.

The new law is a teacher of perfection. It is concerned chiefly
with directing and regulating the new life. While it does not
ignore external acts, it deals mainly with those whose opposites
are contrary to the constitution of internal grace and its proper
use. It places most emphasis upon the internal life of man.
This is manifest in the Sermon on the Mount where our Lord
touched briefly and pointedly on the individual's own internal
life, his relations with his neighbors, and the manner of fulfilling both classes of duties. For himself, the individual is to
avoid evil, not only in its outward forms but in his thoughts
and desires, and even to keep away from the occasions from
which evil arises. He is to do good, not for his own glory, not
for earthly reward, but to the end that he might be perfect,

even as his heavenly Father is perfect. In his dealings with his fellows, his judgments are to be charitable since he himself is not without faults. He is to place the things of the spirit above the things of the world. The use that he makes of temporal things is to be in view of the goal for which he was created. It is to this supreme height of human perfection that the new law points but never without respect for the freedom of man to choose and to act for himself.

Normally, he who is in Christ does that which is right under the guidance and the influence of the Holy Spirit because he himself is essentially, though not perfectly, right. Never here below will he be entirely free from conflicts because there remains in him a lower nature that is hostile to God and holiness. But the less he yields to this lower nature, the more he brings it into subjection through the help of God, the more he grows in spontaneous submission to the will of God, and the more he grows into the likeness of God. That is to say, there is a growing sense of harmony between the conception of that which is best and the expression of the desire of the soul. Thus what he ought to do becomes that which he desires to do, and the conflict between the commandment of duty and the tendency to self-will is resolved. This does not mean that obligations are no longer felt but only that the individual becomes alert to recognition of them and finds the completion of his truest self in this recognition.

Christianity is a life. It is a life in fellowship with God. For this life there is a personal norm, the life of Christ. He is the standard. He took on Himself a full share of our mortal nature. Therefore, "we have not an high priest which cannot be touched with the feeling of our infirmities; but was in all points tempted like as we are, yet without sin" (Heb. 2:14; 4:15). The true ethics is lived, and it exerts actual influence on everyday life. Conditions are widely different from one of us to another, and life, especially in its modern complexity, brings to each of us many perplexing problems. But in Christ we have a guide; by His Spirit within us, by the matchless example of His blameless life, by the wonderful teachings of His gospel, and by the manifold indications of His providence,

He conducts us in our earthly pilgrimage through a world unfriendly to Him and a stranger to His grace.

It is our individual responsibility to give heed to our conduct according to our sincere understanding of the will of God for us. Once we recognize any action or a certain mode of conduct to be right for us, we have no choice. We may make mistakes in judgment; we may sometimes allow passion or desire to cloud the issue; but once it is clear to us what we ought to do according to the will and character of a holy God, who does not let Himself without witness to a sincere follower, we have no alternative. We can do only what we recognize as our obligation, but this we should fulfill at every moment with all the powers of our being. Love is the Christian's true law, and love knows no limit. God so loved us that He "spared not his own Son, but delivered him up for us all" (Rom. 8:32).

QUESTIONS

1. Does man anywhere live without a standard?
2. Does the standard vary much from age to age, from society to society, from individual to individual? Why?
3. Have you always chosen your acts and directed your conduct?
4. What is ideal conduct? How do you know?
5. With what is ethics essentially concerned?
6. Why cannot the rules of ethics be rigid ones?
7. Is all knowledge individual and personal?
8. How can the moral standard be universal and the moral life individual and personal?
9. Why can a society not exist without a moral standard? Is American society disintegrating because of the absence of a standard?
10. Which of the four views concerning the nature of the moral standard makes the strongest appeal to your thought? Why?
11. How could ultimate and absolute law be incorporated within man?
12. Is man under one law in moral nature and under other laws in other aspects of his being?
13. When is a human law really a law?
14. Can there be law without an accompanying sense of obligation?
15. Enumerate the views of the concept of objective law.
16. Could conscience function if there were no universal standard?
17. Were evolution a scientific fact, could there be the evolution of a moral standard? Explain your answer.
18. Are people today better morally than ever before?
19. Criticize the criticism of pleasure, or happiness, as the end of conduct.

20. Wherein is Utilitarianism superior to Hedonism?
21. As man goes back farther and farther in his thinking, where must he finally end?
22. What is the moral standard of the universe? What is the ultimate standard of moral goodness?
23. Has God ever changed — does He ever change — in His purposes for man?
24. Why can morality never be determined by necessity?
25. In what ways may man become like God?
26. What laws function, or operate, in the life of a Christian?
27. Why does man need laws other than eternal law, natural moral law, and human law?
28. What law makes it impossible for us to do the good we know?
29. How can we become free from all external law?
30. "Love God and do what you will," said Augustine. What bearing has the statement on Christian conduct?

CHAPTER VIII

The Motives of Conduct

IT IS THE BUSINESS OF ETHICS not only to discover but also to apply the ideal in conduct. It is interested, therefore, both in the ultimate end of human activities and in the right methods of attaining this end. Consequently, it draws from philosophy, theology, and psychology though it retains its own distinctive field and makes its own contributions to the knowledge and to the life of man. The problems discussed in the three preceding chapters, namely, the ultimate ideal or the final end of life, the source of our knowledge of this ultimate ideal, and the universal standard by which all phases of conduct must be tested, are fundamentally philosophical and theological in their implications.

The remaining two of the five main ethical problems are more psychological in character in that they are concerned with the applications of the standard by the individual to the circumstances of everyday living. Involved in these two problems are questions relating to two practical matters: the manner in which ethical principles can be worked out in the life of the individual and in his relations with his fellows; the individual's reactions and ability to carry out ethical principles. One of these two problems has to do with the freedom of the will and is to be considered in the next chapter. The other problem is concerned with the motives of conduct, which constitute the subject matter of the present chapter.

"Nothing walks with aimless feet." For every effect there is a cause. All activity has a cause. No more in human life than in the physical world does anything "just happen." The individual never acts except under certain influences. Every movement a human being makes, every act he performs, every fact he learns, every deed he does, is caused. There is no such

182

thing as an uninfluenced person. Never for a single moment is any one of us free from the influence of environment, material and moral, from which come stimuli that move us to react and respond. We cannot, in many instances, perceive the cause which incites action but it is there, functioning just as surely and just as definitely as it would be if we could discern its full operation. "Naturally good" or "naturally bad" behavior never just happens to come on the scene.

The Self and Its Development

One cannot think long or deeply on the nature and the cause of human action without meeting the question, What is that in man which is motivated to act? This, of course, is a psychological question which is not easy to discuss. It is a matter of common knowledge that man is capable of choosing at least some of his responses and is able to reflect upon the nature and the quality of his own actions. Psychology is obliged, therefore, to accept the possibility of self-consciousness, that is, to assume that there is a self to which are to be referred all feelings, cognitions, and volitions.

There can be no denial of the fact that there is a "central unity to which all possible experience is to be referred. The self-conscious being stands over against all possible objects of experience, and refuses to be included among them. It is the self to which they are related and in which the experience finds its unity." Except for this presupposition, there would be neither a psychology nor any system of ethics. Perhaps the best definition of self that can be given is "the individual as known to the individual." It is the connected whole of consciousness brought into being in the individual through the responses he makes to his environment. Ordinarily, the word "person" is used for referring to a human being without making any particular distinction. "Individual" has the same meaning but emphasizes the person's singleness or aloneness.

Though no one can define it adequately, everyone knows what is meant by the human self. Everyone knows also that there is a development of what we call the self, though the difficulty of studying this development is great. It is not possible to study effectively the development of a child's self by the direct method of questioning. However, other means of study indicate that the child, who seemingly begins life with no awareness of self, distinguishes, at an early age, between the self and the not-self. Development then goes on apace through the years of childhood and adolescence into maturity. On the intellectual side, the mass of ideas representing our own past is formed in the memory. At every moment of life, we look back on a portion, sometimes to events far in the past. On the moral side, the numerous kinds of actions and their results lead us to bring into being for ourselves a system of values and to form convictions concerning ethically right and ethically wrong actions.

Development a Social Matter

Throughout the entire course of development, the individual is constantly relating other selves to himself. We are social beings and cannot reach our height of self-development in isolation from other self-conscious beings. Passage into maturity from adolescence is characterized by abandonment, to a considerable extent, of the childhood habit of dependence on other people and the assumption of responsibility for one's own decisions and for the consequences following upon them. In the wider contacts of life, the person finds that other individuals who, like himself, seek to determine their lives, have claims that he cannot ignore. Though he no longer relies wholly on others, he recognizes that he can determine himself only in relation to others. In that interaction which neither he nor they can prevent, the life of the individual is developed and enriched by harmonious relations with those who, as he, are centers of consciousness. "None of us liveth to himself, and no man dieth to himself" (Rom. 14:7). Mutual respect for the rights of all, mutual giving and taking, and mutual modification of responses to satisfy individual needs and the needs of all who are in relation to one another is the condition of a healthy development of the self.

Things are not sufficient for the self and its realization. We constantly relate the world to ourselves and bind together into a whole of united experience our various items of knowledge of things. No thing or object has reality for any person apart from his consciousness of it. Things are in constant flux and change; only the perception and the knowledge we have of them is enduring. Things in themselves cannot move us to act morally. It is the action of other selves upon us which stimulates us to moral activity and produces that fulness of life in an ordered unity which is possible for a finite self.

When we are not able to maintain harmonious relations with others, we experience a sense of unrest. That is, there is a feeling of inner discord not founded upon fears we may have of opposition on the part of others or of the consequences which may arise from the lack of harmony. This is evidence of the existence of a moral power beyond the ability of man. It has been called by different names, such as "a stream or tendency, not ourselves, which makes for righteousness," "the course of nature," "the cosmic mind," "the eternal spirit," and "God." The thought of man and the nature of man can be satisfied only in the conception and the reality groped after ever since man began to exist, viz., that the final reality is fellowship in a unity of selves within a supreme self free from limitations of finite existence. The human self cannot locate itself in the universe, except as it affirms a supreme being in which the world and all finite selves find a common unity. This means that the moral in man passes over into the spiritual. It means, furthermore, that man is essentially a unity, a being with a body and a spirit united in the mind.

Personality and Character and Motive

Two psychological terms related to the self are personality and character. Personality is most complex and the subject of much confusion of thought. It is the whole individual considered as a whole — the integrated totality of his structures, modes of behavior, interests, habits, attitudes, capacities, abilities, and traits. Therefore, personality is nothing more or less than the self, or the person, in action, living as an individual, fully, completely, and richly, or miserably and wretchedly, functioning in his interactions with other persons, well or poorly, being a source of benefit or of harm to them. At any given moment, personality is the whole man, including all that his past experiences, present circumstances, and future purposes make him to be — the result of all that the world of which he is a part has contributed and is contributing to his life. His bodily sensations, his mental acts, his desires and motives, are not forces separated from himself and foreign to his nature, but essential elements of his very being.

The terms personality and character are sometimes confused with each other. The former is used apparently more to designate the make-up of the individual in respect to mental capabilities, attitudes, and the like; the latter, with regard to conduct — behavior that conforms to what is considered moral or good. Inasmuch as the primary meaning of the term character is "all qualities or features possessed," it, like the term personality, properly refers to the whole individual considered as a whole. Character, therefore, is personality viewed from the standpoint of the ethical or the moral.

The self cannot be isolated from the world in which it lives. The person is the outward manifestation of something inward, a being who comes to know himself through the objective world and whose interests are shaped from the problems he meets in his environment. As an individual agent, he takes his place in the world of human interaction and plays his unique and definite part in the life of the world. He is part of a universe, but a part that is conscious of what he is — a being who can modify his responses voluntarily in the light of some ever-present dim perception of an end to be attained, who is able to refer his actions to himself and to pass judgment on their moral quality, and whose total of habitual reactions crystallizes in character from which others form their estimate of his goodness or his badness.

Whatever the nature of the world as it exists apart from our knowledge and desires, our conduct, our aims and motives and activities, are formed with respect to the world as we interpret it in experience. We cannot have an object of desire or a standard of conduct unrelated to our experience. As a being who thinks and acts, each of us seeks ends, with awareness that they are his own ends, subject to his own choice. All men and every individual man — all selves — have the will to strive for fulness of self-realization in making, each for himself, a world of his own.

Throughout life the self-realizing impulse of the person is always present. Motive is that which causes him to act in a certain manner. Never is any person independent of all motives. While motives are necessary, a motive does not necessitate. It has been argued that the will is as the strongest motive is. However, the will is not the same as desire or inclination. The will chooses motives; motives do not choose the will. The individual can, and does, look his motives over to choose and to act upon any motive he has. The self is the sovereign arbiter of its own acts and of its destiny, not a slave to motives. We carry our motives within us, for they are part of our very being. We cannot create motive, we cannot act without motive, but we can select any motive high or low, weak or strong, worthy or unworthy, which is in the range of interest. It has been truly said that it is not the motive that seizes the man, but the man who seizes the motive. A good man cannot be influenced by a bad motive, nor is a bad man susceptible to a good motive. "A good man out of the good treasure of his heart bringeth forth that which is good; and an evil man out of the evil treasure of his heart bringeth forth that which is evil" (Luke 6:45).

The motive is as the man is, and what the man is, is determined by his character and his will. Character may well be defined as "completely fashioned will." It is through the exercise of the power to will that the conscious, free moral self which each of us is, chooses among motives, molds his personality, fashions his character, and fixes his destiny.

THE NATURE OF MOTIVATION

It is easier to see that motive has a place in the self-determination of personality, character, and destiny than it is to trace the influence of motive in conduct. To answer such questions as, Why do people do what they do? or, What motives prompt a person's conduct? it is helpful to give some thought to the basic sources of motive. All forms of human motivation are exceedingly complex. The path from the simple urges of bodily existence to the lofty ideals of truly ethical conduct is a long one and leads through a maze of inextricable impulses, tendencies, desires, habits, attitudes, motives, and ideals. Motives are most numerous and so complex as to be beyond possibility

of complete and accurate analysis. In many cases the motives
of our actions and of our judgments are very obscure. Much of
our activity is under the control of subconscious impulses and
motives that are quite indefinite. Understanding of the nature
of motivation is much facilitated when the part that purpose,
experience, and need play in human life is kept in mind.

The importance of such understanding is emphasized to
thought when the place of motive in life is seen. Matthew Arnold rightly stressed, at least in principle, the supreme value of
ethical considerations when he gave utterance to the conception that conduct is three-fourths of life. However, conduct is
only the outward expression of character, or personality viewed
ethically and morally. As was said in the preceding section,
personality is the product of the development of a being who
determines his own acts. Motive is one important link in the
chain that begins in will and ends in character. First, there is
a will which chooses, motives from among which choice is
made, an act which is the outcome of the choice of motive,
then personality or character fashioned on the basis of the kind
of motive chosen, and the nature of the act performed. A good
will means a good choice among motives, good actions, and a
good character.

Kant said, "A good will is good, not because of what it performs or effects, not by its aptness for the attainment of some
proposed end, but simply by virtue of its volition." A good will
is that within man which makes an act morally good. Not
what we do, but the reason for which we do it, is the chief de-
terminer of the ethical value of an act. True moral worth inheres in the will, not in the deed done — in the motive and
intention, not in the outcome.

A motive is a tendency functioning on the level of self-
conscious reflective action. Since animals are not capable of
such activity, we cannot attribute motives to them. Apparently,
whatever consciousness an animal has, causes it, when moved
to action that has a goal, to be aware only in a hazy way of the
immediate goal of each step in action and to anticipate vaguely
the consequence of each next step as the preceding step is
reached. Man, on the other hand, foresees more clearly and

over a longer range both the goal and the successive steps that must be taken to reach it. Yet, even in man, complete foresight of the goal and of the means for reaching it are frequently not present. Often, our goal is only dimly foreseen, and often, when we start toward it, the steps necessary to take to reach it are less clear to us than the goal itself. As the animal does, so we may define each step as we go, working by a process of trial and error and meeting each difficulty when it arises. However, even when each step is unclear and we cannot foresee its effects definitely, our groping for the goal is not entirely blind. Always, we have some foresight, some anticipation, however vague, of our goal.

Purpose Inherent in Everything, including Man

Purpose is inherent in the very nature of whatever is. There must be a beginning not dependent on anything else and an end independent of all other ends. The world process must have a beginning and an end. Whatever our conception of the infinite may be, we are obliged to regard the infinite as the source of all finite existence. And, unless we conceive of the infinite as impersonal and unintelligent, we must view the finite as the outcome or the expression of a plan or purpose on the part of the infinite. Whatever is, exists to function; things are for a purpose; the achievement of purpose is action. The world of action is a world of goals, a world which is always in motion toward the achievement of an ultimate purpose, a final goal.

To be human is to have capacity for reason and will, so it is inherent in man's nature to seek ends and to guide himself toward the accomplishment of a purpose. Never is he satisfied except as he comes to some decision concerning the purpose of his existence. Back of all his activities, there is continually some dim perception of the one increasing purpose that runs through the ages. If such were not the case, there would be no source or spring for action. Dewey maintains that ends are endless, which, to him, is to say that there is no end. He holds that living men have many and varied purposes, but that life itself has no purpose other than life. Aristotle, on the contrary, taught that there is an end for the human person and therefore for all men. This end, he says, is achieved in part, but only in part, during our life on earth; since man is naturally immortal, the ultimate purpose demanded lies beyond this life. This sums up in the conclusion that purpose is implied in all action that is truly human — in all moral action. For ethics, then, the motive inheres in the object itself. Actually, the end and the motive are one, and the highest good is to be sought for itself.

The life of any individual is made up of experiences, or actions that have their source and spring in purpose, however little understood it may be. Each experience is a link in a chain forged continually from the day of birth, or before, until the day of death, or so long as the person has normal possession of his powers. The child begins life in a complex world, supplied with few and simple abilities but with an immense number of potentialities. These potentialities become actualities through experience. Every experience an individual has changes his self, making for development in personality and character.

Needs Are the Starting Point of All Activity, Experience and Development

If the self were a static thing, the person would come into active contact with nothing in his environment, and there would be neither experience nor development. Instead, the person is a living, moving, acting being. Within him exists a self which produces change and motion. The human self is an energy system, that is, a being who is continuously transforming energy into action. To be alive means that life force or energy is being expended. The expenditure of life force means activity. As a living system, the human being is always in action of one kind or another.

The starting point of all activity, experience, and development is a sense of need. To be alive implies necessity for sustaining life. From this main necessity stem numerous specific needs. Whenever need is felt, there is a drive, an urge, or a desire to satisfy the need. Development begins, then, with some upset or disturbance of equilibrium, called a need. As the individual engages in activity for the purpose of satisfying the need, he comes into relationship with certain portions of his total environment. Interaction between him and these results in experience.

The needs that stimulate human beings to action are so many as to be almost infinite in number.

Our most fundamental needs are those arising from our body. Basically, as earthborn creatures, we are physical beings subject to the working of the physiological appetites. These begin to function in the newborn child and exert influence upon the individual throughout his entire life. Our everyday acts, our personality, and our character, though they have a certain innate basis, are much the product of the working of drives, urges, or desires, which arise in the body. These are so compelling as to make the infant seem almost like a self-generating agent. The newborn child is moved to action almost entirely by things that happen within his own body. No one would say that the behavior of an infant or even of a very young child gives evidence of the presence of motives, intentions, and ideals. The only explanation possible is that there are inherent in the nature of his body certain demands as fundamental as life itself, and that his activity is the result of responses stimulated by these demands. These primary drives persist throughout life and constitute the basic content of motivated behavior. Through experience and development they become organized into complex interests, motives, and ideals.

The chief inner drives arising from tissue needs are hunger, thirst, for oxygen, for elimination, sex, for rest and the relief of fatigue, to escape pain, and to avoid extremes of temperature. A bodily condition seemingly equivalent to tissue needs is the desire for activity. Indirectly at least, it may be a tissue need; that is, its basis may be conditions in the tissues that make movement desirable and inevitable. Where life is, there is energy, and where energy is, there is the desire to be active. No normal human being ever remains for a long period of time in an inactive state. On the physical side, the desire to be active finds expression in random activity, in manipulation, and in many other kinds of physical undertakings. On the mental side, it is expressed in curiosity and interest, in discovery of the new, and in study and research.

In addition to these general bodily conditions, there are other desires that seem to be just as primary and equally as, if not more, important in their bearing on motivation. Some among these are the desire for new experience, the desire to achieve, the desire to express one's self, the desire for approval, the desire to possess, the desire to compete with others, the desire for companionship, the desire for freedom, and the desire to worship and to enter into fellowship with a higher Power.

Need or Desire, Self, Will and Purpose

But desires do not exist in a vacuum. They belong to a self which is much more than the physical organism. It is a being not under the bondage of mechanical necessity but capable of making deliberate choice of lines of action, a being who directs his activity in the light of goals and purposes. Primary desires are insufficient in themselves to furnish motives impelling men to moral action — that action which is most typically human action. Motives prompting such action have their origin in the complex acts of living and represent the inner purposes of a self that arise through experience in meeting needs.

Desires — primary or other — are a part of the person and are always directed toward things related to the self. They are always for what has value to the person as seen by him. Desires are not mere tendencies forcing the individual one way or another. What we are in character is reflected in the nature of our desires. Never are we moved by an abstract force, outside of ourselves, of so great strength that we cannot resist it. Only as the individual puts himself into the desire or motive does it become the strongest one upon which he acts. Always, what we do, we choose to do. Our motives are a part of us; our actions are never produced by our motives, but by ourselves. Yet we are never uninfluenced by motive.

The will is more than mere desire. A desire is good or a desire is bad, not in and of itself but as it constitutes a determination of the will to act. In the mere desire there is no moral quality. Only as the desire is harbored in the heart and thus becomes a motive leading to the intention to do an act of goodness or of badness does it assume moral worth. This means that only as one identifies self with the desire, that is, puts himself into the desire, does it take on moral quality. Such identification is extremely important in its effect on the self and on character even if the desire never is expressed in overt act. No human being can cherish evil thoughts and wrong desires without experiencing bad consequences in his inner moral life. Development is always in process, and we grow inevitably in the direction of our thinking. As we think, so we are, and what we are becomes manifest in action — sometimes of nature most startling to others and even to ourselves.

Man is a self of purpose, not just a thing of mere mechanical reaction. In common with animals, he has tendencies to action, comes into situations where actions are necessary, and makes reactions to these situations. But man has something that separates him from the animals. He can set before himself ends by which to modify his reactions and make intentional choices in terms of the ends set forth. His ends are within himself and may be known only to himself, except as action betrays their presence. Animal behavior is characterized by three interlocking reactions: a stimulus, received by a sensory organ, results in a current that travels to the brain, where it follows a pre-established path from sensory center to motor center and thence passes out along motor fibers to effect some particular action. This means that animals are under the domination of instinctive behavior which they can do little to modify.

Man also receives the stimulus that starts a current which is carried to the brain. Here it may cross from a sensory to a motor center by a pre-established path, but it does not necessarily do so. The human being has consciousness, which he is able to use in terms of its knowledge content, its emotional attitudes, and its volitions. In terms of these he thinks, feels, and formulates motives and ideals, then chooses the path which the current shall take as it issues in action. Man, far from being under the domination of blind instincts that propel him in a mechanical way, is a self with the power of building ideals as a basis for choosing to do what he will.

It is not the nature of man to be satisfied with merely reacting to the stimuli of basic urges and desires or even with responding in terms of intelligent action when need arises. He is so constituted that he must have some single ultimate end to which all other ends are subordinate. It is universally recognized that the true end of human existence is connected with moral character. As has been noted in preceding chapters, men have, through the centuries, sought diligently but unsuccessfully to state in a single word or a simple concept the ultimate end of moral conduct. "The nebulous ends of action cannot be expressed in terms of one end, such as pleasure, the greatest good to the greatest number, self-realization, observance of law and custom, or the satisfaction of conscience. The ultimate end is not, or has not yet been, amenable to exact definition. It is probably a compromise of the foregoing ends and may perhaps contain elements over and beyond any or all of them."

PLEASURE, PAIN, AND REASON IN MOTIVATION

Life is a great bundle of desires. We are physical beings and must live physically, with a host of appetites and hungers clamoring insistently and perpetually for satisfaction. We are intellectual beings with cravings and longings just as demanding and enduring as the desires for physical satisfactions. We are social beings with imperative outreachings of never-ceasing desires for love and fellowship and companionship. We are personal beings with motives which, while allied with physiological and common social motives, are distinct in themselves and which may have the urgency which characterizes physiological desires.

Pleasure and Pain as Sources of Motivation

Hedonism and Utilitarianism assert that the desire basic to all motives is the desire either to achieve pleasure or to avoid pain. The English philosophers, Hobbes, Hume, Bentham, J. S. Mill, Spencer, Bain, and Locke advanced the theory. Typical statements are these of Bentham, Bain, and Spencer respectively: "Nature has placed mankind under the governance of two sovereign masters, pain and pleasure"; "There is at the bottom of every genuine voluntary impulse, some one variety of the many fears wherein pain or pleasure takes possession of the common mind"; "The unavoidable conclusion is, then, that the intuition does not, and cannot, ignore the ultimate derivations of right and wrong from pleasure and pain."

Pleasure in the sense of a comfortable feeling attends the satisfaction of any native drive. All of us, therefore, do have a basic desire to experience pleasure and to avoid pain. It cannot be denied that this desire has a bearing on human conduct. Every normal human being is interested in securing the satisfaction of the insistent demands of his own nature, and, if he be charitably inclined, he desires for others like satisfactions. Nor is it to be questioned that, all things being equal, we are justified in seeking pleasure and avoiding pain. However, in the complicated development of human conduct, the pleasure principle becomes modified by other forces. The involved situations of actual living make choice more than a matter of simple acceptance or rejection of pleasure or the avoidance of pain.

Tensions in and of themselves are unpleasant though the release thereof may be enjoyable. Their very unpleasantness is the basis of their driving force. Hunger, thirst, and other inner tensions serve as signs or signals of organic and tissue needs. Pain, heat stimuli, or cold stimuli, on the surface of the body, act similarly as a signal of tissue damage. The reduction of inner tension and of that caused by organic stimuli gives relief or satisfaction. The same is true of the reduction of tensions due to intellectual wants, social desires, and personal aspirations. It is more correct, therefore, to say that man seeks to escape from pain or discomfort and to achieve a state of equilibrium in which tension is absent than it is to say that he seeks pleasure. Fundamentally, the forces that motivate a human being are the discomforts arising from a felt sense of need. Pain and discomfort, or the condition of tension, furnishes the momentum or driving force for activity but does not define the direction the activity shall take. It is through development resulting from experience that we discover what we must do to realize satisfaction.

Strictly speaking, then, pleasure and pain are nothing more than feelings. They are passing states of the individual, belonging only to him and pointing to no reality beyond their mere presence. They are affective states, which follow one another in our experience without constituting any unity or whole. We may feel one way at one time and another at another time, for no tangible reason. We are far more, something much

greater, than a mere collection of drives and urges giving rise
to feelings which determine the direction our conduct shall
take; we are creatures that choose our way. No mere series of
pleasures, however lengthy, can bring us eventual satisfaction,
which is found only in achieving the goal of life. Each succeeding pleasure, in itself, leaves us as far away from this goal
as the first. Pleasures are passing; each vanishes in a moment,
leaving us to "stand with heart unsatisfied and hands empty,
driven on and beyond forever in pursuit of a delusion, through
a weary round which never advances."

To be motivated by pleasure, then, is to destroy the possibility of true ultimate satisfaction. We are creatures of aspirations, ideals, social sympathies and interests, and rational
demands. The only life that can satisfy us is that in which aims
and activities are viewed and chosen intelligently in the light of
an over-all purpose. Our motives must be fixed upon objective
ends beyond desires which are pleasurable. There is an order
of the universe of which man's principles of moral action are
the expression. He interprets this order by reason. Conduct
which makes pleasure its end cannot be truly moral, for its
values are only individual. It is in the environment of a world
of ideals, shaped by the self through experience, that our needs
and our motives are developed.

Besides, it is true that the more a person makes pleasure
an end, the less likely he is to obtain it. When the natural impulses are indulged, the tendency is for them to require a
steadily increasing stimulus in order to produce satisfaction. Inevitably, therefore, the indulgence develops into excess. The
more wholesome practice is to think, not so much of pleasure
itself, as of activities and achievements. Actually, pleasure is
a by-product, an end-result of action engaged in to achieve
some goal.

We often follow ideals the pursuit of which we fully realize
will bring us anything but pleasure, immediate or remote. In the
case of pain, or the extreme opposite of pleasure, it is likewise
untrue to much of life that, if we are not seeking pleasure, we
are seeking to avoid pain. Too many people in the history of
the world have deliberately sought out lives of pain, and too

many individuals of the present endure hardships and privations in order to achieve some end, to make the pleasure-pain principle a reasonable explanation of the motive of conduct.

Reason as a Factor in Motivation

There are those who maintain that reason is the only factor in motivation. Undeniably, if the universe is rational, reason must have a part in the control of the lives of men who are rational creatures. However, none of us is without awareness that he can know a good end ever so well and yet not follow it. Reason, therefore, is not the same as motive. Moreover, there are motives which seem to be almost irrational.

The conclusion is that, while any particular motive may have as elements the seeking of pleasure, the avoiding of pain, and the functioning of reason, it is more than a matter of pleasure, pain, and reason. The motives of human conduct cannot be explained in terms of body, mind, and a self known to psychology. Beneath the physical, the intellectual, the social, and the personal desires, with which we can become at least somewhat acquainted, there are other desires of which the individual is not always cognizant. There are longings for something of which he does not have knowledge received through the senses and grasped by the mind. He is restless for that which he does not possess, but he cannot analyze his restlessness. This restlessness is evidence of need that cannot be met by any resources within the human being.

THE CHRISTIAN LIFE AND MOTIVE
Man's Greatest Need

Of all man's numerous and pressing needs, the greatest and the most urgent is his need of God. He has no stronger and more insistent desire than his desire for God. Except as he is in union and fellowship with God, his being is possessed with an insatiable hunger and an unquenchable thirst. Human motivation has its source and spring in the eternal God. Man is not merely a physical mechanism, nor a biological organism functioning through his conscious processes, nor a psychological self acting on its personal determinations. He is all this and more; he is an immortal spirit whose intended destiny is life with God during the ceaseless ages of a never-ending eternity. However much they may be perverted, distorted, or numbed by denial, his spiritual urges and desires are just as actual and real as, and even more urgent than, any other drives of his being.

"The way of man is not in himself." Satisfaction can never be found in what we are or do; it is found only in what God is and does. "It is not in man that walketh to direct his steps." Men everywhere and in all ages have been conscious of the incompleteness and the imperfection of themselves and of their world. Always, they have hoped and toiled on, inspired by the vision of something ahead. An age of material invention and scientific progress, the like of which was never seen in the past, means less than little so far as the spiritual and the moral are concerned. Political and social problems of such magnitude confront men that the wisest confess their inability to cope with them. Better cars, planes, and mechanical structures of all kinds are unavailing when men and women decay — when crime, delinquency, divorce, graft, compromise of principle, economic disorder, racial animosities, and international suspicion prevail. Mastery of fine phrases and adeptness at originating new movements and remedies count for nothing. Glib talk of the four freedoms and the drawing up of charters get us nowhere when frustration and failure are rife. The goal of life is not a human achievement but a divine creation. Man is powerless to build for himself or for his society the kind of a world he dreams, and knows, there ought to be. What he seeks for and is unable to find can arrive — will finally arrive — because of what God creates.

Of ourselves we are nothing, we have nothing, and we can do nothing. Each of us is as a circle with all trace of a circumference removed, a nothing surrounded by God, needing God, capable of God. We can be filled with God, if we will. Ethics deals with ends and must ask what is the end of human life. The answer is: Man's final end, the purpose of his existence, is to know and be united with the eternal God. All created things other than man obey the law of their being and thereby fulfill their nature. Man by self-will lost this power of obedience and set for himself a course that runs athwart of the purpose for which God created him. Only as God makes him a new creature can he be brought into alignment with this purpose and thus achieve his destiny.

The real problem faced by man is not himself, his happiness, nor the conditions under which he lives while he is here on earth. His real problem is his relationship to God in time and in eternity. God is forever the same — holy, righteous, perfect, absolute, eternal. What He once required of man, He requires today. Our wills are free, and we may identify our being solely with self and its interests or with God through dying to self and living to spirit. We are one great bundle of insistent desires and can never be satisfied except through union with God. The self is capable of a stupendous variety of experiences, therefore we are free to gratify our desires for an almost infinite number of possible objects. We can seek satisfaction in the pleasures of gluttony, or intemperance, or sensuality; in money, power, or fame; in property, hobbies, or collections; in study, learning, or art; in profession or vocation; in family, associates, and friends; in a political party, a philanthropic organization, or a church; in our pains and illnesses; in our memories of success or failure, our hopes, fears, and plans for the future; or in God.

Despite its many teachings about conduct, the message of the Bible is primarily about God and man's need of Him. Conduct comes in a secondary and derivative place. Both doctrine and conduct are necessary but each in its proper order. Whenever conduct assumes predominance over doctrine, that is, when man fails to give God the primary place, the whole purpose of the teachings of the Bible is undone. The centering of thought upon himself and his conduct brings man into spiritual pride or spiritual despair, neither of which is anything but a hindrance to him. It is through looking to God that we are born again; it is through looking to God that we are being made holy; and it will be through looking to God that we shall be perfected forever.

Man by Nature Not Capable of Good Motives

Good motives are not a characteristic of the natural man; it does not lie in his power to achieve the moral life. This is

not to say that all men are to be regarded as bestial or vicious;
yet the Bible does say, "No one does good, not even one!"
True conduct is the product of a character that is good as God
knows and measures the good. It is not good fruit that makes
a tree good, but a good tree that brings forth good fruit. With
all his knowledge, with all his yearnings, with all his strivings,
with all his desires for the good, man is incapable of building
himself a new character. This effect is the result of an adequate
cause. There must be a new creation. Only God can create.
The Christian character, the source of truly good motives,
exists only in a life communicated by a creative act of God.

There is an absolute law of right, a perfect norm, a real
moral standard, by which all conduct must be judged, whatever the motive that impels the doer. A sincere motive does
not make a wrong act right in itself. Neither does a wrong
motive change a right act into a wrong one. The moral process
has three parts — motive inducing action, means or ways by
which the motive is carried out, and consequences or effects resulting from the act done. No one of the three can be ignored.
Conduct is right if it is the outcome of a good motive, carried
out through the use of good means, to effects in accord with
the norm or standard.

However, Jesus taught that righteousness and goodness are
as much a matter of inner motive as of outward deed. He
emphasized strongly that a person can be guilty of gross immorality even while remaining blameless in action. For Him
the nature of a man's being determines his moral standing.
Righteousness, or right standing, is goodness, and goodness is
the expression of the nature of God. He alone is perfectly good,
and He is also righteous. Morality, therefore, is not a matter of
slavishly adhering to law, of plastering something on from the
outside, but the expression in thought and act of a new nature.
The essential of true morality is a new man, not just a re-
juvenated man. The truly moral person has a new nature; he is
something he was not before. Being a new creation, he
is the source of new motives. Just as one must be born a
human being in order to have human motives, so one must be

born again before he can have Christian motives. Birth is as essential in the second case as it is in the first.

The means whereby a new creation is wrought, enabling man to live in union with God, are twofold: redemption by God and appropriation by man. God, the ultimate source of all life, the absolutely perfect eternal Being, because of His love for man, in Christ shares man's nature, thereby making possible the union of the divine and the human. Christ on the Cross gave His life in expiation of sin, man's self-will that destroyed his relationship with God and made him incapable of righteousness and goodness. Thus in a human life was made perfect, even unto death, obedience which fully satisfied the demand of the divine ideal. Christ rose from the dead, ascended into heaven, and in the person of the Holy Spirit takes up His abode within the regenerated man. He is the principle of life working in a new creation. By His Incarnation, death, and resurrection, He is the source and the goal of the new life, a life of righteousness and true moral living. Every person who has died to selfness and is living unto God can say with Paul, "I am crucified with Christ: nevertheless I live; yet not I, but Christ liveth in me" (Gal. 2:20).

Such a statement can be truthfully made only on the basis of an active appropriation. God respects the freedom of man and never makes him simply the recipient of His power and activity. Only as man in his need of God reaches out in desire for Him and thus appropriates by his self-determinative activity the life of God, can that life become his own. The work of redemption accomplished by God through Christ does not void man of responsibility as a free moral agent. Each of us is a self who is the active operator in the unfolding of the potentialities, natural and spiritual, temporal and eternal, of his own being. God is no external power moving us about as we move sticks and stones, but a spiritual and moral power dwelling within us. He neither forces nor sets aside our will but stimulates, inspires, and guides it in the choice of right motives.

Our Part in Becoming Capable of Good Motives

Our part in appropriating the new life includes repentance and turning to God in faith and obedience. Repentance, what-

ever it means by way of feeling, is a turning from sin and self
to God, a determination of will to depart from evil and start
a new way of living. Faith is the look of the soul to Christ,
an act of will by which man accepts and appropriates the gift of
eternal life offered by God. Obedience is man's yielding to God
all he is and all he has. We enter into life by giving over to
God our own will and our whole being. Thereafter, as we
continue ceaselessly to live in full obedience to all the will of
God, we grow in spiritual life and advance in moral conduct.

Entrance into the new life and the living of it may, or may
not, be characterized by ecstatic experience. At any rate, the
systematic quest of ecstasy, or of any experience merely for the
gratification it brings, is a looking to self instead of God. The
Christian motive is to do the will of God and to glorify Him,
not to have glorious experiences. The Christian way to live is
to go forward in implicit obedience whether or not one feels
joy. True it is, absence of joy may be an indication of something amiss in moral action. On the other hand, it may be
nothing more than a passing psychological condition. In either
case, to forsake the path of duty in order to indulge a feeling,
however exalting, is wrong. In this connection the words of
Alexander are relevant: "There are many ways in which a man
may become a Christian. Some men have to undergo, like
Paul, fierce inward conflict. Others glide quietly, almost im-
perceptibly, into richer and ampler regions of life. But when
or how the transition is made, whether the renewal be sudden
or gradual, it is the same victory in all cases that must be won,
the victory of the spirit over the flesh, the 'putting off of the
old man' and the 'putting on of the new'" (*Christianity and
Ethics*, p. 174).

There is no way to the life of God but by the life and power
of Jesus Christ in the soul. But Christ cannot become our life
until, in obedience to His call, we deny self, take up the daily
cross, and follow Him. There can be neither evasion nor re-
serve in respect to this; we cannot indulge self and have the
life of God. We can have the most ecstatic of experiences, we
can deceive ourselves, we can profess what we will, we can
pretend to be angels, we can be highly esteemed among men

for our Christian walk, we can claim to be doing the work of God among the children of men, but the fact remains that if self is not being denied, if we live after our own will, ruled by our natural appetites and lusts, senses and passions, in conformity with the spirit of this world, we are dead while we live and a stranger to Christ and the life of God in the soul.

The Moral Effects of the Life of God in the Soul

Without this life, there can be no true goodness in outward conduct. When a man's being is centered in his self, his acts arise from motives that are bad and ugly; when it is renewed in the image of Christ, his acts are the outcome of motives that are good and beautiful. Whether he is good or evil is a matter of the kind of nature he has. The nature of a man's being determines the nature of his actions. The nature of his being shows itself first in his mind. What he longs for and thinks about, what he imagines and feels, is the means through which his nature is expressed. There is a vital relation between thinking and doing. What we do passes through our minds and finds expression in motive and intention before it becomes an act of conduct.

By the new creation in Christ, God restores in man His image which man by self-will destroyed. God's goodness is communicable. It is ours to give all diligence in reacting, responding, and submitting so that God can do the communicating. Man born again can control his conduct and live a conqueror of evil and wrong. In him is a new self. The Holy Spirit dwelling within does not do our reacting, responding and submitting. We are to think, to control, to act; each of us is a feeling, thinking, willing self. The thing for us to do is to live with minds so surrendered to Christ that He may govern them, making our thoughts His thoughts and our will His will. Thus He will be able to work in us both to desire and to do. We will always have problems with ourselves and with other people, but, when we live surrendered lives, He is the answer to all our problems.

The new birth is not the end of the work of God. It is but the beginning of a life that leads to a final climax in our completed union with Christ. God has a purpose and, as He lays hold on our lives, His purpose becomes our purpose. It is ours to bend every effort toward the realizing of "the goal that is set before us." We are to use the world and the things of the world with awareness that it is the guilt of man and the forces of evil that make for discord in this world. Inasmuch as this perversion exists, we need to be watchful. All things are lawful to us, but not all things are expedient. We must ever ponder our way in relation to the redemptive purpose of God and choose our motives, not with a view to our own advantage or pleasure but in consideration of God's purpose.

In matters of ordinary life, we who are new creatures in Christ do much as other people do. But even when we do the same thing as our fellow man, we do it differently, as a child of God whose citizenship is in heaven. The difference of action may be insignificant, but the difference of motive may be vast. A person indwelt by Christ is different and has different desires. The Holy Spirit, who gives these new desires, supplies also the dynamic whereby they can be transformed into motives leading to acts of righteousness and true goodness.

The Holy Spirit supplies the dynamic, but we are responsible beings who must think and control our conduct. The new man created by the miracle of the new birth is at first feeble and unpracticed. In spite of a great yearning for the will of God and for sharing in His righteousness and goodness, the old man is still present with desires for and tendencies toward self, sin, and evil. So long as we live in the body, there will be strife between our flesh and our spirit. "Watch and pray, that ye enter not into temptation: the spirit indeed is willing, but the flesh is weak," said Jesus (Matt. 26:41). It is dangerous to regard the new life as a state of rest, for sin and evil are never at peace with right and good. There is no vacuum in our being; any part of it that we do not bring into subjection to the new man created by God remains under the rule of the old man — the flesh, the self life. By the help of God and the power of His Spirit, we can assert our self as new creatures in Christ Jesus, in spite of our weak human nature. The question is, What motives can we cherish and choose to set ourselves in conscious opposition to the wrong influences affecting us and thereby keep ourselves in that condition in which God can most effectively communicate to us His righteousness and goodness? To a brief consideration of a few of the more basic of such motives the remainder of the chapter will be devoted.

Some Motives of the Child of God

In a very true and real sense, Christ is the motive of the life of God in us.

1. *Christ, the real motive.* He lives in us and we live in Him, hence He is the inspiration of the new life. The ethics of Christian living is inseparably connected with the character of Christ. He, the Son, came into the world to reveal the character and nature of the Father. He not only offers His example as the pattern to which we should conform but by the Holy Spirit He inspires in us reverence and loyalty which motivates us to right conduct. The example of Christ and His teaching coincide fully. What He said and what He did are in full accord. It cannot be said of Him as it so often must be said of human beings, "What you are keeps ringing in my ears so loudly that I cannot hear what you say." He was what He taught; His words were the accurate and direct representation of His nature. In His divine nature He expressed the "good" as it is in God; in His human life He was the perfect representative of the life of goodness that God wills that all men shall live. When we begin our considerations and deliberations with the unchanging Christ who once lived as a man on earth and who ever lives, we come out at the right place.

2. *Living as members of the kingdom.* Jesus proclaimed the kingdom of God which men are to seek above all else. He placed emphasis on the ethical factors of God's rulership even more strongly than did the prophets, thereby presenting the Kingdom as a great moral ideal. Membership in it thus becomes a high challenge to the best of which we are capable. "The kingdom of God is within you," said He, implying that it is in the everyday duties and the common relationships of life that God must rule. Jesus laid stress upon the character of God and the nature of His kingdom, showing that the Kingdom is wholly bound up with the character of God. He also spoke constantly of the character and conduct required of those who would enter the Kingdom, pointing out the necessity

for their being like God and doing as God does. In making the
Kingdom the true end of all living, Jesus gave us a powerful
motive of conduct. But while this is true, the emphasis of His
teaching is upon God rather than man and his conduct — upon
what God is, what He has done, is doing, and will do for His
people.

3. *Doing the will of God.* By example and teaching, Jesus
gave man the motive of doing the will of God. The moral life,
as He portrayed it, involves a vital relationship with the living
God. His ethics was definitely "God-conscious." To Him God
was all in all and absolutely supreme. His will is to be done
on earth as it is being done in heaven. Unity with the purpose
of God is the basis of spiritual life and ethical conduct. The
duties of man are duties to God. Conscious of being in fellowship with God, the Christian has an impelling motive founded
on his desire so to conduct himself as to maintain this relation
unimpaired by doing anything contrary to the will of God.

4. *Response to God's Love.* The central factor in the life of
one born of God is love as a response, a reaction to God's love.
When the human soul experiences the effects of divine love, it
responds with a love which includes God and all mankind.
We love God, not for ourselves, not merely for His gifts, but
for Himself. Love, therefore, is a great compelling power that
causes all our actions to tend toward God. It is a force which
breaks down all opposition and stimulates most intense activity.
Love is not a mere emotion; it is a state of the will, not merely
a matter of the feelings. Love that does not find expression in
action on behalf of the person loved is only empty sound, sig-
nifying nothing. "This is the love of God, that we keep his
commandments" (I John 5:3). It comprises the attitude of
complete dependence, the consciousness that God who is love
is ever near us, and it produces conformity to His will in all
things, within and without.

Love is a compelling motive, not only in conduct directed
Godward, but also in our relations with our fellows. Love to
God and love to man cannot be separated; the two are only
aspects of the same fact. "Everyone that loveth him [God]
that begat loveth him also that is begotten of him" (I John 5:1).
Love for a person causes us to want to please him, to avoid doing

things which annoy or offend him, to seek his highest welfare
regardless of our own interests, and to shield him from harm
and evil. Love is self-effacing and looks to the good of our
neighbor who, as Jesus taught in the parable of the Good Sa-
maritan, is any human being whom we have opportunity and
power to help.

5. *Gratitude to God.* Related to love to God is the motive
of gratitude for salvation. Luther held that the true Christian
experiences such a work of grace in the free forgiveness of his
sins that there arises in his heart a sentiment of gratitude. Because of this, he is moved to thankful devotion to Christ — a
devotion which prompts him not merely to do what he is expected to do but to go beyond and expend himself in seeking
out and doing good works. Out of gratitude, the Christian asks,
not what he has the privilege of doing for his own satisfaction
but what he may do in return for the benefits bestowed upon
him by a loving God who, in mercy, passes over sins without
exacting from him a penalty.

6. *Living as children of a Heavenly Father.* A motive ex-
hibited by Jesus Himself and one to which He made frequent
appeal was that of living as sons of a heavenly Father. Speaking of the Father, He said, "I always practice what pleases Him."
He taught that we should do those things which befit us as
children of God. He appealed to men on the basis of the
fatherly care of God, emphasizing that they ought to recipro-
cate by doing that which glorifies God. He sought to stimulate
men by showing them their exalted position as sons of God.
Both Paul and Peter stress the same thought in their writings.
We are not to serve God merely for what we get but with
vital and active interest in His purposes as children who share
His possessions and cooperate with Him in His undertakings.

7. *Call to do the work of God.* The idea of sonship is connected with the incentive of the conviction of a divine call to
do the work of God. We are in the world for a purpose; we
have personal and individual responsibility as servants of God;
and there is a task for each of us that no other can do. God
trusts us to perform what He wants done. Be his task small
or great, whether his service is noticed or unnoticed by men,
whether or not he sees results, the motive of the true Christian is

to be faithful to God in the place where God has appointed
he is to serve and in the work that God has given him to do.

8. *Rewards.* The motive of reward is clearly and definitely
emphasized in the Bible. It appears at numerous places in
Christ's teachings the main tendency of which was to lead men
to forget themselves by centering their aspirations upon God.
The supreme duty of man is to love God and to live as a subject in His Kingdom, regardless of what might happen to him.
The essence of wrong relationship to God is self-centeredness.
Self-centeredness and God-centeredness are opposites. Never
will the latter develop from the former. So long as man has
self for a center, God cannot be the center of his life; only a
radical conversion makes it possible for a human being to find
his center in God. The one thing that stands between any person and his highest spiritual well-being, between him and the
deepest, most satisfying fellowship with God, is self and its
concerns. Nothing so blights the moral life as self-centeredness
and self-interest in its numerous forms.

Emphasis on reward as a motive appeals to self-interest to
some extent. However, the Bible view of reward differs from
the typical human conception. This last regards rewards as
something due man in the basis of human merit, which plays
no part in the rewards emphasized in the Bible. That is, the
basis of reward, according to the Bible, is not merely personal
and individual but inheres in the very structure of the universe.
The rewards offered are such as appeal only to a person who is
not self-centered. They are to be given, not to him who seeks
them for self-gratification and self-glorification but to him who,
denying self and devoting himself wholly to God, trusts Him
to reward as He will when He will.

Thus Jesus constantly promised reward only to those who
were ready to follow and obey Him from higher motives than
utilitarian benefits. In His teachings about rewards, He shows
clearly that the human conception of personal merit is not their
basis. Examples are the eleventh hour laborers, and the "unprofitable servants" that all of us are. None of us deserves reward. When reward is given, it is of grace, not of human merit.
God in grace offers rewards because it is better that we be

moved to action by thought of them than that we should not. Tendency to self-centeredness is so much a part of human nature that, if there were no rewards, we would fall easy victims of self-centeredness in yielding to the temptation to pride ourselves in our virtue in following virtue for its own sake. The true Christian is self-denying, but no one becomes a Christian because he practices self-denial. Salvation is not dependent upon anything we do or can do but upon what God in grace has done for us.

The practice of self-denial and self-sacrifice for the sake of benefit is as definitely self-centered as anything else we may do with a motive of having merit accrue to us. Humanly speaking, it is not as reprehensible, not as superficial, as actual seeking of reward, but God sees not as man sees. He looks on the heart alone, and to Him such practice is self-centered. To take the position that all consideration of reward is to be avoided is unscriptural, though not as immoral, as to practice virtue for the sake of reward. The latter makes merit its basis just as much as the former does. It causes us to look away from God and leads us to center thought and effort on self and its interests.

It is not, therefore, selfish and unworthy for a Christian to be moved to act upon ideals of lofty conduct and of devoted service by the thought of reward. We need always to be on our guard, of course, against all motions of self-interest and the thought of merit for what we do. We are not to make reward our first consideration. Life in completed union with God is the purpose and end of our being. As we make progress in living the life of God, our aims and our ideals become higher and our incentives nobler. The consequence is that we become less and less interested in self and its concerns and more and more desirous that Christ have ascendancy in our being. Ultimately, the love of God and the glory of fellowship with Him in a perfect union take supremacy over every other motive.

The reward of the Christian life is that which makes appeal only to him who is wholly devoted to the will of God. The most cherished reward, present and future, of such an one is not something external; it is entirely a matter of what he is in Christ as he grows in righteousness and in power of doing good in the sight of God. Paul incites us with the motive of attaining to "unity of the faith, and of the knowledge of the Son of God, unto a perfect man, unto the measure of the stature of the fulness of Christ" (Eph. 4:13). In the same general context, he exhorts "that ye put off concerning the former conversation the old man, which is corrupt according to the deceitful lusts; And be renewed in the spirit of your mind; And that ye put on the new man, which after God is created in righteousness and true holiness" (Eph. 4:22-24).

9. *Perfection in Christ.* The real incentive for true Christian living, with all that it means in terms of morality and spirituality, is the hope of becoming perfect in Christ Jesus, of attaining to likeness to Him who is the origin and the source of the new life, of reaching perfection, the ideal for which we were apprehended of (captured by) Christ Jesus (Phil. 3:12). It is not a selfish motive to seek fulfillment of one's self in God. Not to do so is to give evidence of lack of appreciation of what life really means.

QUESTIONS

1. Is any conduct accidental?
2. What is the self that is involved in all human motivation?
3. Explain why we cannot attain complete development apart from other human beings.
4. Give illustrations to show that things in themselves cannot put us into action.
5. What evidence do we have of the existence of a moral power beyond man?
6. What is your definition of personality? Of character?
7. Show how the self is dependent on the world in which it lives.
8. What are the implications of the statement that it is not the motive that seizes the man, but the man who seizes the motive?
9. Trace as best you can the motive which prompted you to do some particular act that has moral significance.
10. Do you always know what your motives are? Do you ever do anything without a motive?
11. What part of the whole of life, that is, what proportion, do you say that conduct is?
12. What is a good will? How are will and motive related?

13. Is your behavior sometimes like that of the animal? Should it be? Must it be?
14. State your reaction to the content of the first paragraph of the section on the nature of motivation.
15. Explain: "For ethics, then, the motive inheres in the object itself."
16. Examine one or more of your experiences which seems to have had no motive with a view to ascertaining if this really be the case.
17. Did you ever do anything without having a sense of need? Would you ever act if this were not present?
18. How much of you is body? Little, some, or much?
19. Can you differentiate between desire and need? How are the two related?
20. What is it in man that has need or desire? Is this a thing of mere mechanical reaction?
21. What place has value in the process of motivation?
22. Explain why desire, in and of itself, has no moral quality?
23. How does will differ from desire?
24. What is the basic difference between man and animals?
25. Are there good grounds for regarding pleasure and pain as the desire basic to all motives?
26. Why can they not be accepted as such?
27. Can we obtain pleasure by seeking it? What is the usual experience of one who makes pleasure his aim?
28. Do you think that reason is basic in human motivation? Why, or why not?
29. To what extent are you in accord with the conclusion stated in the last paragraph of the section on pleasure, pain and reason in motivation?
30. Cite evidence to support the truth that man's greatest need is his need of God.
31. Is man an utterly helpless being? If so, why does he appear to be quite the opposite?
32. What is man's real problem? Why is he, then, taken up so much with himself and his own pursuits?
33. What do you think is the one and only source of good motives in a human being?
34. If one's motive is sincere, will not the deed prompted thereby be good?
35. Can one overstress the fact that "morality is not plastering something on from the outside?" If not, why not?
36. What does the phrase, "active appropriation," mean when applied to man's becoming a new creation?
37. Explain clearly your conception of what true repentance is.
38. Can one become a child of God without having "an experience?"

39. Give biblical evidence to support the truth that we may do many things in the name of Christ and yet be dead while we live.
40. Can we become "good" in ourselves? Can we become better every day in every way?
41. Wherein do the acts of ordinary daily life differ as between the non-Christian and the person who is a new creature in Christ?
42. In what sense is Christ the motive of the life of God in us?
43. Does Jesus stress conduct in His teachings about the Kingdom?
44. Just what is love? What is it not?
45. Is it wrong to work for rewards from God?
46. Can we ever get away entirely from self-interest? Did Jesus wholly ignore it?
47. What will be our greatest reward when we reach heaven?
48. Can you think of motives other than the nine given, which a child of God may rightly choose to follow?

CHAPTER IX

Freedom

THE FIFTH MAIN PROBLEM OF ETHICS is concerned with freedom, especially with the freedom of what is known as the will. Its basic question may be expressed thus: Is man always and everywhere wholly free to choose his own lines of conduct?

FACTORS THAT COMPLICATE THE PROBLEM

For various reasons the problem is a complicated one. First of all, it is not easy to understand just what is meant by "the will." Our natural tendency, fostered by the persisting influence of discarded faculty psychology, is to think of the will as an entity or a faculty of the mind, which may or may not be free in its activities. However, will is not a faculty or a mechanism, nor is it a thing that performs acts of volition. Spinoza drew an analogy between will and color which is an aid to the understanding of the nature of will. Our particular experiences of seeing green, red, blue, and other colors is the source and origin of our concept of color. However, we never think of color as the cause of green, red, blue, and other color experiences. As is the case with color, so will is a general concept derived from particular experiences. No more is a thing called "will" the cause of our acts of volition than is a thing named "color" the cause of our particular color experiences.

What is called "the will" and what was formerly supposed to be a distinct entity or faculty is nothing more than a way of acting. It is the way we act when we decide among opposing motives, or make difficult decisions, or persist in a purposeful course of action leading to a goal. We do not infer this activity when decisions are made with ease or when behavior is marked by no persistence. Neither do we assume that will exists in animals. Even when their behavior is characterized by persistence, we see it as an attempt to satisfy an urge or a drive. In human beings, the ways of responding attributed to will are expressions of the relative strength of motives. What is known as "will" is a complex outcome of native tendencies and acquired experiences, organic conditions and environmental influences. In other words, we choose those alternatives which, in terms of our innate drives and our past experience, promise the greatest ultimate satisfaction of motives. Will, then, is the way the self acts in determining its modes of conduct.

A second factor which complicates any discussion of the will is the fact that human behavior may be viewed from many points of view: physical, biological, psychological, social, moral, legal, philosophical, theological, etc. There is considerable overlapping and continuous interaction; the different aspects of life can be separated only for purposes of analysis and study.

The problem of the freedom of the will can be, and often is, approached from the point of view of psychology, law, theology, and ethics. The main interest of psychology is in the correct explanation of the experience of freedom of choice, which seems to be contrary to the scientific assumption that all things, including mental experience, are under the control of law and necessity. Law is concerned with freedom in its bearing on the personal responsibility of the individual for doing or not doing what is legally proper and correct. Theology is interested in the problem from the standpoint of man's capability or power as a moral being to give or to withhold, to welcome or to reject, obedience to God, the morally perfect Creator, and thereby make his own experience, form his own character, govern his own conduct — in a sense, determine his own destiny.

Ethics takes as its fundamental principle the freedom of the individual to direct his own conduct. Except as he has power or ability to do this, he is without obligation. To say that man is a responsible moral agent implies that he makes voluntary response to moral demands and that he may be held accountable for what he chooses to do. Apart from this ability or freedom, man would be a mere natural being, with no more capacity for moral conduct than the animals. It is never considered that a person is morally responsible when he is unable to ponder his paths and to make deliberate choice. The little child incapable of discerning between right and wrong, good and evil, is obviously not accountable for its acts. The insane person who lacks power of rational discrimination and the individual who, in time of stress or crisis, acts without opportunity to think and choose deliberately, are likewise without responsibility. It is by virtue of his freedom to make his own choice or to decide his own course of conduct that an individual is to be commended or censured for what he does.

A third factor that complicates the problem is the subtle and difficult question of how the will exercises its freedom. Admittedly, conduct is, and must be, governed by motives, for motive is that which induces action. Very definitely, it can be said that where no motive is, there also is no conduct. Perhaps the difficulty involved here is the result of our ready tendency to think of motive and of the nature of man in too circumscribed a manner. Feelings and desires are elemental components of our nature and very prominent in motive. Accordingly, we are prone to regard man as so subject to the control of his own feelings and desires as to be driven to action by whichever of these influences is strongest at the moment of decision.

However, the motive which governs an act of ethical conduct is not a mere feeling or desire. Man may be brought to action by the stirring of the affective part of his being but he is truly man and his conduct is truly ethical only when he originates his acts through rational thinking directed in terms of a goal to be reached and mobilizes his energy consciously with a view to reaching it. There is a great deal of difference between acts performed under the stress of strong feeling or impelling desire and those done under the guidance of thought ending in deliberate choice. The former are essentially involuntary — sometimes definitely so. The latter are the voluntary acts of the man himself identifying his self with a particular feeling or desire and making it actually his own motive, the self-instigated cause of his conduct.

Ethics is not a mere creation of experience, the outcome of the operation of urges and drives acquired by man in the struggle for existence. Man is not an irresponsible being, a creature of circumstances, a product of motive, under the control of his desire for the agreeable or his aversion for the disagreeable. Ethical conduct does not mean the capability of a thing to be moved but the ability of a person to move. Freedom does not consist merely in the capacity for responding to movement, in acting only when acted on; it implies power to initiate movement, ability on the part of a self-conscious being to direct his own conduct.

Man is lord of the world, made, according to the eighth psalm, "a little lower than the angels" and crowned "with glory and honour," given "dominion over the works" of God, with all things put "under his feet." The purpose of his creation is that he be a ruler and a governor of himself and of God's created things. He was endowed with reason and with capability to make use of all the material creation. He himself is not subject to anything in the world. "He is intelligent, he is free, he is responsible; his life has meaning, it is going to a definite goal that is intimately personal." He was made to "rule the empire of himself." Of all the creatures in the material world, he alone can say that he will or will not take the path that leads to the goal of his life.

We must choose. This is a disquieting fact, for it reminds us that we are human. We cannot but feel that the ultimate responsibility for our acts rests upon our personal and individual choices. Whenever we accept something as right, there is a strong sense of obligation to choose the right. We may think sometimes that it would be easier if we could consider ourselves as machines, if we could lose ourselves in the dreamy delights of emotionalism, or if we were to let down the barriers and act as animals. But we cannot take the easy way, the weak way, or the cowardly way and feel worthy of the dignity of our humanity. We cannot behave as machines and retain our self-respect; we cannot regard our duties as inventions of our emotions because we find ourselves bound in them by the authority of something far above that of our feelings and desires; we must recognize that our human power to will preserves us from resigning ourselves to hopelessness and surrendering to the vileness of unrestrained indulgence. We cannot avoid taking one course rather than another. We have freedom to choose but the act of choosing is forced upon us. When we are not deliberately for a thing, we are thoughtlessly against it and for something else. To be indifferent, to be undecided, to let things go as they will, simply means choosing in favor of the opposite end. At every moment some choice is made, either deliberately or thoughtlessly.

Degrees of Freedom

Men are free within and without to choose so to act as to remake themselves and their world. Man is not mechanically determined. But this does not mean that every human being, whatever his past may have been, no matter what the present situation may be, is absolutely free, at every moment of his life, to choose any one of the alternatives that may confront him. Choice is not that simple. The individual's heredity, all his past experiences, his present environment, his bodily state and current mental attitude, and the strength of the stimulus are some of the factors that enter into the basis of his present choice. This means that man is partly free and partly determined. The essential signification of freedom is that man can himself determine, instead of being subject to determination, by external coercion or restraint. The value of his resulting conduct, whatever bearing it may have in other connections, does not affect the question of his actual freedom.

There are, then, degrees of freedom. Conduct is always influenced in some measure by external factors not subject to control. The relative part these external influences play varies from case to case. Most important in this connection is the fact that the relative strength of the external factors depends on the general condition of the individual who is affected by them. Absolutely speaking, no one is always at his best. The degree of external coercion, that is, the extent to which the individual is free, may vary much, even when the circumstances are the same, or essentially so, and although he is to all appearances also the same.

Determinism is the name given to the theory that if one has complete knowledge of previously existing mental, physical, and environmental causes, he knows fully how a person will, and must act. That is, every act of an individual has causal connections, not only externally with his environment, but also internally with his impulses and motives. A thoroughgoing determinism is fatal to real morality in that it takes away the responsibility of the person for what he does. According to this doctrine, every event is to be explained completely in terms of its antecedents. What one is through his heredity or by temperament or as a result of the influence of his past environment, along with the impinging physical causes and the strength of his motives (he is not a free self), determines how he shall will.

At the opposite extreme is the theory of indeterminism or indifferentism, which holds that the individual is absolutely free to choose between alternate courses. This position strikes at true morality just as definitely as determinism does. The freedom essential to true morality is not absolute freedom to choose any possible line of action wholly apart from the influence of the past and the nature of the doer. Will is not necessitated by motives, but motives are necessary to choice. Real freedom does not prompt to action without a reason for acting. If there were no reason, choice would be an accident. The motives which induce truly ethical conduct — the motives necessary to ethical choice — are the outcome of the operation of the reason of the individual.

Choice or action that is accidental is non-moral because it is not really the act of the person; that is, though it be associated with a person, it is actually a chance product, not the outcome of determination by his self. The activity of a self involves too many factors to admit of explanation in simple terms. Freedom of the will means the ability of a self to choose deliberately between two or more possible courses of action. The person does not act involuntarily, automatically, or accidentally, but makes a decision according to what he, through intelligent and rational consideration, has concluded is best.

In other words, freedom implies the ability to stop and deliberate before one enters upon a particular activity. It means capacity to bring to attention, through the use of memory and imagination, the results of past experience and the thought of lines of action other than those suggested accidentally by the circumstances of the present. True freedom does not consist in the making of decisions apart from the influence of conditioning factors. Free choice is not based on chance or accident. An act, not influenced by anything in the nature of the situation or in the nature of the individual, is not really an expression of choice. Freedom to choose does not mean that he who does the choosing is free from all determining factors within himself but rather that he is free to choose in the light of conditions to which these factors give rise. It is to be able to express the considered preferences of one's own self.

ACTION AND FREEDOM

Impulse to action is the deepest thing in life, animal or human. To be alive means to act. Even if it is believed that animals have mind, it cannot be conceived that the perceptive function in mind is as fundamental as the active impulsive function. Drives to action manifestly impel the animal. Not insight but impulse is the beginning, and action, not insight, is the end of animal behavior. In man also, most fundamental is the impulse to action. We have this impulse before we have consciousness of the world. Schopenhauer built his philosophy on the conception that "the world as will" is prior to "the world as idea." Hoffding goes further and maintains that the existence of consciousness is due to volitional activity. He affirms that in the mental life of man "a purpose and a feeling aroused by this purpose, rule the course of thought" whereas in animals, because there is no self, consciousness is disconnected. He says also that "only through firm volition is actual self-consciousness possible. What is expressed in the unity and the continuity of memory, and in the immediate feeling of self, is completed in the act of will, in which all elements of consciousness cooperate with concentrated force. In our resolves and acts of will, the real unity of our 'self' is most strikingly manifested" (*Outline of Psychology,* pp. 310, 314, 316, 332).

In body and in mind we are organized for action. The circulation of the blood has action for its basis. The object of circulation is to remove waste and provide that renewal of tissue and of oxygen necessary for the maintenance of the normal amount of potential energy. The blood not only nourishes but also stimulates. Our whole neural organization is, from the physiological point of view, only a mechanism for converting stimuli into reactions. The nervous process has its end in action and is never normally complete until action has occurred. The muscular system, made up of more than six hundred muscles and comprising the major part of the body, is built for an immense number, and for the greatest variety, of actions. From prenatal days until the hour of death, the body has need for active expression. The human body is made for action.

The mind of man is organized for action. In all its experiences, it looks to action. Every idea has its motor aspect. Were it not for the presence of other ideas, it is quite certain that the issue of any idea would be some overt act, more or less consciously performed. The idea tends of itself to expression in action and needs only to be held exclusively in attention to so express itself. The implications of this principle are vast for all of life, including moral life. In both slight and grave matters it means that, as a result of concentration of attention upon one idea, we go into action almost as if moved from without — sometimes in a sort of unawareness — into the performance of the act to which the idea looks. Thus the facts of mental life verify the truth of the old saying, "As a man thinketh in his heart, so is he."

That in animals which moves them to action is sense appetite in its various forms. In man the mainspring of action is will — the conscious and deliberate disposition of the self to persist in a purposeful course, in spite of difficulties and contrary inducements. In a comprehensive but real sense, man's purpose is founded upon his tendency or inclination to his full perfection and to all that is involved in this perfection. Accordingly, as Dewey points out, there is in will a factor that has to do with the foresight of results and another that has to do with the depth of hold the foreseen outcome has upon the individual. The will functions most directly in attention. The oft-repeated statement to the effect that a man's environment makes him is not true. However, it is most true that the part of his environment to which he attends has a potent influence in the making of his life.

Freedom and Self-Control

In the power of attention lies the definite sphere of the freedom of the will. We can choose that to which we will attend — anything from the loving suggestions of an infinite and all-wise Creator to the base proposals of the subtle enemy of all that is good, with whatever lies between these two extremes. It is the idea to which we attend that passes into action. "He that would not enter into sin must not sit by the door of temptation." We cannot use bad, evil, or wrong as a sweet morsel of thought and have good or right issue forth in our actions. Our environment need not make us; we can make our environment. As Kant maintained, we *can*, if we ought. "Every man stamps his own value upon himself, and we are great or little according to our will," said another. Our responsibility is to attend, to give our thought wholly to those things that ought to prevail, then they will pass into act. We need not be victims of environmental influence.

Freedom counts for little if it does not eventuate in self-control. Attention lies at the basis of self-control, which is the chief distinction between men and animals, between the sane and the insane, and a root of all moral virtues. The animal, James says, has a "hair-trigger constitution" which results in action following immediately upon impulse; man can hold the present impulse in check, center attention on the foreseen outcome, and deliberate in terms of his foresight. The insane also let themselves go; the sane keep themselves in hand through the direction of attention to outcomes. Manifestly, without self-control, no virtue, not even the least amount of prudence, is possible. Here, also, the impulse to act must be kept subordinate to the considered view of what is best in terms of foreseen results. The exercise of the free will, then, in directing attention is essential in self-control which is a fundamental principle of moral living.

Effective self-control must be positive, not negative. Moral qualities become ours only as we put them into practice. We are beings with intelligence, freedom, and responsibility, but we are made for action. When we use our intelligence aright, we direct our conduct in the light of a philosophy of life that we have carefully thought out and consciously adopted. This means the governing of ourselves from within in the light of ethical ideals freely chosen. The inner control includes a sense of responsibility for our actions and the effects of our deeds, even to the acknowledgment at times of blame or guilt. The intelligently free, responsible person faces facts and reality in his own life as well as in his world, avoiding easy rationalizations, the making of excuses, the tendency to project blame on others, and pleasant daydreaming. Being essentially free to will at every moment, he exerts his will power with sufficient strength to do what he ought, whatever be the circumstances in which he is placed.

Being Inseparable from Doing

Being and doing cannot be separated; being good and doing right are but two aspects of ethical living. The springs of action, the motive, the intention, the spirit in which an act is done, are as important as the overt conduct. Mere formal doing of duty and conformity to set requirements are not truly moral. Nevertheless, sincere doing is an aid to being. A person of good character is one who in motive, in intention, and by practice, does right things. Genuine doing, free from pretense or deceit, aids the building of good character.

Emerson says that every impulse to perform some moral duty upon which we do not act obscures some truth we should have known. Carlyle expressed the same thought in these words: "Doubt of any kind cannot be removed, except by action. On which ground, too, let him who gropes painfully in darkness or uncertain light, and prays vehemently that dawn may ripen into day, lay this other precept well to heart — Do the duty which lies nearest thee." The doing by deliberate act of will reacts upon our thought-life, enriching, strengthening, and modifying it. "A firm resolve, carried out with decision and without hesitation, clears up the whole mental atmosphere and scatters the clouds which dim the clearness of thought." Thus through active expression do we develop firmness of character and come into an increasingly higher moral life.

There is no other way. We must face fundamental facts as they are in the very structure of our daily living, if we would make our moral thinking more than a matter of mere wishing. Emotional longing to be kind, charitable, generous, or anything else in moral life, counts for nothing except as we meet difficulties masterfully and intelligently. Good resolutions have a way of evaporating into thin air. There is no way to achieve a general purpose other than to attain specific purposes through engaging actively in a series of advancing procedures. We do not get an education or build a house by sitting and wishing, but by doing a long series of detailed acts in accordance with a plan. The execution of each particular act helps in attaining the general purpose but lack of attention to detailed steps or failure to take any one of them obstructs the general purpose.

Probably nothing contributes more to lack of success in life's struggle than the failure of men to master themselves. We are so constituted that we cannot get the most and best, even on the lowest levels, except as we keep ourselves in hand, except as our lives are permeated with the element of self-control. We cannot simply let our selves go. This self-mastery must not be merely a matter of restraint; it must be a positive and definite making the lower serve the higher. We cannot copy it, we can substitute nothing for it. The attitude must be genuine. It must be a real self-control born of a deep sense of the dignity of human personality and of a profound respect for its freedom to choose and to act for itself.

The great battlefield of the will is in the attention and one place where the issue is joined is in connection with our feelings. To control feelings and emotions, we must use indirect means through either attention or action. Over feeling itself we can exercise no direct control; it arises involuntarily in the presence of whatever excites it. However, we can determine that to which we will attend. In so doing we train our thinking through the will in attention, and our thinking finally determines our feeling. Likewise, we can act in the line of the feelings we would have and thereby bring to bear on feeling the reflex effect of action. For example, actions of cheerfulness and courage go far in producing the mood of cheer and courage.

These methods of controlling feeling and emotion by attention and by action are positive. Never do we attain to self-control by the use of negative methods. That one impulse can be displaced only by another is a principle of greatest importance in ethics. We gain self-control only as we attain more than self-control. By positive living, not by merely negatively fighting the evil—trying to keep it out of attention, which but serves to center attention more definitely upon it—but by positively attending to the good, we expel the evil by the good. Whatever we can avoid under the conception that it is bad, we can also avoid under the conception that something else is good. Acting continually under the negative conception enslaves us. We assert our freedom when we act under the positive conception of the good. There is no better way to fight evil than to concentrate on good. Making self-control positive involves, then, two things: (1) keeping attention centered on the good, the higher considerations, the future better conditions that ought to prevail; and (2) as a consequence, making the lower serve the higher. Thus the problem of character and its outcome in conduct is ultimately a matter of exercising our freedom of fixing attention.

Freedom a Growth

Man is a moral personality, a self-conscious, self-determining being. But we live in a world which acts upon us and upon which we act. Our self-consciousness and our self-determination are influenced, therefore, both by what the world does to us and through what we do by virtue of our being in the world. The content and the extent of self-consciousness are the result of this interaction between us and our world. What we become in personal and moral life through self-determination is likewise the outcome of this interaction. Each of us comes into the world as a self-propelling being with a bundle of natural impulses or desires which we express under the limiting influence of the world into which we come.

Freedom an Outcome of Interaction between Our Nature and Our World

Our freedom is a matter of cooperation between our native impulses and the necessity inherent in the world that impinges

upon us. If we had no power other than to act as impelled by
our native inclinations, we would be creatures of caprice, not
rational free beings capable of choice. If we were obliged to
respond only when the world acted upon us, and in accord with
its action, we would be merely creatures of mechanical causa-
tion. Actually, we are conditioned by the world in which we
live, but we also take the very conditions amid which we live
and make them over into elements of our character. We are
never free to make moral decisions in total isolation from ideals
and obligations presented in our world, yet the moral self can
act on no impulse, except as it so works upon that impulse as
to make it over into a motive.

Thus we are not born free. At the moment of birth we are
creatures of caprice, the prey of every passing whim, of every
chance desire. We are likewise the passive recipient of the conditions imposed upon us by our world. We can exercise no initiative, make no choices, arrive at no decisions, and engage in no
conduct. We are not born in freedom though we are born to
it. "We are born free as we are born rational; not that we have
actually the exercise of either; age that brings one, brings with
it the other too." Freedom is a development. We must obtain
it by our striving. It cannot be bestowed upon us any more than
can the ability to think. Freedom must be the product of our
intellectual and moral unfettering, which is possible only
through self-activity. We become free only as we exercise our
freedom; we can exercise our freedom only in an environment.

We win our freedom gradually. We undergo a slow process
of induction into the possibilities of freedom, involving a trans-
fer of restraint from the outer world to the inner self and a
progressive increase in capability to choose, as intelligence,
imagination, and experience extend the range of our vision and
increase the number of alternatives we meet. Increasing se-
lectivity and increasing self-direction are the outcomes of
growth in capacity for freedom. Growth is complete in the
measure that we become capable of subordinating our present
impulses to the attainment of more complete and higher purposes. Only when we attain to Plato's standard of becoming
"the spectator of all time and of all existence" or when we can

place all things, to use Spinoza's celebrated phrase, "under a certain form of eternity" are we free in the fullest sense.

We grow in the direction in which we act, and we grow so long as we have possession of our normal powers. Humanly speaking, we make ourselves by our choices and actions, whatever the circumstances may be. We make ourselves in a world where we find values, in a world in which we act and judge as free, ethical, self-determining beings. By our choices and decisions we form our characters which in turn make later choices and decisions of a certain kind both possible and probable. Neither the character of the confirmed wrongdoer, nor that of the person whose conduct is unimpeachable, is ever completely formed. At every moment, both choose and decide and in so doing help form their characters further. The tendency of each is in a different direction, but tendency is not compulsion. It is possible for each to decide at every moment to go counter to the way he has been deciding to go.

No one ever gets so old or becomes so set in his ways as to be unable to will to start in a new direction. However, one may be too old or too set for the decision to have effect on what he does after starting. A confirmed wrongdoer usually decides wrongly, not because it is impossible for him to will differently but because of the difficulty he experiences in making a new kind of decision effective in his body, mind, and world, accustomed as these are to his decisions to go in the old way. It is difficult for him to make his new decision effective in practice because, through the years, he has formed habits which nullify the force of the decision and so affect his body and mind and world as to destroy the effectiveness of his will, unless it be exercised with greater strength than in the past.

In spite of the fact that he is free to will, the confirmed wrongdoer is so bound by the habit of doing wrong that it is not likely he will act otherwise. His habits are against his carrying into effect his resolves to do differently. If he is to do differently, he must persistently exert more than his former force of will to surmount the hold that his past habits have upon him. This it is possible for him to do, though it is not probable that he will do it. In the usual course of living, it is normal for us to exercise our wills only to the degree we have become accustomed through growth to exercising them.

THE CONDITIONS OF FREEDOM

"A man does what he is at the time" is a significant fact but not a more true or a more significant one than this: "A man is at the time what he does." The self is not truly expressed or fully revealed in feelings, basic though they be, nor in sentiments, nor in moral sensibilities, nor in aspirations, nor in principles, nor even in good resolutions. It is action, born of the will, that portrays most completely and most accurately what a person is but only because he is a self, able and, therefore, free to act. The essential element of moral freedom lies in the power of self-determination by which the individual identifies his self with a particular end. The resulting action is, consequently, the most complete revelation of this self that can be made.

Freedom means that the self is a power which produces effects without being determined — or caused — to do so by anything other than itself. Practically, it means the ability of a person to consider, to ponder, to deliberate, then to choose one from among various possible courses of action. Freedom thus implies ability to act thoughtfully and intentionally on the basis of capacity to give attention to the results of past experience, to the products of imagination, and to possibilities of lines of action suggested by these. Accordingly, there are some necessary conditions of freedom.

One of these conditions is health of body and of mind. Obviously, since the body is built for action, anything which impairs the effectiveness of its acting interferes also with the purposes for which it acts. The person is a unity and anything that affects him in one aspect of his life exerts influence also in every other phase of his being. Pain, illness, weakness, malfunctioning of any kind, affects the person not only physically but also mentally, morally, and spiritually. No one can be at his best for thinking and choosing if he is in pain, if he is fatigued, if he is diseased. Good mental health is just as — if not even more — essential to the exercise of free choice as physical health. Starved longings, unfulfilled desires, feelings of frustration, neurotic tendencies, unbalanced natures without self-control, impoverished aspirations — these and other forms of mental maladjustment are barriers to free choice in that they limit capacity to give consideration to possible courses of action.

A second condition of freedom in making choices is many and varied interests. Interest is the basis of attention. Voluntary attention to an unchanging object is possible for but a brief period of time. In order to hold our attention, an object must continuously change. Therefore, to fix attention on anything involves discerning its different aspects and relations. For a thought to keep its power with us, it is necessary that we reshape it frequently and think of it again in new relations and applications. The ability to discern numerous aspects and relations is dependent upon the possession of a large circle of interests.

To be free in action, we must be able to think of many possible things to do. If we can think of only one thing when it is time to act, our freedom is necessarily limited by that one thing. If we can think of a dozen or a hundred possibilities, the range of our freedom is correspondingly greater. If, when temptation is presented, we are unable to give attention to anything other than the allurement it offers, we are thereby committed to yielding. If, on the other hand, we can turn our attention to things true, things honorable, things right, things pure, and things lovely, we are in position to choose a course of action different from that into which the temptation would bring us. The problem of self-control, the problem of all right conduct, is not that of dependence upon sheer power of will. Self-control and good conduct in general depend on attention, and the chief support of attention is strong and many-sided interest.

A third prime condition of freedom is objectivity. Since we are made for action and no experience is actually completed until it issues in action, it follows that the normal mood is objectivity, not subjectivity or morbid introspection. The person who is wholly wrapped up in himself and his own concerns is in bondage to his narrow self-interest; the person who forgets himself in love for others and in matters having to do with their welfare has an enlarged horizon of life which makes for expanded limits of freedom. Where the first person has one or an extremely small number of alternatives from which to choose, the second has numerous and varied possibilities. Thoughts turned inward on themselves provide an inadequate basis for the stimulation of other thoughts and the development of motives. Thoughts directed outward carry the self beyond its original motives of volition, giving rise to other thoughts and the originating of new motives as a basis for choice and action.

In connection with objectivity, work constitutes a means for enlarging the scope of one's freedom. Made for action, we do not come to our best without work. Idleness cripples and cramps; work enlarges and ennobles. Ethical living calls "not simply for activity of some sort, but for work that shall be an expression of our best self in the full range of our being." We need work, not that we may be idly busy or to be busy with halfhearted purpose, but work in which we can forget self. Nor is it the kind of work or the size of the task, but the spirit and devotion shown in the task, that is the measure of him who does it. The full value of work for any of us is to be found only in activity which seems to us worth-while — activity in which we engage with the enthusiasm and the exhilaration of beings who are doing something we have freely chosen to do and something which affords us abundant opportunity for exercising free choices continually. Significant work calls for a plan and a purpose and requires the thoughtful mind that sees things in their true perspective.

Allied to work is wise leisure as a fifth condition of freedom. Fruitful leisure is rather the result of earnest work and in its turn may markedly contribute to the broadening and the deepening of our work. This work demands times of quiet detachment from its unceasing activity. Leisure pursuits of the right kind offer a form of creative release from the demands of work. It has been listed as one of the "spontaneous therapies" of mankind, that is, it is a form of activity with healing value because it gives man freedom to express himself. In wholehearted leisure activity, the individual is more truly adjusted than at any other time. The physical, mental, social, emotional, and moral responses are so interwoven in such activity that they can scarcely be separated. Each contributes to the total well-being of the individual and thus to his ability to choose and to act.

A sixth condition of freedom is ability to evaluate intelligently particular situations and to decide each issue aright in the light of one's values. We favor one thing above another for a reason; it appeals to us more than any other does. True freedom consists in acting rationally beforehand instead of merely on impulse — in viewing the situation intelligently in all its aspects and then making choice deliberately, in the light of a definite set of values, of one's course of action. Each of us is, and ought to be, held socially accountable for our actions, but we are morally responsible only when our actions originate with us — only for what we put ourselves into, freely making it our own. As morally responsible beings, we are limited, fettered, compelled, like all other beings. Back of everything we do is a cause, and sometimes the course of action we take can be charted well in advance. Nevertheless, we are also free — beings who cannot be forced to decide in any given way. It is in the area of our freedom that we need ability to evaluate intelligently, and the capability for doing so is one measure of the extent of our freedom.

Many of our choices are made thoughtlessly, that is, without adequate consideration of the alternatives and the ultimate end in the light of values. A deliberate act of choosing — a really free act — is one in which the alternative and end have been examined and set over against other possible alternatives and ends. Deliberation requires so much time and effort that the best of men choose thoughtlessly many times in the course of each day. Our tendency is to do without attention or thought what has already been done and to let things take their course. In so doing, we promote the end which those things make possible. Thus we have made a choice. At any moment we make some choice, either a thoughtless one or a deliberate one.

A social situation in which it is possible for us to act is an eighth condition of freedom. Under an absolute dictatorship, freedom of the will is frustrated to a large extent. In any social situation where things are so highly regimented that deviation from the usual ways is regarded with disapproval, there is diminished opportunity for the individual to act on his own free will. Only where men cooperate sincerely in seeking the good is there the fullest freedom for all persons to exercise their power to will.

Finally, we are not completely free, except as we have carefully and definitely chosen dynamic goals for living. Going along from day to day with no clear idea of where we are going or why we are going there is not a characteristic of real freedom. We are truly free only as we are gripped by devotion to an objective which so draws us as to cause us to give ourselves, our wills, and our all to achieve it. Paradoxically, we are never freer than when we are held in unswerving loyalty to the highest possible goal — to purpose that completely absorbs us, calling forth all the resources of our being. We can have inner freedom only through wholehearted dedication to knowing the truth and to doing the good, though such dedication costs us tremendously. "Ye shall know the truth, and the truth shall make you free," said He who came into the world "to bear witness unto the truth" and who died because He went about doing good.

CHRISTIAN FREEDOM

The definite attempt thus far in this chapter has been to consider man's freedom from the general point of view. Essentially, what is true of it from this point of view is true of it also in a Christian sense, though what is true of freedom from the Christian point of view is not true of freedom in general. At any rate, for ethics, be it general or Christian, man has the power of self-determination: he is capable of choosing among motives and of directing his subsequent activity according to the motive thus chosen. In other words, man is free to identify himself with a particular end, rejecting other ends, and to guide his conduct in accordance with the end he chooses. This freedom to choose an end and the means to attain it constitutes the essence of moral responsibility. The facts concerning freedom and the conditions of freedom are fundamentally the same, whatever be the standpoint from which it is viewed.

Union with God Brings Man into a Freedom
Unknown by the Natural Man

But there is for man through union with God a freedom that is far higher than any freedom known by man not in fellowship with God. Jesus told the Jews who believed in Him, "If ye continue in my word, then are ye my disciples indeed; And ye shall know the truth, and the truth shall make you free" (John 8:31, 32). To the Jews who found fault with Him because He made this statement, He said, "Verily, verily, I say unto you, Whosoever committeth sin is the servant of sin," and "If the Son therefore shall make you free, ye shall be free indeed" (John 8:34, 36). In Romans 8:21, Paul speaks of "the glorious liberty of the children of God." In II Corinthians 3:17, he says, "Where the Spirit of the Lord is, there is liberty." In Galatians 5:1, he writes of "the liberty wherewith Christ hath made us free." Again in the thirteenth verse of this same chapter, he says, "Brethren, ye have been called unto liberty; only use not liberty for an occasion to the flesh, but by love serve one another." James, in the twenty-fifth verse of the first chapter of his epistle, writes of "the perfect law of liberty," and in the twelfth verse of the second chapter, he alludes to "the law of liberty." Finally, Peter admonishes us to live "as free, and not using your liberty for a cloke of maliciousness, but as the servants of God" (I Pet. 2:16).

Manifestly, the terms "free" and "liberty" in these passages refer to a state of freedom foreign to the natural man. Admittedly, this state is essentially spiritual, a matter of man's relationship to God, the Father of all spirits. But it has moral implications and moral results, especially as these are related to man's power to choose. Volume after volume could be written filled wholly with the testimonies of thousands upon thousands of people — high and low, rich and poor, brilliant and ordinary, of all classes, of all races, of all lands, of all Christian centuries — who by faith in Christ entered into this freedom and found a power to do right such as they never had before. They had power to resist evil, power to overcome temptation, power to love their fellow men, power to forgive enemies, power to choose the good, power to carry choice into action, power to live truly moral lives.

Man, a Twofold Being, Is Free to Choose to Live
after the Spirit or after the Body

Man is a composite of spirit and matter. From the union of
the two comes the lord of the material world, the creature
whose form is supreme among all material forms, the being
who is only "a little lower than the angels." We are not divine, we are not angelic, we are not bestial, but human. We
can live on the animal level, for we have propensities and inclinations, appetites and passions, such as the animals have.
An animal philosophy of life takes as its norm of living the
purely physical; its standard of measurement is brute strength;
its goal is satisfaction of physical needs. In every age there are
men who act and live much like animals. We can live on the
human level, for we are human beings existing in flesh. We
have powers limited by infirmity and hearts darkened by sin,
nevertheless we are human. Our natural appetites are not
manifestations of iniquity nor are they evidences of holiness.
They are human equipment that can be used by us to ascend to
great heights or to descend to equally great depths, as we may
choose. Our power to will is a source of stupendous potentialities and responsibilities presenting appalling prospects of failure and inciting to actions that only a courageous human being
would dare to do. In every age — even when morality in general is at its lowest — there are some men who live as human
beings.

We can live on the divine level. God gave us originally a
nature like His own. He created man in His own image. He
made each of us a living self that He asks us to express,
expects us to express; and He will, at the end of time, judge
us for the way in which we have expressed it, using as the
standard of judging the moral law implanted in our being, the
teachings of His Word, and, above all, our believing knowledge
of Himself and our approximation to the incarnate life of our
Lord and Saviour. We must face the facts if we are to understand human life and if we are to direct our own actions. The
facts are that we have animal-like tendencies, that we are fallen
human beings, and that we are free to choose whether we shall
live as animals, as human beings, or as children of God. By

our choice, God can be ours. In every age there are men who choose to live as saints of God.

Our power to choose is ours to use as we will. No force in the universe can compel us. God Himself does not prevent us from using it, or save us from the consequences of our decisions. No one but the individual himself and God knows how absurd it is for him to say that he was forced to do an act. When we make a choice, two things are involved, so far as the human element is concerned. One is the act of choosing itself. The other is the psychological content present at the time — the various impulses, thoughts, emotions, and feelings which constitute the raw material of the choice. Unquestionably feeling and emotion play a large part in our lives, but that we should come to think of feeling and emotion pushing us and moving us contrary to our will is one of the inexplicables of life. The act of choosing is the act of the will, an expression of a self-conscious being. Of all created beings, we alone have the power to choose to possess God; we alone, of all creatures, have the power to set ourselves against God.

By nature we are in a state of rebellion. Behind our personal choices is the history of the fall of man due wholly to the self-assertion of a free will, which ought to have remained centered in God. Behind this free choice of the self, through which evil entered, lay the condition of innocency which could have continued but for man's act of setting himself in rebellion against God. The admitting of the evil principle into man's nature unfits it for truly moral endeavor. The message of the Bible, corroborated over and over again in human experience, is that there is, at the very foundation of our being, a tendency toward evil which is manifest in our activities, however good they may be as measured by human standards. Inasmuch as this tendency is ours, a constituent of our "self," we are responsible for its expression in conscious choice and action. As individuals, each of us has taken up the spirit of rebellion and chosen to assert our will in opposition to the will of God and contrary to the commands of our own conscience and the dictates of our own reason. Even the good that we have the will to do we do not have the power to do. That is, we are in a state of bondage to our fallen nature. We need to be set free; we need a new birth, a re-creation by God, to be delivered from the principle of evil which rules us. "Old things" must become "new" by the working of the mighty power of God through Christ.

Deliverance from bondage into the glorious freedom of a child of God is by faith. Faith is not some special power or quality that can be possessed only by certain men. Essentially, it is the power of putting self aside that God may work unhindered in us. We have freedom of will, therefore we can will our self-will out of existence and enter into Christian freedom. We are endowed with power either to choose to allow Christ to set us free or to continue in bondage to our corrupt nature. God works in us. We have in our power nothing but the free use of our will. This free will can concur with or resist the working of God. With our free will we can bring nothing into being nor make any change in our nature. Evil will reign there so long as that nature exists. Only as we are "born, not of blood, nor of the will of the flesh, nor of the will of man, but of God" can we have freedom. And we enter into the freedom of the children of God simply by exercising our free will in response to the wooing of the Spirit to accept Christ and trust in His name (John 1:12, 13).

Help Is Available to Us Whatever the Level on Which We Choose to Live

When we choose to live on the animal plane, we receive help so to live. As we maintain harmony with the biological aspects of our being, we experience a sense of liveliness and an awareness of life as good for its own sake. When we take care of our bodies properly, not abusing them in any way, when we do not allow conscious longings and dislikes to interfere with the functioning of our indwelling animal intelligence, but live wholesomely in relation to the physical world, we are helped along the way. The reasons for living and life itself coincide. Life is then its own reward. The joy and the exhilaration of pure animal spirits functioning at their best is a boon to living on the animal level. However, our nature does not allow us to be perpetually content with such a manner of living. It is all right at times, but as self-conscious moral beings we cannot live continually and always in a state of oblivion to the appeal of good and evil.

There is also much to help us along the way when we choose to live on the human level. Persons, social groups, and the inner forces of our own human nature give us aid. In childhood, parents are our ready helpers. Later, teachers, friends, associates, men and women, better and wiser than ourselves provide us with many things that we ourselves lack. Then we receive tremendous help from country, party, community, church, and other social organizations. Our own personal human nature, by way of the ideals, aspirations, and imaginary personifications which it originates, constitutes an important aid to living on the human plane. However, human help, though it may often be wholly good by way of assisting us to reach the ultimate end of life, cannot be relied upon unreservedly because of the innate tendency to selfness inherent in it. In many cases, the help it gives is help toward the achievement of ends quite different from the true end of our existence.

More than this, human nature is beset by limitations and weaknesses. Even the best of men often prove insufficient as helpers when we stand most in need of help. Job's friends sought unavailingly to help him in the midst of his afflictions and troubles. So little can men help that the psalmist gives expression more than once to these words: "Vain is the help of man." Augustine realized the insufficiency of what he could do for himself, saying that to himself he was nothing more than a guide to his own downfall. "The way of man is not in himself: it is not in man that walketh to direct his steps" (Jer. 10:23). So unable is man to help himself in any true sense that Jeremiah makes this strong statement: "Cursed be the man that trusteth in man, and maketh flesh his arm, and whose heart departeth from the Lord" (Jer. 17:5).

But then he also declares, "Blessed is the man that trusteth in the Lord, and whose hope the Lord is" (Jer. 17:7). Likewise, Augustine says, "Thy omnipotency is not far from us even when we are far from thee." When we choose to live on the divine level, we have in the mighty God an omnipotent Helper.

God is "a very present help" not only in times of trouble but at all times, if we will to accept the help He is more than willing to give. It is as true for each of us as it was for the apostle Paul: "My grace is sufficient for thee: for my strength is made perfect in weakness" (II Cor. 12:9). With Paul we can take pleasure in weaknesses and difficulties and realize that it is when we are consciously weak that we are really strong. All around our insufficiency, lack, and weakness flows the great sufficiency of the omnipotent, eternal God, waiting, as it were, for us to get out of the way so that it can express itself. We can boldly say, then, "The Lord God will help me" and set ourselves with fixed determination to do the right (Isa. 50:7).

Perfect Freedom

He who by act of free will makes God his choice becomes the member of a union with God, mediated by the Holy Spirit, a union as close as the union of the branch and the vine. This is no mere dream but a fact that has been actually demonstrated over and over again in the experience of human beings. In our Lord Jesus Christ, there was a perfect demonstration of a life lived on earth in complete subjection to the will of God. He showed that there can be a union of the human and the divine, and many have there been who, through the power of the Holy Spirit, came into this union. The principle of His life, as it is also the principle of the life of every one of His followers, is "I do always those things which please Him," the Father. In the life of complete subjection to all the will of God, He and they realize, as it is impossible for the natural man to realize, the perfect freedom which is the goal of all ethical thinking.

The feeling that it is our duty to do certain things and our doing of them simply and only because of a sense of moral obligation do not have as an outcome a very high level of ethical practice. Union with God means that "it is God which worketh in you both to will and to do of his good pleasure" (Phil. 2:13). There is no antithesis between a binding command and the deed done to fulfill the command. The glorious freedom of the Christian sanctifies obligation; the inner longing of the soul is in complete harmony with the doing of right acts. The new creation wrought by God is a nature like His own, a nature from which good works flow by virtue of what it is in itself (Ephesians 2:10).

Only as we yield ourselves wholly to God and allow Him to rule us do we become truly free. When we thus yield and enter into freedom, our will is no longer divided against itself. Instead, it has come to its home in the will of God. "Our wills are ours to make them thine." Moral necessity reaches its goal when it rules the will. Freedom, likewise, having reached its goal, takes up into itself the element of moral necessity and in unity therewith attains realization. United to God, we are united to good and also within ourselves. In our fallen nature, we are unsettled, at variance with ourselves, and therefore not free; in union with God, we are in our element and enjoy glorious freedom.

The Christian is free in God. Freedom is not license. Milton says, "None can love freedom heartily but good men; the rest love not freedom but license." Being free in God does not mean that we are free to do as we please — except as we please to do the will of God. Union with God, if it means anything at all, means that our free will has united with the will of God, and that this union has wrought in us delight in the good and detestation of the evil. Therefore, evil has lost its power to tempt us. We consciously will the good and reject its opposite; the thought of evil, as the thought of that which is to be renounced, serves only to stimulate us to will the good.

God has never done away with the righteous requirements of His eternal law. On the contrary, our being made free in Christ furnishes the power we need to realize these requirements in life. Often, people speak of breaking the commandments. This cannot be done. We can no more break God's commandments than we can break the law of gravitation. We can violate the commandments — to find that they break us. We can defy the law of gravitation — to find that our bones are broken. The law of gravitation continues to operate as usual, as do also the commandments of God. That we live under grace, that we are free in Christ, does not mean we are free in every way from law of every kind.

The New Testament teaching is not that, because we have been set free, there are no laws for us. Only he who loves license hates regulations. Paul writes to the Galatians about carrying "out the law of Christ." Jesus gave two commands, supreme love to God and universal love to men, and declared that "on these two commandments hang all the law and the prophets" (Matt. 22:37-40). Thus He gathers up the multiplicity of legal precepts into the unity of the single commandment of love. The unity of Christ's law gives a united direction to moral effort. The outstanding characteristic of this law is that it proceeds from within outwards. To Christ no act is good unless it is the outcome of a good disposition. Ethical conduct is not a mechanical form of activity, nor is it formal observance of regulations. To Christ, only those works are good which have their source in good characters (Matt. 7:17). God is the source of good character and "God is love" (I John 4:16).

It has been said that "the two commandments are sufficient without any supplement whatever, as a complete guide to anyone who wishes to live." To take this position is to deny the fact that the Holy Spirit is a guide to man in living.

It has been said also that Christian ethics has no concern with external laws but has to do only with the internal disposition. Jesus taught that good disposition and good intention must be accompanied by good works. That the centering of attention upon external laws is not ethically salutary does not alter the fact that the commands of these laws still hold. In the New Testament are many commands to Christians. The internal law of Christ gives a general direction and movement to the will but does not of itself provide an answer to all the moral problems we may meet. In the Holy Spirit who indwells us, we have a guide whom we may follow with complete assurance of entire safety. It is His office to reveal the law of Christ, to take the things of Christ and show them to us. Never does the Holy Spirit work in any way opposed to the eternal law of God as this finds expression in the moral law of our being, the teachings of the written Word of God, and in the life and example of our Lord Jesus Christ. On the contrary, through the functioning of the Spirit, we find the answer to the question, "What ought I to do now that Christ has set me free?"

By nature we are lawless. As Christians, we have a new nature. Yet we have also the old nature, which has not changed in the least. All our moral and spiritual difficulties arise from this old nature, which is no better than it was prior to our being made free in Christ. Today, and tomorrow, and next day, and through all the days of our earthly life, there will be a battle between the desires of the flesh and the longings of the Spirit. Our triumph is in Christ, our great Deliverer. Never does the new man attain to such unlimited superiority over the old as no longer to require the continuance of the power of Christ for the overcoming and the restraining of the latter. The practical question is, How can His power be made effective in our lives?

First, Last, and Always We Are Free to Choose

To this question there is but one answer: "Walk in the Spirit, and ye shall not fulfill the lust of the flesh" (Gal. 5:16). This necessitates submitting our will to the new nature, the divine life, the Holy Spirit. It means that we choose to deny all the appeals of the old nature, the flesh. The cause of any dereliction in known spiritual or moral duty is want of harmony between our will and the will of God. If they are in accord, nothing in earth or heaven or hell can prevent our doing good in the truest sense of the word.

Every waking moment we must choose between higher and lower, between the worthy and the unworthy, between speaking unkindly, giving way to temper, or bearing malice in our heart and acting in love, between telling the truth and telling untruth, between clean talking and foul speech, between devoting our time and energy to what is uplifting and ennobling on the one hand and what is degrading on the other. We cannot avoid these choices. They may seem small and inconsequential at the time, but the sum total of them makes us what we are. Each act leads us into closer union with God or separates us from Him.

We are free to choose. If we wish to go downward, we may do so; if we go downward, it is because we wish to do so. We cannot avoid the issue; we alone determine our place. Leanness of soul and flabbiness of moral perception result from wrong choices, whatever be the outward show. Sooner or later, persistence in rejecting the good and the true and in choosing the things of self and evil manifests its effects in the external life. We cannot exercise within the citadel of our will, where we reign supreme, our freedom to make wrong choices and keep the results forever hidden from view.

If we wish to go upward, we need only choose at every turn the highest and the best. To us has been given plain and clear direction so that no one of us can mistake the way. "Seek the Lord, and his strength: seek his face evermore" (Ps. 105:4). A man of God once said, "You are as holy as you will to be." The will has all power to determine whether life shall be superlatively good, noble, and beautiful or absolutely bad, degraded, and unholy. God has so made us that we can continually make ourselves more able to receive His grace and goodness. By the power of our will we are free either to enlarge or to restrict our capacity for, and the operation of, His grace.

The real and fundamental difference between a morally good man and a morally bad man does not lie in the fact that the one wills what is good and the other does not. It lies alone in this: the one has chosen Christ and entered into life while the other willed not to come to Christ that he might have life. The difference between one who merely is called by the name Christian and one who lives in Christian freedom, without in any sense or at any time making his freedom a pretext for failure to do his whole moral duty, lies in a difference in devotion to the consuming purpose of doing all the will of God. The spirit of the second is expressed in this consecration statement of Betty Stam, a martyr for Christ in China: "Lord, I give up all my own plans and purposes, all my own desires and hopes, and accept Thy will for my life. I give myself, my life, my all utterly to Thee to be Thine forever. Fill me with Thy Holy Spirit. Use me as Thou wilt; send me where Thou wilt; work out Thy whole will in my life at any cost, now and forever." Nothing less than such an act of free will makes it possible for us to become participants in the freedom that is in Christ and thereby to live as truly free moral beings.

QUESTIONS

1. What do you understand is meant when we speak of "the will?"
2. Is your understanding helped or hindered by the thought of the will's being "nothing more than a way of acting?"
3. Is there moral obligation apart from freedom to direct one's own conduct?
4. Differentiate clearly between "the capability of a thing to be moved" and "the ability of a person to move."
5. Have you ever wished that you did not need to choose? If so, why?
6. How can there be degrees of freedom?
7. What is determinism? Can it be complete?
8. How is indeterminism opposed to true morality?
9. What does freedom of the will mean?
10. Can any power in the universe compel a person to act against his will? Discuss pro and con.
11. Is man any less, or any more, disposed to action than is the animal?
12. Give illustrations of the fact that the mind of man is organized for action.
13. In what ways is the power of attention related to the freedom of the will?
14. If one does not control himself, is he free? Is there any such thing as negative self-control?
15. Have you ever deprived yourself of knowledge of some truth by failing to perform a moral duty? Give examples.
16. What is the chief tendency of man, to *be*, or to *do?*
17. Is there any adequate substitute for self-mastery? Why, or why not?
18. What is the one and the only way to control feeling?
19. Do you, or do you not, find yourself in agreement with the statements made in the last paragraph of the section on action and freedom?
20. Give examples to show how we are conditioned by the world in which we live.
21. When do we become free?
22. Why does the habitual wrongdoer find it difficult, if not impossible, to change his ways?
23. In what way does one truly express his self? Are not feelings and sentiments expressions of the self?
24. Wherein has your conception of freedom not been correct or adequate?
25. How do many and varied interests make for freedom?
26. Is there any slavery greater than slavery to self? Explain.
27. Can an habitually lazy person or one who is always idle live ethically?

28. Are we more free when we are at leisure than when we are not?
29. In what sense is impulsive action not free? Is a thoughtless act a free act?
30. Is there lack of freedom in the free world today?
31. Distinguish between spiritual freedom and moral freedom.
32. If you are living as the animal or as a human being, whose fault is it?
33. If you are living as a saint of God, by whose merit is it?
34. Does feeling and emotion ever compel us to act contrary to our will? Explain.
35. If, as is sometimes said, we have a will enslaved by sin, how is it possible for us to choose God?
36. Compare and contrast the help we receive when we choose to live on the animal, the human, and the divine level respectively.
37. In what sense does a person yielded wholly to the will of God experience perfect freedom, ethically speaking?
38. Distinguish between freedom and license.
39. What relationship exists between perfect freedom and law?
40. If freedom be perfect, why must we be forever in conflict within ourselves?
41. Whose is the fault if you are not living in perfect freedom?
42. Do we choose God once for all, or must we be continually choosing God if we would live in perfect freedom?
43. "You are as holy as you will to be." How do you like the thought?
44. Fundamentally, is freedom a moral matter or a spiritual matter? If it is spiritual, does it have moral implications? How, or why?

CHAPTER X

The Responsibility of the Christian

ANY SUBJECT ON WHICH MEN THINK DEEPLY for the purpose of discovering general principles may become a basis for disputes and conflicting opinions. Ethics, because of its bearing on human conduct and life, is perhaps marked more by disputing and arguing than any other subject of this nature. The welter of differing ideas causes uncertainty concerning truth and morality, and the result is deep moral confusion. The Christian, as a resident of the world in which this confusion prevails, cannot escape its influence, though it is his privilege and his responsibility to live above it instead of succumbing to it. Men do not continue to subscribe to the principles of rigid morality long after they have ceased to believe like Christians. Experience, individual and collective, demonstrates clearly that the practice of Christian conduct is the outcome of vital Christian faith. Apart from sincere and wholehearted acceptance of the facts of Christianity and firm belief in the doctrines derived from these facts, there is no such thing as an ethics that is Christian.

Secular education through its agnostic scholarship and its adherence to the theory of organic evolution undermines belief in revelation, the infallibility of the Bible, and the unchanging nature of truth and morals. Humanism with its seductive appeal, intruding itself whenever and wherever it is able to get a hearing, causes indifference to Christian truth, refusal to recognize responsibility to a personal God, and exaltation of man instead of God. Liberal theology with its rejection of absolute truth, absolute morality, an absolute God, and the divinity of Christ, in its emphasis upon love instead of holiness, and in its disregard of ethical values and its tolerance of sin, makes for endless moral uncertainty and loss of moral discernment. Neo-orthodoxy, with

244

its position that the Bible contains no direct revelation for either belief or action and its grounding of the moral law merely in the will of God instead of treating it as an expression of the nature of God, does away with all thought of a final ethical standard for man.

Thus rationalism, agnosticism, humanism, liberalism, and neo-orthodoxy, rejecting the basic truths of Christianity and emphasizing the inevitability of change, come to final agreement concerning the non-existence of any truth save that which man is able to discover for himself. That is, absolutism is replaced by relativism. Consequently, there is no fixed truth in either theology or morals by which men's ideas can be governed or according to which their conduct can be regulated. Everything is relative; nothing is absolutely true; nothing is absolutely right.

Men cannot tamper with truth and play fast and loose with moral law without reaping the consequences. P. A. Sorokin, though he cannot be classed as an evangelical writer, describes relativism well and traces aright its course in these clear-cut words: "From the same system of truth and values comes the doctrine of relativism. Since everything is temporal and subject to incessant change, and since sensory perception differs in the case of different organisms, individuals, and groups, nothing absolute exists. Everything becomes relative — truth and error, moral and aesthetic considerations, and what not. A thing may be good today and bad tomorrow; in a given set of conditions a proposition may appear to be true and under other conditions false. Hence the dictum, 'Everything is relative in this world,' as the motto of sensate truth. Hence its negative attitude toward any absolute whatever.

"But relativism, once accepted, inevitably becomes more and more uncompromising, until finally all relative truths and values are completely 'relativized' and reduced, so to speak, to atoms. Sooner or later, relativism gives place to skepticism, cynicism, and nihilism. The very boundary line between the true and false, between right and wrong, disappears, and society finds itself in a state of veritable mental, moral and cultural anarchy.

No society can long exist under these conditions" (*The Crisis of Our Age*, pp. 97, 98).

Relativism in truth and morality has not been without effect on evangelical Christianity. Its most damaging outcome, at least so far as Christian ethics is concerned, lies in the antinomian separation between creed and conduct which it has brought about. The antinomian position is that we are saved by faith alone; works play no part in salvation. Conduct is works; consequently it is unimportant. So long as we have faith in the atoning merits of a crucified Redeemer, it does not matter what we do. Antinomianism is the placing of such an emphasis on grace that there is no "surrender to God's way of right standing," which most assuredly lays stress on right conduct as well as faith.

Our Personal, Individual Responsibility

"If the foundations be destroyed, what can the righteous do?" (Psalm 11:3). "The righteous" may be a class or a group of people, but "righteousness," "right standing," or "right living" is an individual, most personal matter. Each of us is personally responsible for his own reactions. No one of us is free from blame if he does what his conscience condemns. It is not easy for any of us to live in a world where moral principles are ignored, spurned, mocked, violated, and maintain vigorous moral health. It is hard to live in an intellectual atmosphere of agnostic scholarship and treacherous theological currents without becoming contaminated by false teachings. It is decidedly difficult to live in a society which lacks moral discernment and keep our own moral discernment undimmed. It is not easy to live in what calls itself the Church, where a soft antinomianism prevails, and not become tinged with uncertainty concerning ethical conduct and moral values. No individual finds it easy to live among men who, though professing belief in the Word of God, govern their conduct according to their own conceptions and make their own will their ethical authority, and, in all things, take the will of God as the supreme guide of his life. But as moral creatures responsible to a holy God who gave us being and as individuals redeemed at infinite cost, it is incumbent upon us to so live as to have a conscience that does not condemn, whatever difficulties we may meet.

We are individually accountable to God. Each of us is personally responsible for maintaining the kind of life worthy of a follower of Jesus. His command is so to live that men may see our good deeds and, because they see them, glorify God our Father (Matt. 5:16). Instead of doing as people around us do, we are to do what our Lord wishes and intends us to do. Not commonly accepted standards of responsibility, but His standard, is to be ours. It is dangerous to take the attitude of trying to please men. In a short time, each of us is going to come to judgment, not before our fellows but before God. As an individual who must give account of his deeds to God, it is the responsibility of each of us to discharge faithfully every single moral obligation.

Someone has observed that "nowhere is dishonest and careless thinking more frequent among men, or more immoral, than in dealing with their own morality." One of Christianity's greatest foes is unethical living on the part of Christians. Nothing more quickly or more surely brings a blemish on the cause of Christ than the sight of men and women talking about the grace of God and their spiritual experience who do not practice the virtues of honesty, justice, fair dealing, charity, purity, courage, and loyalty, essential to true and noble living. Upon him who says he believes as a Christian rests the heavy responsibility to behave as a Christian. If we have believed, we owe it to God, to our fellow men, and to our own best interests for time and for eternity, to "be careful to maintain good works" (Titus 3:8). Our responsibility is to show "all good fidelity" to doing the will of our Master so that we "may adorn the doctrine of God our Saviour in all things" (Titus 2:10).

The God who has become ours through the revelation of Christ is a moral Being. He justly claims from us conduct that is moral in all its parts — actions, words, and thoughts. Our relationship to Him is a spiritual relationship. Christianity is not an ethical system but a life, the life of God in the soul of man. Its center is God, not nature, or man, or an ideal society to be realized in the future. Its values being eternal, are not dependent on temporal events, past, present, or future. Spiritual relationship and morality are combined in one in Christianity. The moral law which we have responsibility to obey is the reflection of the eternal law of God's own nature This eternal law, therefore, is not an alien power enforced in an arbitrary manner. The rewards of obedience to it are not something external; in part they are enjoyed here and now. The penalty for disobedience is the natural fruit of sin which ends in the death of the soul. Though revealed, Christian ethics is free and autonomous. The revelation is "the perfect law of liberty." Were we not responsible for keeping law, we would be without liberty.

The Doctrinal and Theoretical Basis of Responsibility

Christianity and morality are inseparables. This is a truth that W. Graham Scroggie stresses as follows: "It is important to observe that in the New Testament literature of the Church, creed and conduct are always related. Doctrine and practice, theology and morality, knowledge and action, are inseparably connected, being related to one another as foundation to superstructure, as center to circumference, as root to fruit, as cause to effect." The fundamental thesis of Christianity is that there is an infinite, all-wise, omnipotent, all-loving, holy, perfect God who has revealed Himself in natural and supernatural ways in creation, in the nature of men, in history, in the written Word, in the Incarnation, and in the heart of the believer by the Gospel. Except as man is in vital relationship with God, he is not able to do the right, he cannot rise when he falls, he lacks comfort in his misery, he becomes a ready victim of evil, and he has nothing to stimulate his efforts. Christianity and morality are inseparables not only in theology, but also in human experience.

The Holiness of God the Unchanging Basis of Morality and the True Standard for Conduct

Jesus begins His ethical teaching with the law of Moses, thus giving it a theological foundation. Man's spiritual life and man's conduct — two inseparables — have as their single object the eternal God, our heavenly Father. Jesus did not hold before men, as reasons for being what they should be and doing as they ought to do, considerations of what would bring them happiness, of what would contribute to their self-realization, or of any other form of expediency. Instead, He set forth the character of God and the claims of God as the basis of life and conduct. The essential attribute of God, His very nature and essence, is holiness. God's nature never changes. Holiness is, therefore, the unchanging basis of morality and the true standard for all conduct.

The holiness of God is the message of the entire Old Testament. From Genesis to Malachi, God is the absolutely Holy One, entirely apart from all that is evil and all that defiles, both in Himself and in His actions. In all His dealings during the times of the patriarchs and with the chosen people, God is manifest to men as One free from all evil-doing. He never did wrong to any of His creatures; He never punished wrongly. "I am the Lord your God: ye shall therefore sanctify yourselves, and ye shall be holy: for I am holy" (Lev. 11:44). The tabernacle with its holy and most holy place, the Law of Moses with its moral categories, the ceremonial laws of clean and unclean things — all these declare unmistakably the holiness of God. Both Job and writers of the Psalms ascribe holiness to God. "Far be it from God, that he should do wickedness; and from the Almighty, that he should commit iniquity" (Job 34:10). "The Lord our God is holy" (Ps. 99:9). "The Lord is righteous in all his ways, and holy in all his works" (Ps. 145:17). To the prophets God was the absolutely Holy One, with eyes too pure to behold evil. They did not judge actions in terms of an ethical code, but their standard was what God had revealed to them concerning His holy nature, His character, and His will for men.

The nature and the will of God is the ultimate basis of morality. From Genesis to Revelation, the Bible insists that the moral requirements of a holy God constitute the duty of man. Nothing is moral which is not somehow or other connected with duty; that is, the concept of duty is essential to the realm of morals. This does not mean that duty is irksome, that it is nothing more than a task performed under constraint—

something burdensome and unpleasant to do. On the contrary, personality is recognized in the concept of duty; apart from personality as an expression of will and understanding, there could be no concept of duty. The idea of duty, though it speaks of that which is morally necessary, presupposes freedom. The necessity of duty is not the necessity of compulsion or of physical law. The characteristic of the law which is involved in duty is the desire for expression through free self-determination. To those who are in accord with the holy God, the source of moral good, duty is a delight, not a task. They find satisfaction in meeting moral obligations; they regard the doing of duty as a privilege rather than as a burden. Even when they find duty difficult, as it must at times be, they perform it with a willingness that makes it a delight.

Jesus always takes for granted the ability of man to respond freely to the call of God to righteousness, which is His holiness as manifested in dealing with the children of men. Acceptance of the call means a transformation, the new birth, a being born of God, the admission into the kingdom of God, the impartation of a new and divine life, the putting on of the "new man, which after God is created in righteousness and true holiness" (Eph. 4:24). This is not within the power of man to effect; yet it never takes place without the consenting will of the individual. In all His dealings with persons, God assumes that they have the power of decision. Never does He intimate that the past could not be blotted out and the bondage of habit be broken. None has ever fallen so low or gone so far astray as to be beyond the possibility of being brought back into right relationship with God.

The Holy Spirit is the source of all good. In grace God invites man to become a partaker of His holiness and thereby to receive a new character whence will issue good conduct. It is our responsibility to respond to the gracious invitation. No human being is unvisited by the Spirit of God, and however undeveloped the moral life may be, the possibilities of growth are unlimited, except as the human will sets limits to development. Every one of us can be as holy as he wishes to be; every one of us can be as perfect in conduct as he wants to be.

Every one of us is absolutely dependent upon the grace of God, but not one of us is without responsibility if we in any way obstruct God's purpose to work in us that which He designs.

God the Source of Moral Law

There is no moral law apart from God. That the moral law is inherent in man is recognized even by non-Christian scholars and writers. Their position is set forth in these words of Demosthenes: "Not only will these principles be found in the enactments of the law, but even nature herself had laid them down in her unwritten laws, and in the moral constitution of men." With his statement agree the words of the apostle Paul concerning the law written on the heart of every man (Rom. 2:14-16). The moral law thus known by man is the reflection in man of the eternal law of the holy character of God and the expression of His will for those whom He created in His image. Jesus did not ignore the natural law written in the nature of every normal human being. He combines reason and revelation in His appeal to men. But He always assumes, without arguing for it, the will of God as the basis for man's life and conduct.

Thus He combines, into a most effective unity, spiritual relationship and ethical conduct. The moral law in us, which is but the expression of the great eternal law of God's holy nature, is the standard God has fixed for us who, made in His image, can obey or disobey Him. When we keep this law, we obey Him; when we neglect or violate this law, we defy Him. Whatever our spiritual experience, whatever we conceive our relationship with God to be by virtue of that experience, no one of us is free to live, except in conformity with the moral demands of God as expressed in our own nature and as set forth in His written Word and in the life of His Son. We are not in bondage to the harsh legalism of law, but we cannot, because of this, frustrate the grace of God by living in antinomian rebellion against God.

Jesus emphatically denounced legalistic formalism in conduct. This consists essentially in rendering outward, routine, mechanical obedience when the heart is not fixed on God. We stand always in danger of doing this; a legalistic view of Christian conduct can easily creep in when we are not aware of the beginnings of a wrong attitude. Jesus was also emphatic in stressing the positive nature and the inward character of goodness. A particular feature of His teaching was that morality is concerned with inner motive instead of outward conduct. Murder and impurity, for example, are evils of the heart. Many of the evil things condemned by Him are too much of an inward condition to fall under any written law. Essentially, they are dispositions or attitudes of mind — an inside condition that makes the person immoral.

Thus Jesus teaches clearly that it is the inner state and condition of the individual which is all-important. No external law can reach the realm of the thoughts. We can keep most laws outwardly without being inwardly disposed to do so, but none besides God knows the heart where originate designs for doing evil. All of Jesus' teachings about conduct go back ultimately to the state of the heart. It was His concern that the spirit of the law, not the mere letter, be kept. The law of the Kingdom is not a code of formal laws. It is rather a statement of principles. The righteousness our Lord demands of us, a righteousness far surpassing that of the scribes and Pharisees, is not a way of living in more strict obedience to set rules of conduct. Neither is it a life of insubmission to the righteousness of God. It is a manner of life in full accord with the principles of goodness that find supreme exemplification in the nature and the character of the holy God, of whom we have been born if we are truly children of God. For this goodness, no set rules for finite man can be made because, as Jesus indicated to Peter who asked for a definite rule concerning the limit of forgiveness, it is a goodness that goes to infinity.

To live as children of God means living with God as the center of life. These words of the apostle Paul show clearly and definitely the manner of true Christian living: "The love of Christ constraineth us; because we thus judge, that if one died for all, then were all dead: And that he died for all, that they which live should not henceforth live unto themselves, but unto him which died for them, and rose again. Wherefore henceforth know we no man after the flesh: yea, though we have

known Christ after the flesh, yet now henceforth know we him
no more. Therefore if any man be in Christ, he is a new
creature: old things are passed away; behold, all things are become new. And all things are of God" (II Cor. 5:14-18). Both
the impetus for moral action and the direction of the course
of the moral conduct of one who lives after this manner have
a threefold source.

Threefold Source of the Impetus for and the Direction of Moral Conduct

First, there is devotion to Jesus who died for all. He established the kingdom of God, founded the Church, and left both
precepts and example for us. Jesus came into the world, not
only to save us by His atoning death but also to provide us with
a standard of personal conduct. By the revelation in Himself
of the holy nature and character of God, He sets before us a
perfect moral example. He is "the brightness of his [God's]
glory, and the express image of his person" (Heb. 1:3). Jesus
fully expressed in His own life the moral principles of the holy
God. Thus He points the way to holiness that, through the
aid of the Holy Spirit, we may direct our course in conformity
with this perfect standard. We are called to live as He lived;
He left us an example that we should follow in His steps
(I Pet. 2:21). It has been said that "a Christianity that worships
Jesus emotionally but does not follow Him morally is a conventional sham, and too much of our ecclesiastical Christianity is
precisely that."

Second, there is loyalty to the corporate relationship of the
body of Christ, the Church which He founded. This He is
building up by the preaching of the Gospel under the leadership of the Spirit, whom He sent into the world when He
ascended into heaven. Every Christian has a place and a function in this body which, as an earthly institution, is made up of
imperfect human beings who are one in Christ. Each individual
member has his responsibility. No one is everything, but all
together, if each is faithful to the Head of the Church in using
the gift bestowed upon him for the edification of the whole
Church, fulfill the purpose of the holy God. This calls for
submission of each to the other, the laying aside of one's own

wishes, and the submerging of self and its interests in love and
in the unity of the Spirit.

Third, there is the inward prompting and guidance of the
Holy Spirit who works in us to help us both to will and to do
for the good pleasure of God. It is by the power of the Spirit
that we are enabled to carry into practice in our daily living
the precepts and the example of our Lord, to fulfill our obligations to the Church which is His body, and to live well-pleasing
to God in all areas of conduct. The deeper and the more sincere
our loyalty to the Lord, the stronger and the more real our
fellowship with His children, the more clear and definite will
be the guidance and the empowerment of the Spirit in our lives
and the more nearly will our moral actions approach the standard of holy living.

The Kingdom of God

The ethical precepts of the Gospel are an integral part of the
total teaching of the Gospel. This teaching, especially that of
our Lord, is primarily concerned with one theme: the kingdom of God. All of His teaching was related to the proclama-
tion: "The kingdom of God is at hand"; "the kingdom of God is
come unto you"; "The kingdom of God is come nigh unto you"
(Mark 1:15; Matt. 12:28; Luke 10:9). The meaning is that
the living God is establishing a sovereignty or rule which,
having its source in His own nature and character, is essentially
holy and righteous. Though this Kingdom has no code of laws,
it has the closest possible connection with the life of man in
all its aspects, from the simplest and most circumscribed to the
most complex and the most universal. Under the sovereignty
of the holy God, the most discordant elements in our lives are
brought into harmony, and we come into right relationship
both to God and to the common duties of daily life.

"The kingdom of God has come to you" is the basis of all the
ethical precepts of the Gospel. They set forth the manner in
which men respond who acknowledge the rule and sovereignty
of God in their lives. The more seriously this is realized, the
better the results. Life in the Kingdom, life under the rule
of God recognized as such, is life at its best in terms of good
conduct, true happiness, and most complete realization of the

potentialities of our being. It all depends on our accepting "the kingdom of God as a little child" (Mark 10:15), that is, accepting in utter simplicity, without resisting and without trace of unnaturalness, the situation in which we are placed, and submitting ourselves freely and fully to the will of God in connection therewith. We are wholly responsible to God, and He takes responsibility for us. Faith is the basis of the acknowledgment of our unconditional responsibility to God. It is also the basis for the kind of fearless courage we must have if we are to do our full moral duty.

How We Can Do Our Full Moral Duty

We cannot even approximate this fulfillment merely by making up our minds to do our moral duty. The eternal law of God is written in our moral constitution, but we are fallen human beings with a nature which is enmity against God and righteousness. "The carnal mind is enmity against God: for it is not subject to the law of God, neither indeed can be. So then they that are in the flesh cannot please God" (Rom. 8:7, 8). True it is, the natural man has some knowledge of the difference between right and wrong but, separated from God, the sinfulness of his nature and environment draws him into evil and wrong, degrading him and making him a source of moral infection in the society of which he is a part. The standards of conduct of the law of God are contrary to fallen human nature and make little appeal to unregenerate man. Alienated from the life of God, the natural man loves his self and seeks the interests of the self. He must be born again before he can respond to the demands of a holy God or be motivated to conduct that is in accord with the holy nature and character of God. The natural man cannot perceive, understand, or yield obedience to the moral requirements of God's law or live a completely effective moral life among his fellows.

To do our full moral duty, we are wholly and absolutely dependent on a power we do not have in ourselves. That power is the power of the Holy Spirit. The creation of the new life in God is the work of the Holy Spirit, based upon the atoning work of Christ. It is "not of works, lest any man should boast. For we are his workmanship, created in Christ Jesus unto good

works, which God hath before ordained that we should walk
in them" (Eph. 2:9, 10). The establishment of this union
involves more than a mere change in, or an improvement upon,
what is already present. It means that what did not exist is
called into being. An actual generation takes place, appearing
"in the form of a re-generation, that is, the present substance of
man is not destroyed, the result of the first creation is not
annihilated, but man as he is, is reborn. . . . The natural man
is taken back as it were into the womb of a new divine creative
power and comes forth from it a new creature. His past life of
sin is wiped out by the forgiveness of sin, and by the Holy
Spirit, a new man, a new beginning, is brought forth endowed
with new powers and faculties which he did not possess before.
Regeneration is a process that takes place in the very center
of life, the heart, and by it the innermost and essential parts
of the human personality are transformed" (Reu-Buehring,
Christian Ethics, pp. 125, 126). Here is where Christian ethics
begins. Until the Holy Spirit has convicted us of sin, of righteousness, and of judgment, and pointed us to Christ who dealt
fully with sin in His own person, we are not ready to respond
in a real sense to the moral demands of a holy God. Until,
through faith in a crucified Redeemer, we have come to "be
partakers of the divine nature" (II Pet. 1:4), we have not
power to do holy and right deeds.

Righteousness is God's purpose for us. Being most just
and holy in Himself, He cannot have a lesser goal for us. It is
the basic and fundamental consideration, not only for time
but also for eternity. It was for this purpose that Christ came
in the flesh and died in our stead. By His obedience He perfectly fulfilled the law and propitiated the justice of God.
When we receive Christ by faith, this obedience is imputed to
us, our sins are pardoned, our person accepted, and we are set
on the way to holiness and eternal glory. It is by virtue of
Christ's having dealt fully with sin in His own person that
this new life and new walk are possible for us.

The law is upheld and honored. Being new creatures in
Christ does not make us lawless. The law is the expression of

God's holy nature and will. We are told in Romans 7:12 that "the law is holy, and the commandment holy, and just, and good." The source of all man's moral and spiritual trouble is in his nature which has tendencies contrary to God's law. The law given man by God failed because man failed, not by virtue of what it in itself was. Man cannot but consent to the fact that its requirements are right even though he lacks power to make his life conform to them.

In grace God makes provision for man in his helplessness. He furnishes power whereby we may be set free from the slavery of sin and death. What the law could not do because of man's failure to keep it, "God sending his own Son in the likeness of sinful flesh, and for sin, condemned sin in the flesh: That the righteousness of the law might be fulfilled in us, who walk not after the flesh, but after the Spirit" (Rom. 8:3, 4). God did not change His eternal law, but He does change us. Thereby the impossible becomes possible, and the law is honored and upheld. The ethics of the gospels and the epistles are the ethics of the commandments of the law of God. We are not under the legal system in the matter of our relationship to God, but, if we obey the Spirit in regeneration and yield completely to the Spirit in living the life of union with God, the righteous requirements of God's eternal law and of the moral law of our own being will be fulfilled in us.

To fulfill God's holy requirements, we must therefore "not live by the standard set by our lower nature, but by the standard set by the Spirit." That is, we realize the goal through the Spirit's power. In Galatians 5:16 we are told, "Walk in the Spirit, and ye shall not fulfill the lust of the flesh." This lower nature — the flesh — is ever with us. "The man in Christ is not in the flesh but it is in him, and the problem of salvation is not how to transmute the flesh into something good, but how to live with this very thing every day without being overcome by it. The presence of the Spirit solves the problem." The practice of living by the Spirit is the privilege and the responsibility of everyone who is in Christ. It is ours to choose how we shall live. When we live by the Spirit, the will of God is done

in our lives, and He gets glory from the good works thereby
produced.

MEETING RESPONSIBILITY

First comes theory, then practice. We think; then we act.
Apart from thought, conduct is never really moral, for, by
definition, conduct is action directed toward a perceived end.
How we regard life determines how we live. Whether we be
epicurean, stoic, mystic, realistic, idealistic, altruistic, rationalistic, atheistic, or Christian is determined by our view of life.
For Christian ethics, first comes the doctrinal, then the practical; first the basic facts, then the application of these facts to
daily living; first the provision of God, then our appropriation.
The great facts of our faith are the basis of Christian doctrines
which furnish the foundation for Christian living. The practical grows out of the doctrinal.

The practice of living by the Spirit involves manifesting the
life of God in the numerous relationships of our lives. We are
not independent, isolated beings but social entities connected
with a common humanity from which it is impossible for us
to separate ourselves. We have relationships with God, the
world, society, the state, the church, the community, the family,
individuals, chance associates, the weak, the strong, the high,
the low, the good, the evil, and so on, almost without end. We
are under obligations to live according to the standards set by
the Spirit in each and every one of our relationships.

We cannot grasp adequately the meaning of our obligations,
let alone meet them, apart from the power of the Holy Spirit
operating to effect a close union between us and God. It is
part of the work of the Spirit to enlighten our understanding;
it is part of the work of the Spirit to produce in us the obedience of faith; it is part of the work of the Spirit to empower
us to do what we know we ought to do. To be a Christian
means to have the life of God in the soul; to live as a Christian
means to maintain a vital union with God. Christian moral
experience, then, is a matter of the Spirit of God uniting His
help to our weakness and insufficiency. The Holy Spirit, far
from being a mere influence or an alien force, is the divine person at the very basis of the Christian's personality.

The Practical Importance of Our Relationship to God

Plainly, therefore, our relationship to God is of the greatest practical importance. It is basic and far-reaching. When it is right, all else must be right; when it is wrong, nothing else can be essentially right. The root of much unethical Christian conduct is wrong relationship to God. We cannot fulfill our obligations in the other relationships of life when we are not in right relationship to God. To have everything else fall into its proper place, we must be right at the center. Man as man is now as he ever has been since he chose to set himself in opposition to God. The changes of which men boast are external — not changes in man himself but merely in his mode of activity and in his environment. God has not changed. He is the same today as He always was and as He ever will be. All that men have done, all the advances they think they have made, do not in the least affect the nature and the character of God or bring about an iota of change in His laws or in His attitude toward evil and wrongdoing. In that neither God nor man has changed, the relationship which we should sustain to God is the same as it has been through all time.

Our difficulties and troubles originate in ourselves and what we are. Our attainments in learning, in economic status, in amassing wealth, in respect to situation or position, in social life, cannot save us from ourselves. Our troubles are the direct outcome of wrong relationship to God caused by rebellion against God and disobedience to God's law and God's will. In setting himself against God and disobeying God, man broke the law of his own nature and brought upon himself the awful spiritual and moral effects of sin. So long as we refuse to recognize our corruption and persist in rebellion against the only Being who can help us, we rob ourselves of all that is truly good. Whatever we may do, until we come back into a relationship of complete obedience to God, we will never be capable of right conduct. Though we gain the whole world of wealth and knowledge and though we attain to high standing in the estimation of our fellows, it profits us nothing if we are not rightly related to God.

That, without which our relationship to God cannot be right,

is our absolute surrender to Him. "Know ye not that . . . ye are
not your own? For ye are bought with a price"; "Ye are bought
with a price; be not ye the servants of men" (I Cor. 6:19,20;
7:23). Paul regarded himself as Jesus Christ's slave. From that
hour when, on the Damascus highway, he asked, "Lord, what
wilt thou have me to do?" until the day of his death, he maintained that he belonged to God and served God. When once we
are brought to an end of ourselves and have given ourselves
completely into the hands of God, then, and only then, can God
begin to show forth in us the glory of His work. Never can
two be in union except as they are agreed, and it is not for the
Creator to come into agreement with the creature.

Living as a slave in absolute surrender to God has two practical
aspects. For one thing, it involves the submission of life to God.
When we are servants of God, His wishes and purposes are
supreme with us. It is not our ideas nor the ideas that are
prevalent about us which appeal to us. Paul's question, "What
wilt thou have me to do?" is the one great question in every
situation. This makes for simplicity instead of complexity in
living, for it means adjusting to one unchanging standard and
to the wishes of one person. Moreover, it is substituting for our
finite and limited view the omniscient point of view of the infinite God. In His written Word we have presented to us the
Master's will, plans, and purposes for us. Living in complete
submission to Him implies taking His ideas and judgments as
our own. The devoted slave is not concerned about what others
think; his aim is to ascertain his Master's will. The slave brings
his thoughts into captivity to the thoughts of his Master; it is
his passion to have the good and perfect mind of his glorious
and all-wise Master.

Not only is the slave eager to know the mind of the Master
but his intense desire is to do the Master's will. His one aim
and purpose is to serve his Master. Never would he think of
knowing His will and doing nothing about it. Not his is
participation in a general relaxing in diligence toward doing
the will of the Lord of the universe or a smug satisfaction with
partial obedience to Him. Not his is it to choose which commands he shall obey and which he shall disregard. The doing

of the Master's whole will follows immediately upon his perception of what that will is. By thus doing, he places himself
in line with one of the greatest principles in the moral and spiritual realm: we learn only as we endeavor to obey. We must do
to know — to know the mind of God, to know the truth, to know
the duty that lies next. As we obey, light is given us to know
what next step to take. In proportion as we obey, we come to
possess noble elements of character. These exist in our hearts in
intangible form until they are made definite through acts of
obedience.

When God gives the Holy Spirit, His great object is the
formation of holy character. God, who is the only source of
existence and power and goodness, claims absolute surrender
from us, works it in us, and maintains it, if we but allow Him
to work as He will what He will. All this He does to the end
that we may have the Holy Spirit sanctifying our whole inner
life, giving us a holy mind and spiritual disposition to enable
us to live for His glory.

"Love is the fulfilling of the law." That is, love perfectly
satisfies the law, which is holy. "The fruit of the Spirit is love."
This is true because God is love. The Holy Spirit is the Spirit
of God; therefore the Holy Spirit is love, and the product of
His operation is love. Christ's redemption restored love to this
world. When man sinned, selfishness triumphed; he put self
in the place of God. Selfishness does not love; when self and
sin entered, love to God and love to man fled away. God's Son
came to show what love is. He lived the life of love; He died
the death of love. When He ascended to heaven, He sent down
the Spirit of love. Before He left earth, He told His followers
that they were to love one another even as He had loved them.
He also told them that all men would know those who were
His by the love which they have one to another.

Love is the perfect satisfaction of the holy law of God, and
wherever and whenever the Spirit works, there is love. Nothing but love can eliminate and overcome our selfishness. Self is
the blight of life, the source of wrong relation to God and
others, and the enemy of our own real welfare. Christ died
to redeem us from the curse of self. When we practice living

by the Spirit, love is manifest in the common relations of daily life. In our life and conduct appear the graces and virtues in which love is expressed: joy, peace, longsuffering, gentleness, goodness; absence of sharpness or hardness in tone, of unkindness and self-seeking; the presence of meekness in the sight of God and man, humbleness of mind, and patience. "Love is the fruit of the Spirit all the day and every day," in every way, shown to every person. The fruit of the Spirit is love, so, when the love of God is in the heart, we love even the unlovely person. The Spirit of God dwells in us to make our daily life a revelation of divine power and a manifestation to the world of what God can do for His children. To us who bear the name of Christian is given the responsibility of living in such a spirit of surrender to God as to make possible this achieving of His purpose.

Our wills are free. We are always at liberty to seek to gratify self or to die to self. Paul said that he died daily. Dying is not agreeable. It is neither easy nor pleasant to forego our own plans, to cease from our own works, to give up our reputation, to be set at nought by those we would help. Yet dying is the necessary condition to having the life of God shown forth in our behavior and conduct. Jesus gave no promise or expectation that those who wholeheartedly live unto Him will ever be in the majority. The world is not a friend to help us on to God. Jesus tells us plainly that we will suffer at the hands even of those who claim to be servants of God. If we would be His servants, we must "stop being servants to men" — ourselves and others. "Except a corn of wheat fall into the ground and die, it abideth alone: but if it die, it bringeth forth much fruit. He that loveth his life shall lose it; and he that hateth his life in this world shall keep it unto life eternal" (John 12:24, 25).

The Place of Compromise

Whatever the cost, there can be neither evasion nor compromise in the matter of self-surrender to the Holy Spirit. This surrender must be absolute and complete so that we are possessed entirely by the Spirit. Unless we are totally consecrated to all the will of God, known and unknown, we will lack the ethical sensitivity we need to see readily the will of God and to discern the inherent morality or immorality of human ways. However, the application of the principles of morality to everyday living sometimes necessitates compromise. In itself, the word compromise is morally suspect, being suggestive of laxity in connection with standards. There are situations in which compromise is clearly and definitely wrong. Whenever the slightest sacrifice of moral principle is made merely for the sake of indulging personal desire, compromise is wrong.

On the other hand, some sort of give and take is frequently advisable and necessary. Conflicts of obligation or of loyalties may present themselves to individuals or to groups. It may be necessary to make compromises in order to adjust to new circumstances. It is not a mark, either of moral perfection or of Christian love, to refuse ever to consider points of view different from our own. On the contrary, it is morally wise to weigh, with an open mind, the pros and cons of matters of policy and to try to find out what is fair to all parties concerned. When men discuss a question freely, they are likely to settle it rightly. The Christian is to love his fellows as himself. When we love others, we are able to look at things in the way they do, even if we do not accept their positions. Loving another as one loves himself necessitates permitting the other's interests and preferences to be considered as much as one's own preferences in determining decision in matters not clearly involving principle. We are never justified in lowering our goals or our ideals. We are always right in weighing all the relevant factors and in making our moral decision in the light of the values involved. We may justifiably go to great lengths in compromising where policy alone is involved. We should never compromise in the least in matters of clear and definite moral principle.

The Christian in Relation to the World

We are responsible for the relationship we maintain to God. A second relationship of much practical bearing on conduct is the one we sustain to the world. Actually, this is for the Christian a relation of separation from the world. By nature and kind, Christians are different. It is common experience of God's people that when they are spiritually normal and healthy, they are not worldly. Their interests, convictions, tastes, principles, opinions, and attitudes toward things in the world, as well as their wishes, hopes, desires, and actions are directly opposed to the world's way of thinking and acting. The teaching of the written Word as to this relationship of separation is clear and plain. In Romans 12:2, Paul says, "Be not conformed to this world: but be ye transformed by the renewing of your mind, that ye may prove what is that good, and acceptable, and perfect, will of God."

This verse — one of many New Testament verses on the subject — speaks in no uncertain terms. What is the world which we are to shun and to be unlike? It is not the physical world of plains and mountains, oceans and rivers, earth and blue skies. It is the world or age made up of sinful human beings— men and women who think, act, and live in rebellion against God. Four definitions from a number that could be given are in general agreement. "The world is fallen human nature acting itself out in the human family"; "The world is human society as it organizes itself without thought of God and the spiritual life"; "By the world is meant everything in it that is antagonistic to the truth or to the life of God in the soul of man"; "The world is a system of organizations, philosophies, and pleasures in which God is given no place." It is the ethical atmosphere created by those who do not have the life of God. Each sinful heart, group, organization, and philosophy makes its particular contribution, and all together produce an atmosphere opposed to God and holiness.

This world knew not the Only-begotten Son whom God sent to be its Saviour. It slew Him, and it knows not His followers. It is ruled by a subtle prince, even Satan, whose purpose is to originate and expand moral currents of such strength as to cause pressure too great for human power to resist. Such expressions as these are typical of his mode of appeal and are attractive to numbers of people: "Don't be mid-Victorian"; "Don't be a wet blanket"; "Don't be a wallflower"; "Don't go to extremes"; "Everybody's doing it"; "When in Rome, do as the Romans do"; "It's the smart thing to do"; "Join the crowd";

"Keep up with the age"; "This one time won't hurt"; "What's right is a matter of opinion."

We cannot serve two masters. If we are God's children, we give no place to the prince of this world of whom Jesus spoke plainly when He said, "He is a liar, and the father of it" (John 8:44). The question for us is not what any human being says but what our Lord says. Not man's opinion but God's revelation is the Christian's standard. If we are truly Christian we are unworldly; if we are worldly we are un-Christian. "Love not the world, neither the things that are in the world. If any man love the world, the love of the Father is not in him. For all that is in the world, the lust of the flesh, and the lust of the eyes, and the pride of life, is not of the Father, but is of the world. And the world passeth away, and the lust thereof: but he that doeth the will of God abideth for ever" (I John 2:15-17). If God be anything to us, He must be everything.

The responsibility laid upon us by God is to cease to conform to the world and its godless ways and to transform ourselves continually by the new ideals which He implanted in us when He made us new creatures in Christ Jesus. In regeneration He gives us the mind of Christ that we may possess Christ's thoughts (I Cor. 2:16). When we practice living by the Spirit, we think the things suggested by the Spirit instead of the things suggested by our lower nature (Rom. 8:5). Always, emphatically, and inevitably, we become as we think. "Set your affection on things above, not on things on the earth" (Col. 3:2). "Whatsoever things are true, whatsoever things are honest, whatsoever things are just, whatsoever things are pure, whatsoever things are lovely, whatsoever things are of good report; if there be any virtue, and if there be any praise, think on these things" (Phil. 4:8). Transformation, or a change of form from the earthly to the heavenly, not conformation to the earthly, is God's design. Transformation begins within; it is an internal renewing of the life of God. This renewing we need continually, because, though we are not of the world, we are in the world and subject more or less to its influence.

The strategy of the prince of this world, the persistent, unrelenting, everlasting enemy of our souls, is to keep the mind occupied with lower and inferior things so that we have no time to think God's thoughts. It is our responsibility to take ourselves in hand and to maintain a way of living by means of which the life of God in the soul may be nourished. This life will never flourish except as we think the things suggested by the Spirit. Day by day unceasingly, week by week persistently, month by month with unflagging zeal, year by year untiringly, we must, in order to transform ourselves, mold our minds with thoughts inspired by God. He has given us His written Word with its revelation of abiding and eternal reality. He has sent His Spirit to take the things that belong to Christ and tell them to us (John 16:14). There are literally thousands of things — wonderful and glorious things — upon which we may think, if we will. If the life and light of heaven are to be manifested to the world through our life and conduct, we must supply heavenly material for nourishing that life and feeding that light.

DISCIPLINE

Each of us lives under three influences baneful to the supplying of this material: the temptations of a subtle enemy of righteousness, the effects of the evils and the blandishments of a world that knows not God, and the motions of his own corrupt lower nature. Regardless of how these influences may affect our thinking, life in Christ can be a full, rich reality. Whatever may seem to be true, this life is manifested in inwardness of character, not in outwardness of pomp and circumstance. It consists in what one is, not in what one has. Whatever we get — education, money, position, anything — tends to contribute to self-sufficiency, something most abhorrent to God and very injurious to our life in Christ. The health and the blessedness of this life consist not in what we have, but in what we do with what we have, to bring glory to God. First, last, and always, the material must be subordinated to the spiritual, and primary emphasis must be placed upon inward, in contrast to outward, good. Self is not to rule in our inner life; it is not to dominate either our thoughts and words or our hearts whence these issue.

Necessity for Discipline

A divided life is utterly impossible. Without severe discipline we cannot have that singleness of heart and oneness of aim which are the essence of a life hid with Christ in God. Strength of character and truly moral conduct can come only from discipline. We must discipline ourselves in spirit, and mind, and body. We must submit cheerfully to the disciplines of life as these are administered by society and by the circumstances of daily living. We must be willing subjects of God's disciplines. There is definite and perpetual opposition between the world and the self on the one hand, and the spiritual and the moral life on the other hand. The quality of our Christian life, inner and outer, unseen and seen, depends on the place that Christ has in the inner depths of our being in contrast to the interests of the self and the appeals of an unfriendly world. In comparison with the realization of the blessedness of being in union with Christ, the privations and the sufferings of discipline seem quite insignificant to him who has tasted of the good things of such a relationship.

Never must we forget that both the blessedness of the union and the fruit issuing therefrom are produced by the Holy Spirit. Through the grace of God manifested in Christ, we have a new nature, a nature with which the life of God is incorporated and made our own. The atoning work of Christ is the cause of our new nature and the efficient cause of whatever holiness we shall ever have. It is not a matter of believing in Christ and then adding something else in order to enter into the new life. We do not receive a new nature through faith in Christ, then add something of our own for holiness. We can add nothing either for justification or for sanctification. One word — Christ — is all. Every phase of God's work manward is summed up in Christ, the source of all good, the source of all grace.

Yet we are responsible for dealing with the gifts of this new creation. These are as talents entrusted to us to be used for the glory of Him who bestows life. Only through communion with the Holy Spirit, from whom we receive the new nature, and through His power, can the new life be maintained. However, we are not mere vessels to receive but persons with impulses and desires which we are free to use to cooperate in its maintenance. "Whosoever hath, to him shall be given, and he shall have more abundance" (Matt. 13:12). Never at any time or in our own strength, can we, wholly apart from God, do anything that is good. Never does anything we do effect our standing before God. On the other hand, we are not as inanimate objects, mere passive channels for God's will to flow through. In every Christian is a new personality created to be the focus of a higher life which he is to live.

This new life is shielded by no absolute decree of God. Only as the believer determines to be defended from harm by the influences of evil can he be defended and so defend himself. In the present life, there is neither truce with the enemy nor completion of the conquest. Each advance is but a step to another. Movement never ceases. Each victory helps some other to win. Never can we lay our weapons aside and discontinue the waging of war with present foes without and within. For one thing, though we are united to God through Christ, we are always more or less feeble and unpractised. We must attain "unto a perfect man, unto the measure of the stature of the fulness of Christ" (Eph. 4:13). The process of growth and attainment is never completed in this life. Furthermore, the new and the old are together in us. The enemy, therefore, still has dominion over a part of our being. We can assert ourselves as new creatures in Christ only by setting our will in conscious opposition to the influences of our archenemy, of the world, and of our own lower nature.

The inward process of casting off the influences of evil and separating ourselves from them goes constantly deeper and deeper and costs us painful self-denial. Evil has no power in our new nature but only by unremitting self-discipline can we resist the evil of the old nature that forever cleaves to us. As such discipline is persistently and rightly applied, the new nature grows stronger through its continuing subjugation of larger areas of the old nature. There is no vacuum in our lives. Either self or God fills them. The more there is of self, the less there is of God; the more there is of God, the less there is of self. Never does the old nature yield of its own accord. Mortification or deliberate dying to self is the price we must pay in order to fulfill our spiritual and moral obligations. Between the development of the new man and the death of the old, there is a close connection. It is by purification and self-discipline that we preserve faith, love, and hope and thus maintain the growth of the new life. Only at the cost of the old man can the new one live and thrive.

Compromise with evil, compliance with forces that make for unrighteousness, practical materialism, worldliness, and the negation of discipline are contrary to the laws of the life of God in Christ. Ours it is to undergo rigorous training and to take life far more seriously than we would if we were not children of God. We cannot live in self-indulgence and win spiritual and moral victory. Success in this realm, as in every other, involves labor, pain, and sacrifice. Only at a price can anything worth-while be achieved.

We have in our power nothing but the free use of our will, and our free will can do nothing but submit to, or resist, the working of God. Our will is ours to will our self-will out of existence so that He may accomplish His purpose in us. The life of God becomes ours by grace through faith, but we must deny self and take up the cross. We live in union with God by faith, but we must practice self-denial and mortification, or deliberate putting to death of what is earthly in us. It is by sacrifice of the self-life through doing away with self-will, self-interest, self-centered thinking and wishing, that we make it possible for the new nature to grow and increase.

Discipline Not an End in Itself

Self-denial and mortification are indispensable means for clearing the way for God to work in us, but they are never ends in themselves. They have absolutely no virtue in themselves. They confer no benefit, produce no merit, have no power. They are entirely without holiness or goodness. Their only worth is that they keep the self-life from interfering with, and hindering the operation of, God in us. The one thing that can bring the life of God to the soul and cause growth and increase in this life once it is in the soul is the operation of God. In creation, it was God who gave life; in redemption, it is God through Christ

who restores life. After life is restored, it is God who nourishes
the life He gave, who works in us to help us to desire and to do.
We must receive, we must respond to Him, but it is God who
gives increase in holiness and righteousness. All our activity
in denying ourselves and in mortifying the works of the flesh
has no worth other than to open the way for God to operate in
us.

Self-denial and mortification practiced for their own sake,
as things good in themselves, hinder instead of help the work
of God in us. When we regard them as bringing us merit, as
having virtue for holiness, we rest in them and become exalted
in pride, self-esteem, and self-appreciation. Thus, we enter
into the snare of living for self instead of dying to self. This
hinders the operation of God in us. There is only one way to
avoid this damaging error and that is to impress indelibly upon
ourselves the great fact that nothing we do or can do has any
good in it or works any good in us.

Only One can do this — the Man of God's own choosing.
Mortification and dealing with ourselves, when perfect, bring
forth simplicity. It is not easy to be simple. We are out of
joint because we have separated ourselves from God to live in
self-will. When we give up self-will and yield ourselves to
God to work as He will what He will in our bodies, souls, and
spirits, we enter into the simplicity expressed by Paul, "Yet
not I, but Christ." The single motive of the simple heart is to
please God, regardless of all else. When we are totally indifferent to all selfish considerations, our desires, our words, and
our actions become perfectly simple and natural, for we have
a single purpose. Such simplicity is the essence of living after
the Spirit and the new nature because God, His will, and His
pleasure, is its sole object.

All that Mary did toward the conception, the prenatal development, and the birth of Jesus was to exercise simple faith
and complete resignation to the will of God. "Behold the hand-
maid of the Lord; be it unto me according to thy word" was
her submissive attitude to the announcement of the angel.
This is all we can do toward the birth of Christ and the growth
of His life in us. It is far more easy to acknowledge this truth

with our mind than it is to believe it in the depth of our being. But, blessed is he who believes, for he shall have fulfilled in his experience all that the Lord has promised, none of which can ever become real through futile struggle with the self that blights the glory of Christian living and the good issuing therefrom.

Firmly believed, this truth will have two practical effects. First, it will keep us fixed on God and continually turned to Him in faith, trust, confidence, desire, prayer, and yieldedness for all that we would have done in us, to us, and through us. Thus we will always be receiving from Him, who is the only source of holiness and virtue. Second, it will ground us in true and perpetual self-denial and mortification. As we know, see, and realize our own nothingness and our total inability to be good or to do good, self is wholly denied and its kingdom destroyed. There is no room then for self-sufficiency and pride; we will have no thought of a hypocritical holiness, of the worthiness of our own works, or of anything we think we have or take ourselves to be by nature or by grace.

Self-Discipline

This means that we will deny self and discipline ourselves. The life of a Christian is a life of self-denial. Every good thing has its substitute. Satan is a great substituter. Under his influence, men have always made substitution one of their favorite practices. We have nothing of our own. In the record of our lives there is only transgression and guilt. In grace God has so provided that we need nothing of our own. He even warns us against trusting in and depending upon anything we call our own. He instructs us to rely solely on the righteousness of the Saviour whom He provides and whose merit He places to our account when we accept Him by faith. Through the new birth God brings us into a state of character which He calls sainthood. Thereafter, He takes us through the process of sanctification by which this sainthood is enhanced and beautified. The outward outcome of the inner process is progressively better deeds in daily living. The work begins with God; the process ends with God. From first to last, from the new birth to complete and final sanctification of life, it is God's doing.

Nothing we do is in itself meritorious and contributory to results in spiritual life.

Yet in us is a deep tendency to substitute for the simple life of faith, the merit we think we derive from self-imposed abstinences and practices. Like many in the past who performed wonders in the way of ascetic exercises, we face the constant danger of attributing holiness to ourselves because of what we do by way of denial of self. It is most easy to mistake the means for the end and to fancy ourselves holy and righteous because we are strict in self-discipline or in self-restraint. It is easy to exalt certain aspects of the personal life at the expense of other aspects. One may live a life of severe self-discipline and great self-restraint and yet be a thoroughly immoral person. The highest virtues may be accompanied by, and even connected with, the evils of pride, envy, covetousness, lust, anger, and uncharitableness. Immorality is much more than a matter of carnal self-indulgence. No act of self-denial, no instance of self-discipline, no case of self-restraint, is meritorious in itself. The Christian is concerned with the total denial of self in all its aspects — those regarded as creditable no less than those which are considered discreditable — and the abandonment of the will to God. We must wage unceasing warfare against the tendency to think of merit inhering in self-discipline, self-restraint, or self-denial of any kind and we must not rely on any such practice as the basis of holiness of life.

Christian discipline recognizes the human appetites and tendencies as real and God-given. It places no emphasis on action which effects nothing, which is of no moral assistance to the individual himself and of no use to others. It does not stress formal or artificial abstinences but realistic self-control. It requires us to discipline ourselves as athletes train for their activities. The Christian life is a vocation, a calling to be followed with all the powers of one's being concentrated for definite accomplishment. The Christian divests himself of anything and everything that hinders him in the pursuit of holiness and he trains himself rigorously for godly living.

Christian discipline means, then, simply a course of training as men train for a race. We succeed in no calling or walk of life except as we focus our energies. We must reject what is superfluous to the achieving of the goal; we must endure hardness; we must renounce much in order to win any one thing we esteem to be of great value. We do not, in the general affairs of life, treat the rejecting, the enduring, and the renouncing, as in itself a good, but distinctly and definitely as merely a means for achieving the goal we have set. It is the recognized means by which the passions and the appetites unfavorable to our progress to the goal must be brought into subjection.

Thus the philosophy of Christian discipline is simple. Because of natural impulses and natural tendencies, we are prone to forms of selfish indulgence opposed to the achievement of holiness and practical godliness. Rigorous discipline of these natural impulses and tendencies is necessary to free ourselves from the temptations and weaknesses due to the flesh. True self-denial is concerned with the strengthening of the life of God in the soul. This means, above all, the training and the strengthening of the habit of faith, which is the impulsive power of this whole life and the one essential to any progress which is real growth instead of merely something built up through formal practice.

To train and strengthen faith we must recognize that we have moods. We do not find God in ecstasies but in obedience. We must maintain fellowship with Him by keeping in constant repair our relationship to Him which is ever subject to impairment from the impurity of evil within and from the inducements of evil without. We must deliberately hold before our mind every day, in contemplation, meditation, prayer, and reading, the teachings of God. Without continually training ourselves in faith, we drift away from our faith. Earlier experiences, old anointings, and past blessings do not suffice for present needs. Today we must be in vital relationship with God who is the source of our life. Conflict and victory call for constant renewal. We never make progress toward the goal by carrying on our work from mere force of habit due to what occurred in the past. We must forever keep in training, not let ourselves try to live on the strength developed yesterday. Any

power for good we have derives from present living connection
with the one and only source of good, the eternal God who
gives and sustains life.

Self-imposed abstinences and practices have moral value when
they are means for breaking the dominance of the lower nature and for bringing into ascendance the higher nature. Except as these occur, faith neither continues nor grows. Self-
denial, self-restraint, and self-discipline may justifiably be practiced for the purpose of self-improvement, because this is a
necessary basis for all good living. Such practices are morally reprehensible when they are not helpful to the individual or without worth to others, when they harm the body, and when they
are mere manifestations of power, as ends considered good in
themselves. An action accomplishing nothing at all, done
merely for its own sake, is not moral action.

Discipline by God

For the Christian, everything including self-denying practices of whatever sort must be founded on faith. "Whatsoever
is not of faith is sin" (Rom. 14:23). The delight of the Christian is that the life of God grow in him more and more. To
this end he is careful to remove all hindrances, as far as he has
power to do so. Whatever he does, he does not to be seen of
men but by his Father who is unseen that he may be rewarded
by Him who sees what is secret. Far from being occasions for
display of pride and vanity, the self-denials of the Christian
are humbling experiences in that they are evidences of the
training he yet needs while he is following on to reach the
perfection of the ideal for which he was taken captive by
Christ Jesus.

"He which hath begun a good work in you will perform it
until the day of Jesus Christ" (Phil. 1:6). What God begins,
He completes; He begins it because He intends to complete it.
God disciplines us in order to bring us to where He wants us to
be — to make of us what He purposed when He redeemed us.
As a kind Father who loves us, He cannot allow us to go un-
corrected. To do this would be to tolerate in us that which is
contrary both to His purpose and our own best interests. His
purpose in making us His children is to secure in us entire

conformity to His character and will. He disciplines us to eliminate from our character all that is unlovely and unholy — all that is foreign to His character. He says, "My son, despise not thou the chastening of the Lord, nor faint when thou art rebuked of him: For whom the Lord loveth he chasteneth, and scourgeth every son whom he receiveth. If ye endure chastening, God dealeth with you as with sons; for what son is he whom the father chasteneth not? . . . . He [chasteneth] for our profit, that we might be partakers of his holiness" (Heb. 12:5-10).

The discipline of God is the discipline of perfect love. Human parents sometimes say they love their children too much to punish them or correct them. What is thus called love is not really love. One who truly loves another seeks what is best for the loved one, whatever the means necessary for attaining the best. Love does not refrain from administering discipline because discipline is painful. Love looks to the end-result and uses correction, reproof, instruction, punishment, or anything else, unpleasant though it be, if it gives promise of bringing about the outcome desired. God disciplines everyone He loves. The love that dictates His discipline is the infinite love of a perfect Father who sees all, knows all, yet continues to love. His fatherly love imposes no more discipline than is required but it does impose all the discipline necessary to bring us to the perfection of holiness of character for which He destined us when He made us His children.

Discipline as practiced among men is always defective. Even at its best, it cannot be otherwise because men are limited in knowledge, understanding, love, ability, time, and in every way. The discipline of God is perfect. We are under His authority all our days. He knows fully and definitely what He desires us to be. He is infinite in love and wisdom; He is omnipotent in power; therefore, He is abundantly able to accomplish a perfect work of training and discipline. He knows just the kind and the amount of discipline to impose and how to impose it to obtain best results.

Our responsibility is to submit to His discipline with a glad obedience and with the full trust of a child who knows that the way of the Father is best. When we are aware that all things work together for good to those who are called in accordance with God's purpose, we can realize that He permits nothing to come into our lives, except what will further that purpose. It is foolish to think that submission to God means restriction and limitation. Actually, it means just the opposite. The more we submit, the more fully and the more nobly we live. Far from despising His discipline, thinking lightly of it, or giving up when He corrects us, we need to submit patiently to our Father so that He may work His work in us. It is thus that we can reap to the full the fruit which grows from upright character. We have nothing to fear or dread when we yield ourselves fully to His control.

God disciplines us through affliction, pain, illness, bereavement, loss, frustration, disappointment, trial, and suffering of one kind or another. He has a purpose in every pain and loss He allows us to experience. Christ bore the penalty for our sins, so we are forever relieved from their penal consequences. But God often disciplines us for our wrongdoing, not that we expiate the wrongdoing by suffering but that we may be led to see it in its true light. When we undergo pain, we are impelled to examine our past and thus to view the carelessness, the unwatchfulness, the unfaithfulness, and the prayerlessness of our lives. We see where we have been going astray, how we have grieved the Holy Spirit, and what a gulf has been formed between us and God. Times of affliction lead to heart-searchings and awareness of sins of which we had no knowledge. In affliction we also learn that fellowship with the sufferings of Christ and that sympathy for others which are characteristic of true Christians. Even Christ "learned from what He suffered how to obey." Our suffering is discipline for our correction and instruction with a view to our sanctification. When we accept the experience of suffering as sent by our loving Heavenly Father we enter experientially into more of His love, wisdom, patience, goodness, power and become more like our Lord.

God disciplines us through His Word. It is useful for reproof, for correction, for training in doing what is right as well as for teaching, so "that the man of God may be perfect, throughly furnished unto all good works" (II Tim. 3:16, 17). Unbelief in the Word of God and unclear conceptions of right and wrong go together. Lack of knowledge of the revealed will of God is the source of wrong action. We cannot neglect the Bible and refuse to accept the discipline of the written Word except at our own moral peril.

God disciplines us by His Holy Spirit. The Spirit prevented the preaching of the Word in Asia and would not permit Paul and Silas to go into Bithynia. "They that are after the Spirit" do mind "the things of the Spirit" (Rom. 8:5). We are admonished not to grieve the Holy Spirit (Eph. 4:30) and not to quench, or stifle, the Spirit (I Thess. 5:19). In the leadership and the discipline of the Holy Spirit within the moral standards of the Word of God, we have the true basis of Christian ethics. It is an ethics without legalism, yet not contrary to the eternal law of God, but in the spirit of the law of God. True morality and ethics, as acknowledged by all who have thought deeply on the subject, must be inward. The Holy Spirit makes the precepts of the law live in the heart and control the motives of the heart. When the leading and the disciplining of the Holy Spirit are accepted and followed, there is a refined sensitivity that lifts ethical practice above all mere legalism.

Finally, God disciplines us by prayer. He who prays sincerely — whose thoughts and words go up instead of remaining below — lives above known evil and wrong moral practices. Our hearts are most deceitful, and our minds are subject to endless rationalizations. Often we are misled by our own selves. Many are the disguises of self-interest and subtle are its manifestations. Only as we submit to the searchings of God can we see ourselves as we really are, know the depths of our depravity, and not become easy victims of the guile and hypocrisy of our own hearts and the dupes of our own desires. We cannot know ourselves by ourselves. Forever and always, we are fooled to the limit by things we view after our own sight. When we pray sincerely, we pray in the spirit, if not in the words, of Psalm 139:23: "Search me, O God, and know my heart: try me, and know my thoughts: And see if there be any wicked way in me, and lead me in the way everlasting."

Character is seen in conduct. While holiness of character is being wrought in us by the discipline of life and the disciplines of God, the fruit of righteous conduct becomes more and more manifest in our lives. The rigors of training seem painful, but the fruit of good conduct grows from upright character as a satisfying return for the privations and sufferings which mark the discipline. When we are in union with Christ whom God has made redemption, our consecration, and our means of right standing, the issue in our lives is bound to be a progressive practical holiness, or holiness of personal character. As it advances, it becomes manifest in outward conduct. Not the degree of holiness we claim to possess but the measure in which the fruit of righteousness appears in our conduct is the standard for judging our inward character. As we joyfully submit to the training our God gives us, we experience the blessedness of life hid with Christ in God and the inevitable results in right conduct. Then our strengthened lives are a benefit to others and bring glory to God. The straight paths in which we keep our own feet, instead of turning our fellows out of the way, offended, crippled, broken, will be an encouragement to them to follow on, a source of strength for their faith.

QUESTIONS

1. Why are the present-day moral practices of Christians as loose as they are?
2. How has relativism affected evangelical Christianity? Have you personally observed instances of the effect?
3. Is difficulty ever a valid reason for not doing our full duty?
4. Can a follower of Christ be too careful in his moral living?
5. Explain: "Were we not responsible for keeping law, we would be without liberty."
6. Why can Christianity and morality not be separated?
7. What is holiness? Righteousness?
8. Can morality and duty be separated? How does the idea of duty presuppose freedom?
9. In what sense is the Holy Spirit the source of all good?
10. Show from the teachings of Jesus that He did not ignore the natural law written in the nature of man.

11. How did Jesus combine effectively spiritual relationship and ethical conduct?
12. Are you free from a legalistic view of Christian conduct? If not, how does your lack of freedom manifest itself?
13. What is the antidote for such a view?
14. Is your Christianity "a conventional sham"?
15. Are we justified in berating the Church and calling attention to its imperfections?
16. What is the essential meaning of the Kingdom of God? What bearing has the Kingdom on ethical living?
17. What is the first thing a person must do if he wants to do his full moral duty?
18. Why did the positive law given by God fail?
19. Has it been changed? How does God provide for its effectiveness?
20. What is the continuing thing a person must do if he would do his full moral duty?
21. What do we mean when we say that the practical grows out of the doctrinal?
22. Do you think that evangelical Christians in general realize the importance of the work of the Holy Spirit?
23. What is the root of a great deal of unethical Christian conduct?
24. What is the basic essential to right relationship to God?
25. How does absolute surrender to God simplify living?
26. "Let go and let God." What glorious truth does this statement express?
27. Can one live morally who is not ruled by love?
28. Do you sort of shy away from the word "compromise?" Why?
29. Can we live good moral lives without compromising? Explain your answer.
30. When are we justified in compromising? Under what circumstances or conditions should we be totally uncompromising?
31. What is your definition of "the world?"
32. Basically, what must the attitude of the Christian be toward the world?
33. Are there more than three influences that work against our nourishing the life of God in the soul?
34. Can we live morally merely by disciplining ourselves, that is, apart from discipline by any other agent?
35. Explain why we do not add something to the new nature for our holiness.
36. Is the growth of the child of God spiritual or moral or both spiritual and moral?
37. Is self-denial a moral virtue?
38. Is it of any use if we are disciplined by agents other than ourselves, if we do not also discipline ourselves?

39. Under what circumstances does the discipline of self-denial hinder the work of God in us?
40. Do you know of instances — in yourself or in others — when the highest virtues were accompanied by sordid evils?
41. What is immorality if it is much more than a matter of carnal self-indulgence? Do you accept as fact that it is much more than this?
42. What is the "realistic self-control" that Christian discipline stresses?
43. Show wherein Christian discipline is simple.
44. Why does God discipline us? How does He discipline us?
45. Should we look within or at our conduct to determine whether or not we are making progress in ethical living? Why do you answer as you do?

Index

INDEX

Ability to evaluate a condition of freedom, 230
Adolescence, 184
Aim, 13
Alexander, 59, 174, 202
Altruism, 127
Animal, 16, 129, 159, 188, 193, 214, 219, 220, 233
Anthropology, 92
Antinomianism, 246
Aquinas, Thomas, 21, 103, 107
Aristotle, 17, 99, 104, 106, 107f., 127, 141, 189
Arnold, Matthew, 188
Atonement, 65
Augustine, 15, 25, 77, 102, 103, 153, 236
Authority, 19, 87, 102, 150, 163, 166f., 178, 275

Bacon, 106
Bain, 194
Behavior, 13, 19, 123, 186, 214
Being, 13, 119, 131, 203, 222f.
Belief, 128, 130, 145, 244, 267, 271
Bentham, 194
Birth, the new, 69f., 78, 81, 82, 83, 96, 131, 200, 203, 235, 253, 255, 265, 271
Body, the, 63, 65, 159, 187, 191, 197, 219, 227, 233f.
Bryant, 119
Butler, 143, 166

Calvin, 105
Carlyle, 222
Categorical imperative, 142, 143, 150
Character, 13, 71, 84, 114f., 119, 132, 171, 173, 185f., 191, 261, 275, 278
Choice, choosing, 20, 39, 43, 79, 188, 193, 214, 216, 217, 218, 230, 231, 234, 236, 240f.
Christianity, 82, 94, 101, 106, 116, 130, 131, 132, 146, 179, 245, 248
Communism, 158
Compromise, 262f., 269
Compulsion, 14, 178f., 215
Conduct, 13, 19, 20, 27, 28, 31, 32,
50, 71, 86, 92, 94, 113, 116, 144, 145, Chapter VII, Chapter VIII, 214, 217, 247, 253, 263, 278
Conflict, 85, 145, 263
Confucius, 49
Conscience, 45, 48, 49, 78, 80, 84, 144, 147f., 163
Control, 91, 204, 221f.
Conviction, 93, 138, 207
Custom, 14, 42, 145

Demosthenes, 251
Descartes, 106f.
Desire, 123, 169, 180, 186, 192, 194, 197, 215
Determinism, 21/f.
Dewey, 189
Development, 183, 184
Discipline, 266ff.
Doctrine, 28, 29, 82, 130, 258
Doing, 13, 131, 138, 206, 222f.
Dorner, 60, 76, 151
Doughton, 107
Dudley, 134
Duty, 14, 86, 97, 110, 152, 154f., 222, 237, 249, 250, 255

Ecstasy, 202, 273
Einstein, 94
Emerson, 222
Empiricism, 140
End, goal, 13, 17, 20, 21, 42, 70, 112, Chapter V, 159, 165, 168, 175, 189, 193, 194, 198, 204, 209, 231, 263
Epictetus, 100
Epicureans, 100
Erasmus, 105
Esthetic School, 166
Ethics
General, 14, 28, 93, 95, 96, 97, 98, 107, 111, 122, 126, 128, 159f.
Natural, 17, 26, 81
Philosophical, 17, 27, 28, 94
Evolution and morality, 167f., 244

Fact, facts, 15, 140
Faith, 32, 33, 34, 66, 88, 113, 132, 151, 202, 232, 235, 256, 272, 274

281

Fault, 71
Fellowship, 55f., 133, 175, 179, 194
Freedom, 19, 23, 37, 46, 87, 92, 138, 151, 158, 168, 201, Chapter IX, 269

Gnostics, 102
Good, goodness, 18, 25, 41, 42, 60, 61, 71, 124, 125f., 132, 133, Chapter VI, 149, 169, 174, 200, 203, 234, 252, 269
Gospel, 13
Government, 39, 45, 49, 58
Grace, 43, 45, 52, 67, 70, 72, 78, 79, 80, 97, 177, 237, 238, 250, 257, 267, 271
Gratitude, a motive, 207
Growth, 226, 268

Habit, 226
Hammond, 82, 150
Happiness, 16, 24, 44, 100, 133, 135, 169f., 199
Health a condition of freedom, 227
Hedonism, 127, 169f., 194
Hegel, 141
History, 14, 24, 49, 58, 68, 87, 102, 142, 196
Hobbes, 106, 194
Hoffding, 219
Holiness of God the basis of morality, 248f.
Holy Spirit, 73f., 77, 79, 80, 82, 83, 85, 86, 110, 112f., 153, 179, 204, 237, 239, 240, 250, 254, 257, 258, 261, 265, 266, 267, 276, 277
Honesty, 15, 18, 247
Humanism, 104, 244, 245
Hume, 194
Huxley, Thomas, 167

Ideal, 18, 87, 97, 128, 132, 139, 168, 196, 209, 263
Image of God, 40, 41, 79, 135
Incarnation, the, 60f., 76, 131, 205, 248, 253
Indeterminism, 218
Individual, the, 91, 122, 135, 157, 160f., 183f., 190, 250
Intercessory work of Christ, 66, 67
Interest a condition of freedom, 228
Intuitionism, 127, 141

Judgment, 14, 44, 45, 53, 54, 68, 81, 86, 110, 124, 125, 142, 152, 158, 162, 180
Justice, 18, 41, 60, 247

Kant, 127, 141, 142, 143, 144, 161, 165, 188
Kingdom of God, 67-70, 72, 73, 74, 95, 96, 205, 206, 254f.

Lao-tze, 49
Law, 20, 21, 24, 39, 58, 78, 114, 142, 157, 162, 163f., 169, 176, 214, 239, 250, 252, 254, 256, 261
  Eternal, 22, 23, 25, 52, 60, 77, 78, 83, 86, 94, 147, 148, 164, 175f., 238, 251, 255
  Human, 15, 24, 165
  Moral, 14, 15, 16, 23, 25, 41, 42, 52, 77, 78, 138, 139, 164, 171, 175f., 248, 251f.
  Mosaic, 50f., 59, 61, 115, 248
  Natural, 21, 23, 175f.
  Physical, 14, 21
Leisure a condition of freedom, 229
Locke, 194
Love a motive, 206
Luther, 53, 105

Marcus Aurelius, 100
Melancthon, 105
Mill, John Stuart, 170, 194
Milton, 238
Montaigne, 106
Moral attributes of God, 46
Moral Sense School, 166
Mortification, 269f.
Motive, motives, 19, 172, Chapter VIII
Mystery, 31, 110, 160

Naturalism, 127
Naziism, 158
Needs, 190f., 197f.
Neo-orthodoxy, 245
Newman, Cardinal, 43

O'Brien, 15
Obedience, 68, 77, 85, 87, 115, 135, 199, 202, 248, 251, 259, 261, 273
Objectivity a condition of freedom, 228
Obligation, 25, 124, 139, 154, 158, 165, 180, 216, 237, 258
Ovid, 16

INDEX

Paradise, 37
Passion, 42, 180, 203, 273
Perfection, 16, 172, 178, 210
Personality, 13, 45, 59, 62, 87, 185f., 191, 268
Philo, 100, 101, 102
Philosophy, 13, 22, 58, 102, 159, 182, 273
Plato, 17, 22, 49, 99, 101, 108, 127, 141, 225
Pleasure, 16, 100, 169, 194f.
Plotinus, 102
Pope, 144
Pride, 15, 42
Problem, 18, 78, 94, 101, 112, 198
Profession, 117, 118, 202, 278
Progress, 15, 168, 198, 209, 273
Proofs of existence of God, 34f.
Prophecy, 53f., 205, 249
Protagoras, 99
Psychology, 182, 214
Purpose, 16, 17, 21, 31, 32, 33, 36 48, 50, 53, 55, 74, 86, 91, 92, 123, 133, 138, 172, 173, 189f., 198, 209, 256, 274, 276

Rationalism, 141, 245
Realism, 106
Reason, 20, 24, 26, 34, 41, 81, 84, 86, 98f., 101, 104, 105, 108, 109, 111, 142, 146f., 155, 194, 197
Redemption, 26, 43, 44, 87, 201, 278
Reformation, the, 105
Relativism, 140-141, 144, 158, 245-246
Religion, 25
Renaissance, the, 104
Repentance, 201
Resolutions, 223
Reu-Buehring, 256
Revelation, 14, 26, 28, 31, 41, 46, 49, 53, 59, 67, 81, 87, 102, 103, 104, 105, 108, 150, 247
Reward, rewards, 208f., 235
Right, 13, 14, 17, 38, 83, 86, 93, 98, 124, 132, 137, 144f., 149, 153, 179, 200, 215, 259
Righteousness, 64, 69, 75, 83, 87, 185, 200, 210, 250, 252, 256, 278

St. Bernard, 40
Sanctification, 75, 87
Satan, devil, 36, 39, 65, 66, 67, 265, 266, 271
Sauer, Erich, 47, 48

Science, 13, 17, 22, 29, 86, 91, 95, 139, 159
Scroggie, W. Graham, 248
Self, 23, 38, 44, 62, 131, 147, 155, 183f., 192, 197, 199, 201, 203, 208, 209, 227, 261, 266, 268
Skepticism, 100, 106
Smyth, 104, 109, 151f.
Socrates, 17, 49, 99, 127, 141
Sophists, 99
Sorokin, P. A., 245
Soul, 15, 35, 63, 75, 82, 138, 161, 202, 203f.
Spencer, Herbert, 167, 194
Spinoza, 107, 141, 213, 226
Spirit, 22, 35, 37, 79, 81, 138, 172, 199, 233f.
Spirituality and morality, 118
Stalker, 97
Stam, Betty, 241
Stoics, 100, 166
Sturm, 105
Summum bonum, 18, 127, 132, 134, 160, 163

Temperance, 41, 110
Temptation, 116
Tennyson, 84
Tests, testing, 45f.
Tension, 195
Theology, 29, 130, 182, 214, 244, 245
Thinking, 17, 92, 157, 244, 258
Thought, 17, 58, 62, 104, 106, 138, 171, 215, 258
Truthfulness, 18

Utilitarianism, 127, 170, 194

Values, 123, 161, 192, 274
Virtue, 19, 27, 100, 262, 269, 272

Will, 37, 40, 84, 165, 177, 187, 188, 192, 213f., 220, 223, 224, 233, 234, 237, 241, 263, 269
of God, 38, 52, 54, 77, 78, 88, 97, 110, 131, 132, 144f., 171, 173, 206, 209, 249, 260, 270, 275
Work a condition of freedom, 229
World, the, 263f., 266
Wrong, 13, 14, 17, 19, 83, 86, 93, 98, 132, 145, 146, 153, 200, 215, 221, 259

Zarathustra, 49
Zeno, 100
Zwingli, 105